THE FBI WAR ON TUPAC SHAKUR

STATE REPRESSION OF BLACK LEADERS
FROM THE CIVIL RIGHTS ERA TO THE 1990S

JOHN POTASH

MICROCOSM PUBLISHING
Portland, Ore

THE FBI WAR ON TUPAC SHAKUR

STATE REPRESSION OF BLACK LEADERS FROM THE CIVIL RIGHTS ERA TO THE 1990S

© 2007, 2021 John Potash

© This edition Microcosm Publishing 2021
First edition - 3,000 copies - October 12, 2021
ISBN 9781621064558
This is Microcosm #538
Edited by Sarah Koch

To join the ranks of high-class stores that feature Microcosm titles, talk to your local rep: In the U.S. **COMO** (Atlantic), **FUJII** (Midwest), **BOOK TRAVELERS WEST** (Pacific), **TURNAROUND** (Europe), **UTP/MANDA** (Canada), **NEW SOUTH** (Australia/New Zealand), **GPS** in Asia, Africa, India, South America, and other countries, and **FAIRE** in the gift trade.

For a catalog, write or visit:
Microcosm Publishing
2752 N Williams Ave.
Portland, OR 97227
microcosm.pub/FBI-Tupac

Did you know that you can buy our books directly from us at sliding scale rates? Support a small, independent publisher and pay less than Amazon's price at **www.Microcosm.Pub**

Library of Congress Cataloging-in-Publication Data

Names: Potash, John L., author.
Title: The FBI war on Tupac Shakur : the state repression of Black leaders from the civil rights era to the 1990s / John Potash.
Description: Second edition. | Portland : Microcosm Publishing, [2021] | "Second edition"--Introduction. | Includes bibliographical references. | Summary: "Since the first day after the tragedy was announced, controversy has surrounded the death of rap and cultural icon Tupac Shakur. In this work, preeminent researcher on the topic, John Potash, ... ts forward his own theories of the events leading up to and following ... murder in this meticulously researched and exhaustive account of the ... . Never before has there been such a detailed and shocking analysis ... e untimely death of one of the greatest musicians of the modern ... he FBI War on Tupac Shakur contains a wealth of names, dates, and ... letailing the use of unscrupulous tactics by the Federal Bureau ... igation against a generation of leftist political leaders and ... Based on twelve years of research and including extensive ... ources include over 100 interviews, FOIA-released CIA and ... ts, court transcripts, and mainstream media outlets. ... th the birth of the Civil Rights Movement in America, Potash ... ways in which the FBI and the United States government ... e down and dismantle the various burgeoning activist and ... ups forming at the time. From Martin Luther King Jr. to ... Hampton, the methods used to thwart their progress can ... ain and again in the 80s and 90s against later ... , musicians, and, most notably, Tupac Shakur. Buckle ... ocking, and unbelievable tale as John Potash ... elly of our government and their treatment of ... d black icons"-- Provided by publisher.
... 381 | ISBN 9781621064558 (trade paperback)
... s. Federal Bureau of Investigation--Corrupt ... Central Intelligence Agency--Corrupt ... s--Government relations. | African ... ment. | African American radicals. | ... Discrimination in law enforcement--United ... tions.
... 5 2021 | DDC 363.250973--dc23
... c.gov/2021022381

MICROCOSM PUBLISHING is Portland's most diversified publishing house and distributor with a focus on the colorful, authentic, and empowering. Our books and zines have put your power in your hands since 1996, equipping readers to make positive changes in their lives and in the world around them. Microcosm emphasizes skill-building, showing hidden histories, and fostering creativity through challenging conventional publishing wisdom with books and bookettes about DIY skills, food, bicycling, gender, self-care, and social justice. What was once a distro and record label was started by Joe Biel in his bedroom and has become among the oldest independent publishing houses in Portland, OR. We are a politically moderate, centrist publisher in a world that has inched to the right for the past 80 years.

Global labor conditions are bad, and our roots in industrial Cleveland in the 70s and 80s made us appreciate the need to treat workers right. Therefore, our books are MADE IN THE USA.

CONTENTS

INTRODUCTION
TO THE SECOND
EDITION

I started researching this subject regarding the FBI targeting of Tupac's Black Panther family in 1991, and specifically started researching Tupac in December of 1994. I first published initial conclusions in a local magazine in the Spring of 1995, before Tupac's death.

In 1999, I published a more comprehensive article in the award-winning *Covert Action Quarterly*, started by CIA agent whistleblower Phil Agee. Tupac's political mentors, such as his former Black Panther business manager, Watani Tyehimba, and his national lawyer, Chokwe Lumumba, urged me to turn that article into this book.[1]

Over twelve years of investigation revealed the murderous targeting of not only Tupac Shakur but other prominent members of the Civil Rights Movement and Black musicians. This investigation included primary source information along with my personal interviews with hundreds of eyewitnesses to these events, including the five police-linked attempts to murder Tupac Shakur before his death. Thousands of pages of government documents also support this claim and I have meticulously footnoted these sources for examination.[2]

Some may question the central thesis of this book, based on the information they've been given from television news programs or other mainstream news sources. For that reason I've included an in-depth analysis of what I believe to be an American oligarchy of the wealthiest families, the U.S. intelligence agencies they mostly control, and the mainstream media over which they have the most influence. I quote both U.S intelligence and media insiders on these topics.[3]

These far reaching agencies and their unconscionable actions have had an irreversible effect on the Black community and the Civil Rights Movement. When I researched this book, national Black Panther

---

1 John Potash, "2Pac Shakur's Shooting: A Police/FBI Setup?" *Claustrophobia*, Summer 1995, Issue 6. John Potash, "Tupac's Panther Shadow: The Political Targeting of Tupac Shakur," *Covert Action Quarterly*, Spring-Summer 1999. Personal interviews, Watani Tyehimba and Chokwe Lumumba, 5/10/00.

2 Note, the FBI refused to release 97% of their 4000+ page FBI file on Tupac Shakur. Told to this author with information on Freedom Of Information Act (FOIA) response, by Tawanda Monroe of the FBI headquarters on 5/10/2000. FOIA request on these documents released 99 pages, FBI letter to this author, May 18, 2000, Request no. 911992, Re: Shakur, Tupac. Also see court documents from New York vs. Tupac Shakur Ind. No. 11578/93, and Handschu, et al vs. Special Services Division a/k/a Bureau of Special Services, U.S. District Court, S.D.N.Y., 71 Civ. 2203 (CSH) Memorandum Opinion and Order, December 16, 1981.

3 Examples include former CIA assistant director Victor Marchetti, Victor Marchetti and John D. Marks, *The CIA and the Cult of Intelligence* (New York: Dell, 1974), and FBI Cointelpro agent Wes Swearingen, M. Wes Swearingen, *FBI Secrets: An Agent's Expose* (Boston: South End Press, 1995). They also include Pulitzer Prize-winning Dean of the University of California Berkeley School of Journalism, Ben Bagdikian, *The Media Monopoly*, 4th Ed. (Boston: Beacon Press, 1992) and longtime CBS national news anchor Dan Rather, seen in *Why We Fight* (2005) Sony, dir. Eugene Jarecki.

leaders such as national Spokesperson Kathleen Cleaver told me in an interview that after all the attacks, traumas, and friends murdered at the hands of U.S. intelligence groups, she needed counseling. She reached out to several counselors about a group she could attend. They told her that the only applicable group they could recommend was one for Jewish Holocaust survivors.[4]

I would later be able to help Kathleen Cleaver with a court case just after my book came out by sending her copies of my source information. A Black Panther "late-comer," Elaine Brown, sued Cleaver and Los Angeles Panther leader Elmer "Geronimo" Pratt (later Ji-Jaga) for defamation in December of 2007. That year, Kathleen and Pratt were concerned that Brown was working to take away votes from their friend, Congresswoman Cynthia McKinney, who was running for President in the Green Party elections. Cleaver and Pratt accused Brown of working for U.S. intelligence when she entered the Panthers in 1968. A judge dismissed Brown's claims of defamation in January of 2009.[5]

Since I published the first edition of this book in 2007, segments of police forces nationwide have increased their brutality against the Black population in particular, often using similar tactics that will be outlined later in this book. While the names of so many victims would take up many pages, some of the more notable unarmed deceased victims include Eric Garner, Sandra Bland, Michael Brown, Freddie Gray, Alton Sterling, and Philando Castile.[6]

Black Lives Matter (BLM) activists have organized to protest police and other government officials' involvement in these deaths. The FBI has now placed them on watch lists as possible "Black Identity Extremists," whom they call a greater threat than Al Qaeda and white supremacists. The BLM movement has inspired athletes such as Colin Kaepernick to protest murderous police brutality, and see the National Football League settle with him out of court after they blacklisted him. Lebron James and other athletes had Eric Garner's famous last words,

---

4 Personal interview with Kathleen Cleaver, November 15, 2002.

5 CNS, "Can't Old Black Panthers Just Get Along?" Courthouse News Service, 12/5/07. courthousenews.com/cant-old-black-panthers-just-get-along/ Greg Land, "Former Black Panther to Appeal Dismissal in Libel Case," Law.com 1/26/09. law.com/almID/1202427713045/?slreturn=20190725104240

6 P. R. Lockhart, "Black people are still suffering from police violence. Is America still listening?" Vox, 5/24/19. vox.com/identities/2019/5/24/18636305/police-violence-eric-garner-sandra-bland-black-lives-matter

"I can't breathe" repeated eleven times, emblazoned on their protest shirts. It would take five years for the police officer fatally choking Garner to be fired from the police force (though not charged with murder).[7]

These attacks are tragic and must be stopped. Though such events are not the central theme of this book, a number of the activists discussed in this book mention the attacks on their Black communities as fueling their activism. This book has always hoped to put more of a spotlight on such racial and social justice issues, partly through the community activists and musicians working to change them.

In recent years, more mainstream media organizations have slowly but steadily begun accepting some of the information presented in this book. For example, CSPAN's American History TV covered my 20-minute presentation on the FBI's murderous targeting of Malcolm X and Tupac Shakur in 2014.

Then, the first widely released biopic on Tupac, *All Eyez on Me* (2016), which made $54 million at the film theater box office, included the statement of the information I found from a Freedom Of Information Act filing that there were over 4,000 pages in the FBI's file on Tupac. In the last four years, other media organizations that have covered my research as covered in this book include VH1, A&E, RT, The Reelz Channel, and The Real News Network.[8]

Reviews of the 2007 book have included former Philadelphia Black Panther-turned-acclaimed radio journalist, Mumia Abu-Jamal, who said, "It's truly remarkable work." Former LA Black Panther-turned KPFK radio host Deodon Kamati said, "John Potash is arguably

7 Benjamin Fearnow, "FBI Ranks 'Black Identity Extremists' Bigger Threat than Al Qaeda, White Supremacists: Leaked Documents," *Newsweek*, 8/8/19. Eric Levenson, Shimon Prokupecz, Brynn Gingras and Mark Morales, *CNN*, "NYPD officer accused of choking Eric Garner five years ago has been fired," 8/19/19. Edvard Pettersson, "Colin Kaepernick Settles Blacklisting Lawsuit with the NFL," Bloomberg News, 2/15/19. bloomberg.com/news/articles/2019-02-15/colin-kaepernick-settles-blacklisting-lawsuit-against-nfl

8 "Life and Assassination of Malcolm X," C-SPAN American History TV, 2/21/14, c-span.org/video/?c4538045/john-potash-tupac-book . On the FBI's file on Tupac, see the first footnote of this book for more information. On *All Eyez on Me*, see *The Numbers*, the-numbers.com/movie/All-Eyez-on-Me#tab=summary . Ben Smith, "A Guide to the Notorious B.I.G. and Tupac Shakur Murder Conspiracy Theories," VH1 News, 3/9/16. vh1.com/news/249769/notorious-big-tupac-murder-conspiracy/ A&E *Who Killed Tupac?* (2017 TV Mini-Series) youtube.com/watch?v=DvzI_BVFq0M . "Hollywood, D.C." Watching the Hawks, RT, 3/2/18. youtube.com/watch?time continue=3&v=nqADZa2BeLE *Case Closed with AJ Benza: Tupac and Biggie* (2016) The Reelz Channel, youtube.com/watch?v=z00fKzLio5I

"Tupac Shakur's Commitment to Resistance and Revolution Began in Baltimore," The Real News Network, 7/7/19 therealnews.com/stories/tupac-shakurs-commitment-to-resistance-and-revolution-began-in-baltimore . "Happy Birthday Tupac Shakur: Unraveling the Politics of his Life and Assassination," The Real News Network, 7/17/15. therealnews.com/stories/tupac0616

the definitive voice on Tupac Shakur's death." Delaware State University Professor Ahati N. N. Toure said the book is "Enlightening, stimulating, incredibly detailed and painstakingly researched... a masterly presentation." And former U.S. intelligence contract worker Mill Butler said, "My friends and I from the U.S. intelligence community all read this book and picked it apart to try and find errors in it, but none of us could find any."

In my first edition, I continually added the names of TV and radio programs that interviewed me, or magazines that published my articles on these subjects. I'm sorry that I don't have the space to continue this in the second edition of this book, except to give thanks to several, such as the Pacifica Radio network in New York, Washington, and Los Angeles, *Coast to Coast AM* and Zoomer Radio, Baltimore's WFBR 1590AM, *Z Magazine* and *The Free Press* in Columbus, Ohio for continual support.

I'm now releasing a second edition of this book in the hopes of better distribution and of reaching a wider audience with this information. I also hope to polish and streamline the presentation of this work for attracting more readers. I have further updated some of the information and events around this story in the Epilogue.

INTRODUCTION TO THE FIRST EDITION

Years of accumulated evidence supports that the FBI orchestrated the murder of rap icon Tupac Shakur, and that they used similar tactics to murder other leftist black leaders. Thousands of pages of U.S. Intelligence documents, court testimony and agents' disclosures reveal how the FBI and other intelligence agencies have waged war on Black leaders. A review of Black Panther progeny, Tupac Shakur's life, and times highlights how the FBI maintained the use of these targeting tactics throughout the last four decades of this war. It also shows how U.S. Intelligence focused on musicians and on aiding conservative corporate control of the media. In this work, I will show how U.S. Intelligence murderously targeted political and cultural leftist leaders, including Malcolm X, Martin Luther King, prominent Black Panthers, and activist rappers and musicians.

By looking at the U.S. Intelligence targeting of Tupac and his Shakur family, we are provided with a window into intelligence targeting of leftist Black leaders from 1965-2005. U.S. Intelligence (Defense, CIA, FBI, and police intelligence) historically opposed leftists—those working to make changes in society to gain a more equitable sharing of wealth and resources.[1] The CIA's leadership, the director of all intelligence agencies until 2001, was composed of the wealthiest American families. I will argue that their founders also participated in saving thousands of Nazis and supervised these Nazis as they worked on intelligence projects.

To stop leftists from achieving their goals of opposing America's wealthiest, U.S. Intelligence used tools ranging from propaganda to violence.[2] With historical prejudices not too dissimilar from the Nazis they protected, U.S. Intelligence brandished particularly brutal violence against many Black leftists. Evidence also supports their violent targeting of ethnic leftist leaders linked to Tupac's activism.

---

1 See, for example, Michael Parenti, Inventing Reality, (New York: St. Martin's Press, 1986), p. 233. Carl Bernstein, "The CIA and the Media," Rolling Stone, 10/20/77; Stuart Loory, "The CIAs Use of the Press: A Mighty Wurlitzer," Columbia Journalism Review, September/October, 1974, pp.9-18. Cited in Parenti, pp.232-3. Morton Mintz & Jerry Cohen, Power Inc. (New York: Bantam Books, 1976), p.364. The New York Times, December 25, 26, 27, 1977. Ralph McGehee, Deadly Deceits: My 25 Years in the CIA (New York: Sheridan Square Publications, 1983).

2 For example, see police intelligence's brutal beatings of striking workers in Philip Foner's The Autobiographies of the Haymarket Martyrs (New York: Monad Press, 1977), pp. 1, 2, 10. Referenced in Huey Newton, War Against the Panthers, (New York: Harlem Press/Writers & Readers, 1996), pp.6-8, 15-16. Also see the origins of the Secret Service and the Bureau of Investigation (later FBI) for these purposes, detailed in U.S. Congress.

These include Latino gang leaders-turned activists, as well as Robert F. Kennedy and environmental leader Judi Bari.

The Shakurs worked in many legitimate radical political organizations in the '60s, from Malcolm X's OAAU to the socialist Black Panther Party. U.S. Intelligence's murder of Malcolm X and many Panthers led the Shakurs to a more revolutionary perspective by the time Tupac was born in the '70s. Tupac Shakur's Black Panther mother, Afeni Shakur, raised Tupac as her "revolutionary Black prince." Afeni's radical activist partner, Mutulu Shakur, and her Black Panther friends also served as Tupac's mentors throughout his childhood. This helped Tupac gain his own revolutionary leadership position before his rap career.

Tupac left this position for the entertainment world, but U.S. Intelligence focused more on him as he used his fame to further his political agenda. When Tupac's career took off immediately, U.S. Intelligence increased their tactics in proportion to his increasing wealth and influence. Tupac used his success to aid a national revolutionary group of former Panthers, led by his business manager, Watani Tyehimba, and national lawyer, Chokwe Lumumba. He hid his revolutionary agenda behind a "gangsta rap" façade as part of a political plan to aid the growing movement of gangs' leftist politicization.[3]

Media-censored eyewitness accounts support Tupac Shakur confidantes' reports of how U.S. Intelligence targeted Tupac. Evidence suggests that this targeting included up to six police intelligence murder attempts before he was jailed on an apparent frame-up. Prison "penal coercion" and police agents that filled the ranks of Death Row Records then helped manipulate Tupac in order to distort his political goals and create conflicts among rappers. Upon Tupac's signaled departure from Death Row, evidence supports that intelligence agents killed Tupac to stop him from aiding his extended family's goals, to curtail gangs'

3 Personal interview with Tupac Shakur's long-time family friend and business manager, Watani Tyehimba, 5/10/00. Tyehimba was a Black Panther in Los Angeles who was a founding Director of Security for the New Afrikan People's Organization. On gangs' leftist politicization that started mostly with the Bloods and Crips gangs peace truce, see Alexander Cockburn, "Beat the Devil," The Nation, June 1, 1992, pp.738-9. Mike Davis, "Who Killed LA? A Political Autopsy," New Left Review, 197, 1993, p.7. Mike Davis, "Who Killed LA? Part Two: The Verdict is Given," New Left Review 198, 1993, p.34. c, p.53. Mutulu Shakur reportedly started organizing the truce in the Lompoc Penitentiary. hitemup.com/tupac/family.html.

activist conversions, and to aid the police rap units' targeting of many top rappers with political links.[4]

A review of the last four decades details U.S. Intelligence's use of overlapping tactics and agents against the Shakurs and other Black leaders. While this review attempts comprehensiveness, it remains merely a sampling of targeted leaders and attacks on the Black community. The sampling stopped many months before this book's publication date and a diverse range of left-leaning to socialist, local to national, cultural and political leaders. A subtext of this book also examines how wealthy, prejudicial conservative forces have controlled virtually all of mainstream media in order to veil or hide most of this information.

---

4 On Penal Coercion, see "Biderman's Chart on Penal Coercion," *Amnesty International Report on Torture, 1983.* Reproduced and discussed in Ward Churchill and Jim Vander Wall, *The Cointelpro Papers: Documents from the FBI's Secret Wars Against Dissent in the United States* (Boston: South End Press, 1990) pp.321-323. On use of Death Row Records as police intelligence front to continue Penal Coercion tactics as well as orchestrate Tupac's murder upon his leaving the company, see FBI agent and police detective disclosures in Sundance Award-winning documentary filmmaker Nick Broomfield's documentary, *Biggie and Tupac* (2001), as well as their disclosures in Randall Sullivan, *LAbyrinth: A Detective Investigates the Murders of Tupac Shakur and Notorious B.I.G., the Implications of Death Row Records' Suge Knight and the Origins of the Los Angeles Police Scandal* (New York: Atlantic Monthly Press, 2002). On targeting rappers, see New York's rap intelligence unit, Dasun Allah, "NYPD Admits to Rap Intelligence Unit," *The Village Voice*, 3/23/04.

1

CIVIL RIGHTS, BLACK LIBERATION, AND THE FBI

Years of accumulated evidence supports that the FBI orchestrated the murder of rap icon Tupac Shakur, and that they used similar tactics to murder other leftist Black leaders. Thousands of pages of U.S. Intelligence documents, court testimony, and agents' disclosures reveal how the FBI and other intelligence agencies have waged a war on Black leaders.[1] By looking at the U.S. intelligence targeting of Tupac and his Shakur family, we are provided with a window into this targeting of leftist Black leaders from 1965-2005.

U.S. Intelligence (Defense, CIA, FBI and police intelligence) have historically opposed leftists—those working to make changes in society to gain a more equitable sharing of wealth and resources.[2] To stop leftists from achieving their goals of opposing America's wealthiest, it can be argued that U.S. Intelligence have used tools ranging from propaganda to violence.[3] With historical prejudices, U.S. Intelligence brandished particularly brutal violence against Black leftists.

The FBI and other intelligence agencies employed many devious tactics to "neutralize" Black activist leaders. For example, they used undercover agents to spread false information and they forged letters to be sent to Black leaders who were geographically separated. They sent letters in the names of these leaders to each other or signed them as anonymous sources.[4]

1For example, the FBI refused to release 97% of their 4000+ page FBI file on Tupac Shakur. Told to this author with information on Freedom Of Information Act (FOIA) response, by Tawanda Monroe of the FBI headquarters on 5/10/2000. FOIA request on these documents released 99 pages, FBI letter to this author, May 18, 2000, Request no. 911992, Re: Shakur, Tupac. Also see court documents from New York vs. Tupac Shakur Ind. No. 11578/93, and Handschu, et al vs. Special Services Division a/k/a Bureau of Special Services, U.S. District Court, S.D.N.Y., 71 Civ. 2203 (CSH) Memorandum Opinion and Order, December 16, 1981.

2 See, for example, Frances Fox Piven and Richard A. Cloward, *Why Americans Don't Vote* and *Poor People's Movements* (New York: Vintage, 1977) pp.99-100. For example, see police intelligence's brutal beatings of striking workers in, Philip Foner, *The Autobiographies of the Haymarket Martyrs* (New York: Monad Press, 1977), pp. 1,2,10. Referenced in Huey Newton, *War Against the Panthers*, (New York: Harlem Press/Writers & Readers, 1996), pp.6-8, 15-16. Also see the origins of the Secret Service and the Bureau of Investigation (later FBI) for these purposes, detailed in U.S. Congress. Senate. Book II: Final Report of the Select Committee to Study Governmental Operations with Respect to Intelligence Activities, 94th Cong., 2nd sess. 1976, p.21, and Michael R. Belknap, "The Mechanics of Repression: J. Edgar Hoover, the Bureau of Investigation and the Radicals 1917-1925," *Crime and Social Justice* (Spring-Summer 1977), p.50. Both referenced in Newton, *Panthers*, pp.16,17,24. And finally, see Charle Lane, "Book Details U.S. Protection for Former Nazi Officials," *Washington Post*, 5/14/04, p. A2.
Frances Stonor Saunders, *The Cultural Cold War: The CIA and the World of Arts and Letters* (New York: The New Press, 1999),

3 See, for example, Michael Parenti, *Inventing Reality*, (New York: St. Martin's Press, 1986), p. 233. Carl Bernstein, "The CIA and the Media," *Rolling Stone*, 10/20/77; Stuart Loory, "The CIAs Use of the Press: A Mighty Wurlitzer," *Columbia Journalism Review*, September/October, 1974, pp.9-18. Cited in Parenti, p232-3. Morton Mintz & Jerry Cohen, *Power Inc.* (New York: Bantam Books, 1976), p.364. *The New York Times*, December 25, 26, 27, 1977. Ralph McGehee, *Deadly Deceits: My 25 Years in the CIA* (New York: Sheridan Square Publications, 1983).

4 "The FBI...sources." See, for example, published copies of FBI documents on this strategy against the Panthers and SNCC in Churchill and Vander Wall, *The COINTELPRO Papers*, pp.126-8, including FBI memorandums dated 10/10/68 and 7/1068. Also see FBI memorandums from SAC, Chicago to Director, 1/10/1969, 3/24/69, 4/8/69 in *Agents of Repression*, pp.43-4, 49, 66. And, 10/10/68 memorandum. *COINTELPRO Papers*, pp118-19,127.

Some called this "divide and conquer" strategy, which they used against the Black Panthers in the 1960s, an East Coast versus West Coast feud. Particularly when they pitted the Oakland, California National Office against East Coast leaders.[5] They first pitted the Oakland office against leaders of the Student Nonviolent Coordinating Committee (SNCC).[6] In later chapters, I will argue that the FBI drafted fake letters and used undercover agents to create that divide and to turn other national Black Panther leaders against each other.[7]

They further used these strategies to pit the Oakland National Office against Tupac's mother, Afeni Shakur's New York Panther leadership when they were in prison in the late 1960s.[8] Accumulated evidence supports that U.S. Intelligence again used these strategies to help cover up their involvement in the assassination of Tupac Shakur. The term assassination usually applies to official heads of state government, but historians have also applied it to Black activist and religious leaders such as Malcolm X and Martin Luther King Jr. As to be detailed herein, Tupac Shakur was indeed an elected national activist leader before he became the 25-year-old national cultural leader that he is known as today.

In the 1900s, American racist oligarchs and their linked U.S. Intelligence first targeted Black leaders such as socialist W.E.B. DuBois. Du Bois founded the NAACP (National Association for the Advancement of Colored People) as an interracial organization in 1909. Mary White Ovington and Moorefield Storey aided Du Bois in starting the NAACP. The group worked to advance justice, economic

5 "But a...effort." See text of FBI COINTELPRO memorandum from G.C. Moore to W.C. Sullivan, dated 5/14/70, copied in Churchill and Vander Wall, *The Cointelpro Papers*, p149.

6 "The FBI...leader." On Brown as 60s Cointelpro target, see FBI memorandum from SAC Albany to Director, FBI, August 25, 1967, "COUNTERINTELLIGENCE PROGRAM, BLACK NATIONALIST-HATE GROUPS," Copied in Churchill and Vander Wall, *The COINTELPRO Papers*, pp.92-3d. Also see important FBI document of concern that SNCC's Charmichael or Brown, SCLC's MLK, RAM's Max Sanford, or NOI's Elijah Muhammad could become the new Black "messiah." See "AIRTEL, To: SAC Albany, From: Director, FBI (100-448006), COUNTERINTELLIGENCE PROGRAM, BLACK NATIONALIST HATE GROUPS, RACIAL INTELLIGENCE, 3/4/68. Copied in Churchill and Vander Wall, *The COINTELPRO Papers*, pp.108-111, particularly Brown et. al. at p.111. On Brown's honorary East Coast panther status, see Churchill and Vander Wall, *The COINTELPRO Papers*, p.126. The writer of this FBI War on Tupac book also saw Seale say this in a documentary. Newton's printed speeches officially declared SNCC's Carmicheal an honorary field marshall, in Huey Newton, *To Die for the People*, pp.7-9. The "Nonviolent" in the SNCC title was changed to "National" around 1966.

7 "The FBI...figures." See copies of FBI memorandums dated 2/2/71 sent to about 30 offices that attempts to split Newton and Cleaver as well as an Airtel memo that attempts to split Newton and Afeni Shakur's New York Panther 21, Churchill and Vander Wall, *The COINTELPRO Papers*, pp.160-1. M. Newton told how this was turned into an East Vs. West Panther war, *Bitter Grain*, p.203. For FBI manipulation of the media in this regard, see copy of FBI memorandums dated 8/5/68 in which Albany, NY comments on Miami's success with a television station's Panther coverage that was sent to approximately 40 other cities' offices. Also see 10/10/68 memorandum. *COINTELPRO Papers*, pp118-19,127.

8 "U.S. Intelligence...cities." Newton, *Bitter Grain*, p.38, 173. Churchill and Vander Wall, *The COINTELPRO Papers*, p.126. *Agents of Repression*, p.64, Newton, *Bitter Grain*, p.38

advancement, and social awareness for African-Americans and their plight. For example, the NAACP recorded nearly 5,000 lynchings of Black people from 1900-1950. Du Bois also submitted to the United Nations "An Appeal to the World," petition linking racism in the U.S. to colonial imperialism. Unsurprisingly, U.S. agents spied on Du Bois and revoked his passport.[9]

Other top Black activist leaders included Jamaican born Marcus Garvey. Garvey had originally founded the Universal Negro Improvement Association (UNIA) in Jamaica in 1914. He then established a new branch in Harlem in 1916 and chapters opened up across America.[10]

The UNIA gained widespread appeal in the 1920s and '30s, reaching a million members amongst northern U.S. Black people.[11] Garvey originally started his UNIA with its Black pride activism in Kingston, Jamaica before restarting it in Harlem. Garvey's life appeared to reflect the effect of government oppression of many Black leaders and groups that would come after him. He first supported socialists and anti-colonialists worldwide. He had a successful international shipping company that helped distribute his *Negro World* newspaper to the Caribbean and Africa, where other UNIA chapters started. When both British and U.S. Intelligence officials (including emerging FBI leader J. Edgar Hoover) corroborated against him, he took on a more conservative, capitalist but nationalist stance to allow himself back into the U.S. Nonetheless, Garvey was shot, imprisoned, deported, and exiled for his activist work, eventually dying in 1940.[12]

9 "Top Black...1900-1950." Top intellectual and socialist, W.E.B. Du Bois, had started the longest-running Black improvement organization, the NAACP, in 1910. The Federal Bureau of Investigation's predecessor, the Bureau of Investigation, quickly dubbed the NAACP's journal *Crisis* as inflammatory. Ed.s Mari Jo Buhle, Paul Buhle, and Dan Georgakas, *Encyclopedia of the American Left* (Chicago: University of Illinois Press, 1992), p.203. On 5,000 lynchings, Piven and Cloward, *Poor People's Movements*, p.186. loc.gov/exhibits/civil-rights-act/world-war-ii-timeline.html
10 "Earl Little...suicide." Malcolm X, *The Autobiography of Malcolm X*, as told to Alex Haley (New York: Ballantine, 1964,'65,'99), pp.1-11. Afeni's accounts from North Carolina in the 50s, *Look for Me in the Whirlwind*, pp. 49-50. Also see other similar accounts of varying degrees of racism in that book from Boston to New York. Also see
11 "Afeni...Black people." First sentence explained later. Malcolm's birth and father, Malcolm X, *The Autobiography of Malcolm X*, as told to Alex Haley (New York: Ballantine, 1964,'65,'99), pp.1-9. On Afeni's father in law in Garvey's group, Jasmine Guy, *Afeni Shakur: Evolution of a Revolutionary* (New York: Atria, 2004), p.70. On James Coston's name and change, Lumumba Shakur, Afeni Shakur et al, *Look for Me in the Whirlwind: The Collective Autobiography of the New York 21* (New York: Vintage, 1971) pp.22-3. On million members in Garvey's UNIA, see Michael Lewis, "The Negro Protest in Urban America." In *Protest, Reform, and Revolt*, edited by Joseph Gusfield (New York: John Wiley and Sons, 1971), p.158. This source and fact is cited in Frances Fox Piven and Richard A. Cloward, *Poor People's Movement: Why They Succeed, How They Fail* (New York: Vintage, 1979), p.203.
12 "Garvey...work." Ed.s Mari Jo Buhle, Paul Buhle, and Dan Georgakas, *Encyclopedia of the American Left* (Chicago, Illinois: University of Illinois Press, 1992). Also see his accomplishments listed on a Marcus Garvey commemorative poster, Harlem 1947, in Timothy White, *Catch a Fire: The Life of Bob Marley* (New York: Owl/Henry Holt,1996), p.104. On Garvey's reach to countries such as Belize, see Peter Eltringham, *The Rough Guide to Belize* (New York: Rough Guides, 2004), p.296.

While the UNIA appeared to end with Garvey's death, the NAACP continued their Civil Rights work. Another Black activist who collaborated with the NAACP, A. Phillip Randolph, worked as a labor leader in the 1940s. He proposed a March on Washington to demand fair employment for African Americans. Randolph also created the National Council for a Permanent Fair Employment Practices Commission in 1942, and organized the Committee against Jim Crow Military Services and Training in 1945.[13]

In 1942, an interracial group of 50 activists founded the Congress of Racial Equality (CORE). They worked closely on Civil Rights work with Black activists such as Bayard Rustin in the 1940s and 1950s. In the 1950s, Black activists Ella Baker, Rustin, and Martin Luther King Jr. worked together on many Civil Rights actions, and together founded the Southern Christian Leadership conference in 1957.[14]

13 loc.gov/exhibits/civil-rights-act/world-war-ii-timeline.html
14 Nishani,, Frazier, (2017). *Harambee City : the Congress of Racial Equality in Cleveland and the rise of Black Power populism*. Fayetteville: University of Arkansas Press. Branch, Taylor (1988). *Parting the Waters*. Simon & Schuster.

②

MALCOLM X

"You are out of touch with reality. For a few in several smoke filled rooms, you're calling that remaining free while the masses of the people—white and black, red, yellow and brown and vulnerable—are suffering in this nation…. The seal and the constitution reflect the thinking of the founding fathers that this was to be a nation by white people and for white people. Native Americans, blacks and other non-white people were to be the burden bearers for the real citizens of the nation."

>—Malcolm X speech excerpted and played in Tupac Shakur's, "White Man's World," under the alias Makavelli, *Don Killuminati: The 7 Day Theory*, 1996.

"No Malcolm X in my history text, why is that?
'Cause he tried to educate and liberate all Blacks."

>—Tupac Shakur, "Words of Wisdom," *2Pacalypse Now*, 1991.

Born in 1925, Malcolm X saw his town's horrible race relations in Lansing, Michigan, in the town's segregationist and racist rules, even including banning Black people from East Lansing after dark. Malcolm X also saw bold Black leadership as his father, Earl Little, worked as a preacher while also leading a Lansing chapter of Marcus Garvey's Universal Negro Improvement Association (UNIA), during the 1920s.[1]

When leaders such as Earl Little organized for change, they were threatened by racist whites. For example, the White Legion, Lansing's Ku Klux Klan, threatened Little and then burned his house down in 1929. In 1931, when Malcolm was 6, his father was found dead with a crushed skull and his body almost cut in half, reportedly due to being laid on street car tracks. Malcolm's mother, Louise Little, was forced to pay for the funeral through a small insurance policy. The larger company wouldn't pay on Little's life insurance because they ruled his death a suicide.

The FBI began their surveillance file on Malcolm X (a.k.a. El-Hajj Malik El-Shabazz) early in the 1950s.[2] Malcolm's influence first began to grow when he became the national spokesman for the Nation

1 "Earl Little…suicide." Malcolm X, *The Autobiography of Malcolm X*, as told to Alex Haley (New York: Ballantine, 1964,'65,'99), pp.1-11. Afeni's accounts from North Carolina in the 50s, *Look for Me in the Whirlwind*, pp. 49-50.
2 Clayborne Carson, *Malcolm X: The FBI File*, p.18.

Of Islam (NOI). From the late '50s on, Malcolm X's leadership of the New York NOI mosque led him to meet with third world revolutionaries and African leaders in the New York-based United Nations. The CIA started to be concerned about Malcolm's growing influence and his contact with these leaders, some of whom would eventually host Malcolm X and have him take part in many of their political decisions. By the 1960s, U.S. Intelligence wrote up to several reports a week on Malcolm X and his activities.[3]

Africa has struggled against imperialism for hundreds of years. From the mid-1800s to the mid-1900s, European nations had invaded and forcibly taken Africa's riches of oil, diamonds, and other minerals until independence movements drove some of these European colonizers out. After WWII devastated most European countries, it expedited the chances for African independence movements to gain control of their countries and U.S. corporations saw a chance to gain control of African wealth through more subtle means. Malcolm's input about racism in the U.S. threatened to sabotage these multinational corporations' hundred-million-dollar deals.[4]

Malcolm X criticized America's capitalist system as exploiting people in general, but he believed that its historical racism kept people of color particularly disadvantaged. And, with a huge media presence, he expressed his ideas to large forums. However, NOI leader Elijah Muhammad disagreed with Malcolm's leftist political activism and he restricted Malcolm's political activities, leading Malcolm to split with the NOI in 1964.[5]

African leaders helped fund Malcolm's travels and he started a new activist group in '64, which he named the Organization of Afro-American Unity (OAAU), in connection with the Organization of African Unity (OAU).[6] African presidents invited Malcolm as the only American allowed in their OAU meetings because they recognized him as the leader of Black American interests.[7] Malcolm also maintained his

3 "By the...activities." On FBI document, FBI memorandum, March 4, 1968. In Clayborne Carson, *Malcolm X: The FBI File* (New York: Carroll and Graf, 1991), p. 17. Also see, Kenneth O'Reilly, *Racial Matters: The FBI's Secret Files on Black America, 1960-1972* (New York: The Free Press, 1989), pp.112, 217, cited in Ward Churchill and Jim Vander Wall, *The COINTELPRO Papers: Documents from the FBI's Secret Wars Against Dissent in the United States* (Boston: South End Press, 1991), p.170.

4 "The CIA grew...deals." On United Nations and CIA concern, see Douglas, *Assassinations*, pp.379-80. On European nations and Africa, see, for example, Ed.s William Harris and Judith Levey, *The Columbia Encyclopedia*, (New York: Columbia University Press, 1975), pp. 29-30. On threatening multinational corporations' deals with African leaders, see Malcolm X's speech titled by one editor, "I Don't Mean Bananas," in the Audubon Ballroom, 1964. *New Left Reader*, pp.208-222. Other bibliographical information on this previously copied source unavailable.

5 "Malcolm...1964." Malcolm X, as told to Alex Haley, *The Autobiography of Malcolm X* (New York: Ballantine, 1965), pp.316 & 322, for example.

6 FBI Memo, 9/17/64, Carson, *The FBI Files*, pp.289, 299.

7 Evanzz, *Judas*, pp.249-50. Cited in Douglas, *The Assassinations*, p.396.

position of militant self-defense while he began directly collaborating with Martin Luther King's group and other Civil Rights movement leaders.[8]

While the OAAU chapters were growing, U.S. Intelligence agencies were also ramping up their infiltration tactics. Undercover police agent infiltrator Gene Roberts joined the OAAU at its inception and rose to the leadership ranks of its Harlem-based security force. By working for the New York Police department's Bureau of Special Services (BOSS), Roberts also worked for the FBI's Counter Intelligence Program (Cointelpro) against Malcolm X and the Black Panthers, all while CIA superiors supervised the entire U.S. Intelligence apparatus.[9]

U.S. Intelligence had made several attempts on Malcolm's life early in his political career. As early as 1958, New York detectives shot up Malcolm X's office, for which the city settled with Malcolm in a $24 million lawsuit.[10] FBI undercover agent, John X Ali, who infiltrated the Nation Of Islam (NOI), possibly provided the floor plan of the building since he was living with Malcolm at the time.[11]

Agent John X Ali also reportedly played a part in orchestrating the firebombing of Malcolm's house in 1965. Ali had risen to a national secretary assignment, one of the highest leadership positions in the NOI.[12] NOI leader Elijah Muhammad's son, Wallace Muhammad, said

8 See Corretta Scott King, *My Life with Martin Luther King, Jr*, revised edition (New York: Henry Holt, 1993), p.238. Cited in Douglas, *Assassinations*, p.403. Also see PBS's *American Experience*, "Malcolm X : Make It Plain," Archival footage of Malcolm pledging his group's support for Martin Luther King in an interview. Ossie Davis discussed Malcolm's day-long strategy meeting with other civil rights leaders. And in an interview Pacifica radio held with Mississippi-based Fannie Lou Hamer, she said Malcolm was her best friend and mentored her during her civil rights work.

9 "Information revealed ...Panthers." See, for example, an NYPD BOSS undercover agent's memoir on his dual work with the FBI against Malcolm X, Tony Ulasewicz, with Stuart McKeever, the President's Pirvate Eye (Westport Connecticut: MACSAM Publishing), p.145, cited in James Douglas, "The Murder and Martyrdom of Malcolm X," James DiEugenio and Lisa Pease, eds, *The Assassinations: Probe Magazine on JFK, MLK, RFK and Malcolm X* (Los Angeles: Feral House, 2003) p.390-1. One historian said BOSS agents reported in. Zimroth, *Perversions of Justice* called the intelligence as "the little FBI and the little CIA." Frank Donner, Protectors of Privilege (Berkeley: University of California Press, 1990), p.155. B.O.S.S. Cointelpro-type tactics were described by a federal judge in *Handschu, et al vs. Special Services Division a/k/a Bureau of Special Services*, U.S. District Court, S.D.N.Y., 71 Civ. 2203 (CSH) Memorandum Opinion and Order, Mar. 7, 1985, p.26. Against the Panthers, B.O.S.S. agents worked closely with the FBI-paid Roland Hayes, a key to the frame-up of the Panther 21. In his book *The Briar Patch: The People v. Lumumba Shakur Et Al*, a National Book Award winner, Murray Kempton said that Roland Hayes provided the FBI with five reports a week, and BOSS accompanied the FBI on raids. *The Briar Patch*, p.73-4. Former assistant district attorney Peter Zimroth said that federal law-enforcement officials told him that Hayes was on the FBI payroll when he helped frame the Panther 21 by transporting dynamite to the Panther office, after which BOSS agents reported it. Zimroth, *Perversions of Justice*, p.193. For other reports on Roberts work for BOSS, see Peter Zimroth, *Perversions of Justice: The Prosecution and Acquittal of the Panther 21* (New York: Viking, 1974) p.48. Murray Kempton, *The Briar Patch: New York vs. Lumumba Shakur et al.*(New York: Delta, 1973) p.202.

10 Karl Evanzz, *The Judas Factor: The Plot to Kill Malcolm X* (New York: Thunders Mouth, 1992) p.73 and Karl Evanzz, *The Messenger: The Rise and Fall of Elijah Muhammad* (New York: Pantheon, 1999) pp.187-8, 192. Also see, Louis Lomax, *To Kill a Black Man* (Los Angeles, Holloway House, 1987) p.103. All cited in Douglas, "The Murder and Martyrdom of Malcolm X," DiEugenio and Pease, eds, *The Assassinations* (Los Angeles: Feral House, 2003), pp.380-1.

11 See Louis Lomax, *When the Word is Given* (New York: Signet Books, 1964), p.82 and the firestorm his claim created but was later confirmed by FBI documents cited in Evanzz, *The Messenger*, p.317. Cited in Douglas, "The Murder and Martyrdom of Malcolm X," DiEugenio and Pease, eds, *The Assassinations* (Los Angeles: Feral House, 2003), pp.378-79.

12 See interview of Nation Of Islam Captain Joseph X in Spike Lee, *By Any Means Necessary: The Trials and Tribulations of the Making of Malcolm X* (New York: Halperion, 1992) p.63 and *On Brother Minister: The Assassination*

25

several FBI undercover agents in the NOI national staff helped Ali make that rise, as also attested to by FBI documents.[13]

Malcolm X believed that U.S. Intelligence further set up his near-fatal poisoning in Cairo, Egypt, late July of 1964. He said CIA agents made their presence obvious to try and intimidate him as he traveled through Africa. They didn't want him to present a planned United Nations appeal to African leaders that the U.S. was violating Black Americans' human rights. At a Cairo restaurant, Malcolm stated that just as he felt the poison take effect, he realized that he recognized the waiter as someone he saw in New York.

Rushed to the hospital, he was barely saved by a stomach pumping. The attending doctor confirmed that there was a toxic substance in his food. Malcolm had been concerned about NOI death threats, but he knew that they didn't have a global spy capacity. Malcolm implied that only U.S. Intelligence could employ an agent to spy on him in New York, fly him to Egypt, and to then get a job as a waiter in Cairo.[14]

Several other disclosures support Malcolm's belief that this was a CIA attempt on his life. A high level African diplomat later said that the French Counter-Espionage Department reported that the CIA planned Malcolm's murder, and France barred Malcolm from entering the country for the first time in fear of getting scapegoated for the assassination.[15] The FBI Director wrote a confidential memo on Malcolm's travel plans through Britain and France. He sent it to the CIA Director, the Army Intelligence (Intel) chief, the Naval Intel Director, and the Air Force Counterintel chief, as well as Intel chiefs in London and Paris.[16]

One such memorandum on Malcolm and African leaders went directly to the CIA Director of Covert Action, Richard Helms, who had reportedly produced a "blueprint" for the "elimination" of Congo's

---

of Malcolm X, a 1997 film directed by Jack Baxter and Jefri Aallmuhammed. Also see Fire Marshall Victor Canty informing Malcolm X that fire department officials tried to frame him for that, in press statement, 2/18/65, "We Are Demanding an Investigation," *Malcolm X: The Last Speeches*, ed. by Bruce Perry (New York: Pathfinder, 1989) p.179. All cited in *Assassinations*, pp.381, 406. A PBS documentary on Malcolm X showed NOI Capt. Joseph X and Philbert X who also said John X Ali was the National Secretary of the NOI in the last years of Malcolm's life.

13 "NOI leader Elijah...by FBI documents." Author James Douglas' interview with Wallace Muhammad, now W.D. Muhammad, 2/2/99 and Evanzz, Messenger p.317, both cited in Douglas, Assassinations, p.379. Wallace himself, accepted FBI money for information after fearing his half-siblings actions for Wallace aiding Malcolm X.

14 "Malcolm X believed...capacity." Jan Carew, *Ghosts in Our Blood* (Chicago: Lawrence Hill, 1994) p.39. Cited in *The Assassinations*, p.396.

15 African diplomat's statement made to Eric Norden, "The Murder of Malcolm X," *The Realist*, 2/67, p.12. Cited in The Assassinations, p. 404

16 FBI Director J. Edgar Hoover, February 4, 1965, memorandum. Besides the intelligence agencies mentioned, Hoover also sent this memo to the Attorney General and the Foreign Liaison Unit, Zak A. Condo, *Conspiracies: Unraveling the Assassination of Malcolm X* (Washington: Nubia Press, 1993) pp.271-2, endnote 491.

Patrice Lumumba. Helms also worked in this position during what a U.S. Senate Select Committee found were at least 8 CIA attempts to assassinate Cuba's leader Fidel Castro.[17]

Furthermore, FBI and police behavior around Malcolm X's assassination on February 21, 1965, supports their role in it. An FBI document said [undercover agent] John Ali met with Talmadge Hayer (a.k.a. Thomas Hagan), one of the gunmen who shot Malcolm X, the night before the assassination. Hotel information on Ali's stay in New York supports this claim.[18] At the Audubon Ballroom hall where Malcolm X gave his last speech, uniformed police left the area despite usually filing inside and outside the halls where Malcolm gave speeches.[19]

When cross-examined at the New York Panther 21 trial in 1971, undercover police agent Gene Roberts said he was the first to arrive at Malcolm's body and he "proceeded to give Malcolm X mouth-to-mouth resuscitation."[20] But Roberts revealed more, in interviews decades later, which would support the claim that his real role may have been to check Malcolm X's vital signs to confirm the assassination's success. Roberts described the actions of Joan Roberts who was with him at the event. When Malcolm X was shot, Malcolm's wife Betty Shabazz first tried to cover her daughters and screamed, "They're killing my husband!"[21] When the shooting stopped, Shabazz, a nurse, went to run to her husband, but Joan Roberts grabbed her. Shabazz struggled to get free, threw Roberts into a wall and ran to Malcolm.[22] Gene Roberts

17 August 11, 1964, CIA memorandum fro Deputy Director of Plans, titled "ACTIVITIES OF MALCOLM POSSIBLE INVOLVEMENT OF AFRICAN NATIONS IN U.S. CIVIL DISTRUBANCES," cited by Zach Kondo, *Conspiracies: Unravellling the Assassination of Mlacolm X* (Washington: Nubia Press, 1993) pp.49 and 242 endnote 280 and Evanzz, *The Judas Factor*, p.254. In *Assassinations*, p.398-9 endnote 118. On Helms, see Leonard Mosley, *Dulles: A Biography of Eleanor, Allen, and John Foster Dulles and Their Family Network* (New York: The Dial Press, 1978), pp. 462-463. From his notes, Mosley's source for this appears to have been Richard Bissell. This note came from the article by Lisa Pease, "Midnight in the Congo: The Assassination of Lumumba and the Mysterious Death of Dag Hammarskjold," *Probe* March-April, 1999 (Vol. 6 No. 3) kennedysandking.com/articles/midnight-in-the-congo-the-assassination-of-lumumba-and-the-mysterious-death-of-dag-hammarskjold

Regarding Castro, "Alleged Plots Involving Foreign Leaders", U.S. Senate, Select Committee to Study Governmental Operations with Respect to Intelligence Activities, S. Rep. No. 755, 94th Cong., 2d sess.

18 Peter Goldman, *The Death And Life of Malcolm X* (Urbannam, Illinois: University of Illinois Press) 2nd ed.1979), pp.314. Also in the *New York Times*, 3/3/66, p.24. Cited in *Assassinations*, p.410-11.

19 On police conspicuously absent from the scene, see eyewitness Patricia Russell's account she wrote for *The Baltimore Afro-American*, 2/27/65, in George Breitman, The Assassination of Malcolm X (New York: Pathfinder, 1991) pp.58-9. In Earl Grant, "The Last Days of Malcolm X," *Malcolm X: The Man and His Times*, ed. by John Henrik Clark (New York: McMillan, 1975), p.96 and Lee, *By Any Means Necessary: The Trials and Tribulations of the Making of Malcolm X*, p.42.

20 Kempton, pp.200-201. "What appeared to be twenty minutes later," Roberts finished "police finally got there and took him over to the medical center." This disclosure contradicts police officer Henry's attempt to call backup officers and Police Inspector Taylor's claim of 20 police officers at the Ballroom.

21 Malcolm X's daughter, Ilyasah Shabazz, in Corey Kilgannon, "Remembering Malcolm X In the Place Where He Fell," *The New York Times*, 2/21/05, p.B1.

22 On Joan Roberts restraining Betty Shabazz and Shabazz throwing her into a wall, see Eugene Roberts interview in the 80s with Elaine Rivera, "Out of the Shadows: The Man Who Spied on Malcolm X," *Newsday*, 7/23/89, cited in James W. Douglass, "The Murder and Martyrdom of Malcolm X," in ed.s James DiEugenio and Lisa Pease, *Assassinations* (Los Angeles: Feral House, 2001) p.413. Roberts said he calmed Joan Roberts down and escorted her

said he was there checking Malcolm's pulse. He turned to Shabazz and declared Malcolm dead.[23]

Roberts' admission bore even more importance due to its historical parallels. As previously noted, attorney William Pepper extensively documented revelations on the role of undercover infiltrator, Military Intelligence agent Marrell McCullough, in Martin Luther King's assassination. McCullough disclosed how he raced to and knelt over Martin Luther King as he lay bleeding from the fatal shooting. Pepper noted that McCollough was "apparently checking him for life signs," making sure the assassination was successful and signaling to Military Intelligence that "the army snipers there as backup shooters [weren't needed as]...the contract shooter [hadn't]...failed to kill King." They then communicated to the Special Force Group snipers, who were waiting for their shooting orders, that they could disengage.[24]

Police officials' admissions and later events supported the malevolent roles of Roberts. Without Gene Roberts' disclosure at the Shakurs' Panther trial that would take place six years later, no one would have known he worked undercover for the BOSS police intelligence unit. New York's *Herald Tribune* also said a "high police official" confirmed that several undercover BOSS agents were in the Ballroom audience at Malcolm's assassination.[25]

And finally, despite some admissions, police and media's cover-up actions were extensive. For example, New York's *Herald Tribune* and *The New York Times* reported that just after the shooting of Malcolm, police calmly filled the hall within fifeen minutes, without drawing their guns. Furthermore, police detained two people that the crowd had grabbed. A later *Herald Tribune* edition said the crowd only grabbed one, without acknowledging their earlier account. The *New York Times'* later edition dropped the second suspect from its subheading, but still quoted Patrolman Thomas Hoy who said that, while one subject was grabbed by Malcolm's supporters, he grabbed a second suspect being chased by some people. Hoy further said, "the crowd began beating me

to a taxi after the incident, suggesting he was with her but didn't take the taxi home with her because he had more to do at the scene.

23 On checking Malcolm X's pulse, see author Douglas' interview with Gene Roberts, 7/7/2000, in Douglas, *Assassinations*, p.413. On turning to Betty Shabazz and saying Malcolm's dead, Murray Kempton, *The Briar Patch: New York vs. Lumumba Shakur et al.*(New York: Delta, 1973) pp.200-203.

24 Roberts admission...disengage." William Pepper, *Orders to Kill: The Truth Behind the Murder of Martin Luther King, Jr.* (New York: Time Warner, 1998), pp.128, 431, 481, 485.

25 "A police...assassination." As quoted from the *Herald Tribune*, 2/23/65. Cited in Breitman, Porter & Smith, *The Assassination of Malcolm X*, p.54.

and the suspect" in the Ballroom. In the following days, no mention was made of the second suspect in the mass of media's accounts.[26]

The media also largely ignored the circumstances around the death of Malcolm's close ally, Leon 4X Ameer. Mainstream media alleged that he died of an overdose of sleeping pills less than twenty days after Malcolm's assassination. This happened just after Leon 4X announced plans to produce tapes and documents belonging to Malcolm proving the government was responsible for his assassination.[27] Soon after Malcolm's murder, a partially deleted FBI memo noted the CIA's desire to get rid of Malcolm. It said a *Life* magazine reporter agreed with a source that the reporter should "check out Washington and the CIA because they wanted Malcolm out of the way because he 'snafued' African relations for the US"[28] risking deals worth vast amounts of money for top American corporations.

26 "For example, New York's *Herald*...accounts." See copies of New York's daily *Herald Tribune*'s 2/22/65 front page early edition headline and description of two men being grabbed and beaten by the mob before police took custody of them. This was changed without explanation in the later edition. Also see *New York Times*, 2/22/65. All in George Breitman, Henry Porter and Baxter Smith, *The Assassination of Malcolm X* (New York: Pathfinder, 1976,'91), p.52-4. As elaborated on below, U.S. Intelligence stated in their internal documents having censorship control over media organizations. For one of many examples, see, Joseph Crewden, "Worldwide Propaganda Network Built by the CIA," *New York Times*, 12/26/77, p.1. Also, former 25 year CIA operative Ralph McGehee obtained documents from 1991 through the Freedom Of Information Act (FOIA) in which the CIA's Public Affairs Office (PAO) said, "PAO now has relationships with reporters from every major wire service, newspaper, news weekly, and television network in the nation. This has helped turn some 'intelligence failure' stories into 'intelligence success' stories... In many instances, we have persuaded reporters to postpone, change, hold, or even scrap stories...." As referenced from Lisa Pease, "The Media and the Assassination," *The Assassinations* (Los Angeles, CA: Feral House, 2003), p.311. Also, Earl Grant, "The Last Days of Malcolm X," Malcolm X: The Man and His Times, ed. by John Henrik Clark (New York: McMillan, 1975), p.96 and Lee, By Any Means Necessary: The Trials and Tribulations of the Making of Malcolm X, p.42.

27 Breitman, Porter and Smith, *The Assassination of Malcolm X*, p.16.

28 FBI teletype, 2/23/65, FBI Files, p. 368.

3

MARTIN
LUTHER KING

"Human progress never rolls in on the wheels of inevitability. It comes through the tireless efforts and the persistent work of dedicated individuals. [Many] say the Negro must lift himself by his own bootstraps. They never stop to realize that no other ethnic group has been a slave on American soil. [They don't] realize that the nation made the Black man's color a stigma"

> —Martin Luther King, Jr. 1968. Excerpt "Remaining Awake Through a Great Revolution."

While formerly on the other end of the spectrum regarding civil rights struggle tactics, Martin Luther King began to be pushed closer to Malcolm X's more radical perspective by 1968. This can be explained by the increasingly racist and repressive tactics used by U.S. Intelligence agencies to stifle his social movement. Martin Luther King Jr. had first won a Nobel Peace Prize in 1964 after close to a decade of non-violent civil rights organizing. Martin Luther King Jr. (hereafter, "King" or "MLK") helped spearhead many marches and rallies to end segregation and gain voting rights that were denied to so many poor Blacks in the American South.[1] The fact that civil rights work, marches, and sit-ins led to arrests and vicious beatings by local police appeared to radicalize MLK. CIA documents and later admissions by FBI agents reveal that U.S. Intelligence stated their goal was to destroy the increasingly radical MLK. They made MLK their number one Black activist target.[2]

Historians have debated what most helped get national civil rights legislation passed during King's life. Top sociologists Piven and Cloward effectively argued that riots contributed the most to the passage of national civil rights laws. Mainstream history texts rarely cover the vast violence by racist whites that spurred riotous reactions by Black communities. For example, in 1963 a gunman killed Medgar Evers, a high-profile secretary of the Mississippi NAACP. Also

1 See Frances Fox Piven and Richard A. Cloward, *Why Americans Don't Vote*.
2 "CIA...target." Clayborne Carson, David Gallen ed, *Malcolm X: The FBI File* (New York:Carroll and Graf, 1991), p. 17. On efforts to "destroy King," see memorandum in CIA file for Chief, Security Research Staff, from Allan Morse, one Jay R. Kennedy report. 6/9/65, p.7, in this writer's possession (Thanks to New Haven Black Panther founding member, George Edwards, for providing copies of these documents, originally obtained in a FOIA filing by filmmaker, Lee Lew-Lee. Also see, Wallace Turner, "FBI Taps Called Plan to Discredit Dr. King," *The New York Times*, Monday, May 21, 1973, p. A18. William Pepper, *Orders to Kill* (New York: Warner Books, 1998), p294-295.

in Mississippi that year, the Ku Klux Klan, with the aid of the police force, killed one Black and two Jewish SNCC activists. Between June and October of 1964, twenty-four Black churches were bombed in Mississippi alone. These murders and terrorist attacks would spark riots across the country. Partly in response to these events, Americans held 1,412 separate demonstrations in 1963, according to the U.S. Justice Department. Researchers documented a nationwide series of riots after police brutalized Black leaders at peaceful demonstrations. The largest of the riots were in New York, Chicago, Maryland, Philadelphia, and New Jersey in the first half of 1964. Whether responding to riots or sincere about civil rights, President John F. Kennedy initiated the Civil Rights Act just before his assassination in November of 1963. Congress passed the Act and President Johnson signed it in July of 1964.[3]

Despite police continually arresting and brutally attacking him, MLK called for nonviolent civil disobedience. Some of the Black community went along with MLK, while others responded to police brutality and government oppression by rioting in a number of cities in the summer of 1967. MLK refused to condemn the rioters, instead defending them by saying, "A riot is the language of the unheard."[4] U.S. Intelligence interviewed over 500 jailed Black protesters in the largest of these riots—a violent outburst in Detroit. When U.S. Intelligence asked the rioters who most inspired them, Intelligence analysts stated their surprise that most responded with MLK rather than younger SNCC firebrands such as Stokely Charmichael and H. Rap Brown.[5]

A friend and fellow activist with MLK eventually found that King's inspiration to rioters contributed to U.S. Intelligence's motives for assassinating him. Several decades after King's April of 1968 assassination, his widow Coretta Scott King and most of the Kings' adult children hired attorney William Pepper to represent them. Pepper aided them in filing a civil lawsuit against Memphis' rooming house owner Lloyd Jowers and his government co-conspirators in MLK's assassination. They filed this lawsuit mostly due to a 20-year

3 "Historians…1964." Frances Fox Piven and Richard A. Cloward, *Poor People's Movements: Why they succeed, how they fail* (New York: Vintage, 1979) p.244-8.
4 Lewis Killian, *The Impossible Revolution?* (New York: Random House, 1968), p. 601.
5 "Blacks…Brown." William Pepper, *Orders To Kill: The Truth Behind the Murder of Martin Luther, Jr.* (New York: Warner Books,1998). p. 446.

investigation that Pepper, a former friend of MLK, had undertaken in order to identify the real perpetrators of King's assassination.

William Pepper worked as a journalist in Vietnam, an experience that led to him engaging in anti-war activism beside MLK. Jr. Pepper then went to law school and, after MLK's death, had initially accepted the official version of the assassination. In 1977, MLK's closest civil rights associate, Rev. Ralph Abernathy, asked Pepper to represent long-believed sole assassin James Earl Ray who was serving a life sentence for allegedly shooting King from the third floor bathroom of Lloyd Jower's rooming house. Ray hoped that his case could be reassessed and Abernathy believed that Pepper would help them find out who really orchestrated the assassination.

Pepper took the case and first published a book on his MLK assassination investigation in 1995, titling it *Orders to Kill*. Warner Books then bought the rights to *Orders to Kill* and published it in 1998 (as Ch.20 suggests, Warner likely had ulterior motives as it appeared to decrease the book's circulation). *Orders to Kill* detailed the U.S. Intelligence documents, government whistleblowers, and other evidence supporting the theory that U.S. Intelligence carried out the assassination of MLK.[6]

In his introduction to *Orders to Kill*'s 1998 edition, MLK's son, Dexter Scott King, argues that U.S. Intelligence orchestrated the assassination of his father in 1968 for several reasons. Their top motive was to stop MLK's civil rights work and anti-Vietnam war organizing. They also wanted to halt MLK's mobilization of an interracial poor people's coalition that planned to camp in front of the White House to redirect money from the war to the poor, and to decrease King's influence over the 1968 presidential election.[7] Pepper and others found government-documented evidence that a dozen government intelligence agencies coordinated their plotting against King before his death. Many witnesses and much evidence supported how they worked with police and contracted the Mafia to aid the fatal shooting of MLK in Memphis.[8]

6 William Pepper, *Orders To Kill: The Truth Behind the Murder of Martin Luther, Jr.* (New York: Warner Books,1998). See Foreward by Dexter Scott King.

7 "King had won…election." This poor people's march was called an "extremely explosive situation." Memorandum from Howard Osborn, Director of Security to Deputy Director of Support. 3/27/68, copy in this writer's possession. Also, the fact that MLK was assassinated on the exact day anniversary of his official anti-Vietnam War announcement attests to that stance as a major reason for his assassination. See more on this tactic below.

8 "Pepper…balcony." See both, William Pepper, *Orders to Kill* (New York: Warner Books, 1998) and *An Act Of State: The Execution of Martin Luther King* (New York: Verso, 2003). Also see, Clayborne Carson, ed. by David Gallen,

On April 4, 1968, a gunman fatally shot MLK. He had just come out of his Memphis hotel room and onto the third floor balcony that faced the back bushy area of Lloyd Jowers' rooming house, whose ground was at about MLK's room level. Pepper published photos of an identified CIA agent lowering himself to the street from the wall extending down from that rooming house backyard within minutes of the assassination. Despite this, the government claimed James Earl Ray shot from that very rooming house's bathroom window. A photo's confirmation helped lead undercover Black Military Intelligence agent Marrell McCollough to admit that he raced to King seconds after his shooting. McCollough was the first to kneel over King, checking him for life signs and reporting his death.[9]

A former Naval Intelligence agent-turned reporter aided Pepper by interviewing two Special Forces Group (SFG a.k.a. Green Berets) snipers, hiding out in separate Latin American countries by the 1980s. The two independently corroborated each other's information that they were stationed atop Memphis' Illinois Central Railroad Building. Other snipers were reportedly located in two different positions, including J.D. Hill who said he was perched on a water tower with his rifle site on King. They all said they were to keep MLK and his associate, Andrew Young, in their rifle sites as they waited for a signal to shoot. One of the three SFG snipers provided a copy of his Army Intelligence orders paper that day which Pepper included in his book. It proved Naval Intelligence aid and top Pentagon command knowledge of the operation. Pepper verified its shorthand through others that worked in the Pentagon.[10]

Pepper said that these Special Forces Group (SFG) officers had been active in the 5th SFG conducting cross-border covert operations in Vietnam, from 1965-66. Throughout 1967, the U.S. Strike Command (CINCSTRIKE), with Army Intelligence, the CIA and FBI members

Malcolm X: The FBI File (New York: Carroll and Graf, 1991), p. 17. Pepper, *Orders to Kill*, p.82. Also see, DiEgenio and Pease, *The Assassinations*, "MLK" pp.432-529.

9 In support…death." On McCollough as undercover Military Intelligence agent, see William F. Pepper, *Act of State: The Execution of Martin Luther King* (London/New York: Verso, 1993) p.74. On McCollough racing to MLK's body to check for life signs, Pepper, *Act of State*, p.160. Also see James DiEugenio and Lisa Pease, *The Assassinations*, p.413. They refer to McCollough as a deep cover operative for the Memphis police, which he was while also working for military intelligence according to William Pepper, p.424 n.191. McCollugh even confirmed the picture of the first person kneeling over the shot MLK was him, a Congressional report. Pepper, Act of State, p.12.

10 "A former Naval…Pentagon." See photograph of these snipers' orders that day in photo no.33, Pepper, *Orders to Kill*, with explanation at pp.424-5. MLK Papers director, Stanford professor Clayborne Carson read from the interview at the trial, Pepper, *Act of State*, pp.129, 283-91. On the third SFG verifying the first two, see, for example, William Pepper, *An Act Of State: The Execution of Martin Luther King*, pp.72-4, 129-31.

responded to the urban riots. CINCSTRIKE deployed these SFG snipers in their 902nd division to do covert operations as part of small "Alpha team" units in cities where riots erupted. Their bosses gave them photographs of Black militants and community leaders that were to be killed if an opportunity arose in the course of the riot.[11]

Coretta Scott King and her children, who had also grown into accomplished Black leaders, had William Pepper represent them in the Lloyd Jowers case in part to draw publicity to Pepper's extraordinary findings. The King family's lawsuit against Jowers and his government intelligence co-conspirators in MLK's assassination came to trial in 1999. That trial brought over 70 of Pepper's witnesses under oath. While Pepper couldn't get all his interviewees to the courtroom, at the trial he presented videotaped messages along with 4000 pages of documents that included declassified government intelligence papers to support the King family's case for a government planned assassination of the civil rights leader.[12]

William Pepper's findings first became public in Britain. The BBC aired a September 1989 documentary on MLK. In that show, Mafia boss Sam Giancana's occasional driver, Myron Billet, claimed to witness the CIA and FBI offering a million-dollar murder contract on King to New York and Chicago Mafia bosses. He said they rejected it.[13]

The BBC documentary also showed James "Ricco" Kimbel, who offered evidence that he worked with the Mafia as a CIA and FBI asset. Kimbel said New Orleans Mafia boss Carlos Marcello accepted the CIA/FBI contract on King. He also stated that he worked with Memphis Mafia bosses Frank and Sal Liberto, who helped carry out the assassination on behalf of Marcello. Kimbel further said that he flew two army snipers to Memphis as part of the operation. Kimbel and Myron Billet signed affidavits on their claims.[14]

As Pepper explained in his book, "the Marcello/Liberto/ Memphis assassination operation provided the Government with a plausibly deniable alternative to the use of its own trained professionals

---

11 Pepper, *An Act of State*, pp.66-7. Also see William Pepper, "An Act of State: The Execution of Martin Luther King: Talk given at Modern Times Bookstore, San Francisco, CA," 2/4/03 p.14. www.ratical.org/ratville/JFK/WFP020403.html
12 See Pepper's *Act of State* book tour talk at Modern Times Bookstore on 2/4/03.
13 "The BBC...it." Pepper helped validate Billet's story by presenting Billet a nameless photo line-up from which he identified various Mafia bosses at the scene Pepper, *Orders To Kill*, pp.145-7, 160, 174, 275. *Act of State*, p.118.
14 "The BBC documentary...claims." Pepper, *Orders To Kill*, pp.145-7, 160-2, 174.

who were waiting in the wings and ultimately not required.... Organized crime [the Mafia] frequently fulfills this need and insulates federal, state, and/or local public officials and agencies from responsibility."[15]

Pepper tried to release this information to the public in a variety of ways. In 1993 he agreed to defend long-believed assassin James Earl Ray in a television trial (Ray never actually had a trial as he was strong-armed into a plea bargain to avoid execution). Home Box Office (HBO) and Thames Production of London agreed to co-produce it. The jury at the trial found Ray not guilty. While the trial lasted for 50 hours over ten days, it was aired in a three-hour show on April 4, 1993, the 25th anniversary of the assassination. Virtually no media covered the event except NBC's *Today Show*.[16]

William Pepper presented much of his evidence, detailed above and below, at this trial. CBS completely ignored the claims of government involvement in Martin Luther King's assassination. NBC only allowed brief coverage once in one particular program, mentioned above, while ABC only followed up the television trial broadcast with a one-time televised interview with Lloyd Jowers.

Out of fear of harsher charges due to Pepper's accumulated evidence, Lloyd Jowers admitted to part of his role in MLK's assassination after the HBO/Thames televised trial. On ABC's *Prime Time Live* in 1993, Jowers told Sam Donaldson that Mafia boss Frank Liberto paid him $100,000 for his part in MLK's murder. Jowers also cleared James Earl Ray. Jowers' employee at the time of the assassination, Willie Akin, supported Jowers' account on *Prime Time Live*.[17]

Jowers gave further details independently to Pepper, Dexter King, and Ambassador Andrew Young. The three tape-recorded their discussion with Jowers and later authenticated it when they replayed it at the 1999 trial. Jowers said that five people involved in MLK's assassination planned it at his rooming house. These included an Intelligence/Mafia liaison named Raul Pereira, Memphis Police Inspector Sonny Barger, Military Intelligence agent Marrell McCollough, and Memphis police sharpshooter Lt. Earl Clark. Besides Jowers, Young, and King, another 1999 trial witness said he heard Liberto tell someone by phone to "shoot

---

15 "As Pepper...responsibility." Pepper, Orders to Kill, p.539.

16 "Pepper...Show." Pepper, *Orders To Kill*, pp.301, 304-305.

17 "Out of...Live." Pepper, *Act of State*, pp.323-5. The *Prime Time Live* show was on 12/16/93.

[him] on the balcony" the day of King's death. Several more witnesses also testified that Liberto admitted his role in King's assassination. And witness James Milner said that Lloyd Jowers told him how a law enforcement officer fired the fatal shot at MLK.[18]

Two women closely connected to some of these named figures in MLK's assassination backed Jowers' account, while also further implicating him. Jowers' girlfriend at the time, a waitress at his rooming house's grill named Betty Spates, said she saw Jowers bring a rifle in from his backyard seconds after the assassination.[19] Glenda Grabow, a long-time associate of Raul Pereira (better known by his first name), signed affidavits to the fact that Raul stated that he killed King. Grabow had also aided Raul's many illegal activities, including gun-running. She said that two of Raul's cousins participated in his illegal activities and told her that Raul played a part in King's assassination.[20]

Other witnesses at the trial testified that Memphis police chiefs cooperated with U.S. Intelligence and Mafia-contracted individuals in the assassination operation. For example, two detectives, one a captain, testified as to how Memphis Police superiors ordered him to withhold the usual Black security team for King.[21] Amongst much more evidence, former Memphis Intelligence officers Jim Smith and Eli Arkin, along with former Fire Department captain Carthel Weeden, testified to their parts in aiding army and military officials with the audio and visual surveillance of MLK prior to and during his assassination. Arkin said these officials were from the 111th Military Intelligence Group (MIG) who had partly based themselves in his office.[22] Undercover agent Marrell McCollough worked for the 111th MIG before getting a promotion to the CIA following MLK's death.[23]

Furthermore, videotape of known police intelligence informant Rev. Billy Kyles showed him seeming to accidentally admit his role in the assassination. In cross-examining Kyles at the trial, one of William Pepper's assistant defense attorneys played a videotape of the reverend making a public speech in 1981 about his being with MLK

---

18 "Jowers gave…MLK." Pepper, *Act of State*, pp.73-4, 110-112, 137-9.
19 Spates gave a deposition and signed an affidavit to this statement. Pepper, *Act of State*, p.138.
20 "Glenda…assassination." Grabow had been injured in a car accident just prior to the trial and couldn't testify in person but her husband testified to the authenticity of her affidavits. Pepper, *Act of State*, pp.53-61, 122-3.
21 "Witnesses…King." Pepper, *Act of State*, pp.73-4, 110-113.
22 "Amongst much…in his office." Pepper, *Act of State*, pp.127-8.
23 Pepper, *Orders to Kill*, p.431.

on the day of the assassination. Kyles said he was standing outside King's hotel room door and knocked to bring King out of his room and onto the hall balcony. Kyles then seemed to get carried away in that public speech and said in the tape, "…only as I moved away so he could have a clear shot, the shot rang out," leaving the judge and jury looking stunned. When the attorney asked him who he meant could have a clear shot, Kyles had a hard time answering but finally said that he supposed it would have been James Earl Ray.[24]

Other testimony came from diverse sources. Due to a scheduling conflict, *New York Times* reporter Earl Caldwell could not attend the trial, but he gave videotaped testimony that included the prosecutor cross-examining him on his statement in a pre-trial hearing. Caldwell said that his *Times* editor shocked him by saying he was sending Caldwell to Memphis to "nail" (write an attack article on) King. Caldwell further stated that he saw a shooter in the bushes behind Jowers' rooming house. Another witness signed an affidavit as to having seen smoke come from that backyard location just after the fatal shot was fired at MLK. For years, officials claimed that James Earl Ray fired from that rooming house's third floor bathroom.[25]

Testimony continued from Cab driver Louie Ward who testified that a fellow cabdriver saw MLK get shot, and then saw a man immediately jump down from the rooming house's backyard wall and run to a waiting police car. Ward said he saw the cab driver repeat the story to police officers twice. The fellow cabdriver at the scene died later on that assassination night, apparently either falling or being pushed out of a speeding car. Also, a police officer claimed to have guarded fresh footprints in the backyard of the rooming house and police made a cast of the prints but never investigated them thereafter.[26]

Two judges later took the stand to add testimony about the alleged murder weapon used in MLK's assassination. Criminal Court Judge Joe Brown, who had presided over several mid-'90s hearings reexamining the assassination evidence, testified that ballistics experts showed how authorities accepted the wrong rifle as the murder weapon. Judge Arthur Hanes, Jr. testified that as a lawyer on James Earl Ray's case

24 "Furthermore, videotape…Ray.'" Pepper, *Act of State*, p.74, 142,. On Kyles as a police intelligence informant, Pepper was told Kyles did that from '67-'68, *Orders to Kill*, 391-2.
25 "Other testimony came…bathroom." Pepper, *Act of State*, pp.117-118.
26 "Testimony continued…thereafter." Pepper, *Act of State*, pp.117-118.

he interviewed a man who had the alleged murder weapon in his store during the assassination, exempting it from the crime. Another witness, James McCraw, had given a deposition saying that Lloyd Jowers showed him the real murder weapon and McCraw's housemate testified that McCraw admitted disposing of the weapon for Jowers. An ignored FBI report also stated that the alleged murder rifle failed an accuracy test and didn't match the fatal bullets found in King.[27]

Amongst several dozen more witnesses, key testimony came out regarding the U.S. Intelligence operatives who disclosed their roles in the assassination operation. Former CIA operative Jack Terell, an expert witness for the ABC television network as a whistle-blower in the Iran-Contra scandal, testified by videotape because he was bed-ridden with liver cancer at the time of the trial. Terell said that in 1975, his close friend, J.D. Hill, seemed to want to unburden himself and admitted his role: having MLK in his gun scope as a backup Army Special Forces Group (SFG) sniper in the MLK assassination. Hill's murder after his admissions sent the other snipers in his unit, described above and below, into hiding.[28]

Stanford History Professor Clayborne Carson, the 15-year director of the MLK Papers Project, read interviews of the other assigned Army SFG snipers, having already noted their historical significance. As part of his trial testimony, Carson read an interview of a sniper who said that fellow government agents "would not be wearing ties," and Marrell McCollough was the only person close to MLK's body not wearing a tie. Clayborne further read the sniper's statements that they would be radioed on whether to fire backup shots or disengage (leave). Apparently, McCollough's job was to rush to the body, confirm the death, and signal that confirmation to the Military Intelligence Group agents conducting the surveillance. They then communicated to the backup snipers to disengage since the first shots killed King.[29]

27 "Two...MLK." Pepper, *Act of State*, pp.30, 119-120.
28 "And finally... hiding." Pepper, *Act of State*, pp.71-3, 129-30. Also see, Ei Eugenio and Pease, *Assassinations*, pp.502-3. Note that at p.71, Pepper tells how Terrell was used by ABC as a highly credible source and how Terrell believed Hill was murdered in what was described as a "professional killing." This caused the two snipers Pepper's investigative team interviewed, 'Warren' and 'Murphy,' to remain in Latin American exile (p.73).
29 "Stanford...King." See interviews with those snipers read at the trial MLK's family held vs. government co-conspirator Lloyd Jowers with Pepper representing them. William Pepper, *An Act Of State: The Execution of Martin Luther King*, pp.67-71,129, 283-91. Also see William Pepper, *Orders to Kill*, pp.418-29, 481. Further see, James DiEugnio and Lisa Pease, eds, *The Assassinations: Probe Magazine on JFK, MLK, RFK and Malcolm X* (Los Angeles: Feral House, 2003) pp.406-7, 502-3. On "friendlies not wearing ties...McCollugh only one close to MLK without tie," see Pepper, *Act of State*, p.286 and *Orders to Kill*, p.476 and photo #36. It further should be noted that a picture of witnesses at the scene appear to be pointing upward at the shooter as if the lethal shot may have come from another location.

McCollough's role gained importance in scrutiny of Malcolm X's assassination since an undercover agent was also the first to arrive at Malcolm's body, showing a possible modus operandi that would later be repeated at the assassination of Tupac Shakur.

Clayborne last read the interview statements of an intelligence agent photographer positioned on a fire station roof who first got pictures of King falling and then took pictures of the actual shooter. He said that the agent gave them to a military Colonel and kept the still unreleased negatives that showed James Earl Ray wasn't the shooter. The military snipers said that Black leader Andrew Young was also a target, but he hadn't come out of the hotel and onto the balcony.[30]

The jury in the 1999 trial delivered a guilty verdict against Lloyd Jowers and concluded U.S. "governmental agencies were parties to this conspiracy." When William Pepper published his last book about the trial and his investigation, *An Act of State: The Execution of Martin Luther King*, Coretta Scott King and the U.S. Attorney General at the time of MLK's assassination, Ramsey Clark, wrote supportive statements for the book's cover. Pepper and Clark have both said how wealthy corporations have too much control over the media in most democracies so that the research and ideas in books such as Pepper's would receive little attention or support.[31] Virtually all American media sources heavily censored this trial. For example, *The New York Times* had an article on the trial's verdict on its front page, but spent much of the article belittling the King family's claims and minimizing the trial's importance.[32] The entire transcript of the trial can be found on The King Center's website.[33]

Some have suggested this came from a sniper on top of another higher building. Pepper shows evidence for several shooters aiming at King, implying a different shooter. Also see photo of Army orders photo no.33, Pepper, *Orders to Kill.*, with explanation at pp.424-5.

30 "Stanford History…hotel." See, Pepper, *Act of State*, pp.129, 283-91. Also see Pepper, *Orders to Kill.*.

31 "The jury…support." On the verdict, see the complete trial transcript at the King Family's The King Center website thekingcenter.org/wp-content/uploads/2018/12/King Family Trial Transcript.pdf. On Pepper and media see Pepper's *Act of State* book tour talk at Modern Times Bookstore on 2/4/03. ratical.org/ratville/JFK/WFP020403.html On Ramsey Clark's view of the media, see his group the International Action Center iacenter.org

32 "Coretta…importance." William Pepper, *An Act Of State: The Execution of Martin Luther King*. Kevin Sack and Emily Yellin, "Dr. King's Slaying Finally Draws a Jury Verdict, but to Little Effect," *New York Times*, 12/10/99, pp.A1, A26.

33thekingcenter.org/wp-content/uploads/2018/12/King Family Trial Transcript.pdf"

THE CIVIL RIGHTS MOVEMENT RADICALIZES INTO THE BLACK PANTHER PARTY

"Racism plus capitalism breeds fascism when the avaricious businessmen refuse to give control to the unemployed workers and their unions... Fascism breeds when the lazy, tricking, demagogic politicians lie and mislead people about the suffering that Black people are subjected to, that Brown peoples are subjected to, that any color or minority group peoples, or any poor White peoples are subjected to... [by brutal] pig cops... 'Pig' [refers to] people who systematically violate peoples' constitutional rights."

—Bobby Seale, 1969,70. Speech and interview excerpts, *The Black Panthers Speak*.[1]

In the 1950s, U.S. Intelligence agencies (CIA, FBI, police intelligence, etc.) began collaborative operations against leftists that were particularly violent against Black communities.[2] The FBI's Counter Intelligence Program (Cointelpro) typefied these collaborative operations that worked on behalf of the interest of the biggest corporate owners to counter these poorer workers, along with countering Blacks struggling for better jobs and Civil Rights. In response to the '50s civil rights movement, southern racists began a long series of bombings of Black churches and civil rights headquarters. Later investigations found that Cointelpro agents took part in many of these actions.

For example, *The Baltimore Sun* reviewed a University of Delaware professor's book, *The Informant*, that used FBI files, trial transcripts, and interviews amongst its sources. *The Sun* summarized that book's chronicling of an FBI undercover agent in the Ku Klux Klan, Gary Thomas Rowe, "in the vicinity of just about every conflagration of racial violence in the virulently segregated Alabama of the early 1960s. He was around for beatings, bombings, ultimately even murder." The book said he virtually never arrested anyone and kept several top Klansmen from getting arrested after their brutal crimes.[3]

1 Bobby Seale, excerpt from speeches and *The Black Panther*, collected in ed. Philip Foner, *The Black Panthers Speak* (New York: Da Capo Press, 1970,95), p.161
2 For example, see Kenneth O'Reilly, *Racial Matters: The FBI's Secret Files on Black America, 1960-1972* (New York: The Free Press, 1989), pp.112, 217, cited in Ward Churchill and Jim Vander Wall, *The COINTELPRO Papers: Documents from the FBI's Secret Wars Against Dissent in the United States* (Boston: South End Press, 1991), p.170.
3 "*The Baltimore Sun*...crimes." Michael Ollove, "The FBI's Mole in Klan was Horrifyingly Brutal as the Rest," *The Baltimore Sun*, 6/5/05.

Saludine "Abbah" Shakur, the patriarch of the activist Shakur family, started his activism as a member of Marcus Garvey's United Negro Improvement Association (UNIA). He and his biological sons, Lumumba and Zayd, then joined Malcolm X's New York City-based Organization of Afro-American Unity before Malcolm X's assassination. Abbah was part of Malcolm X's inner circle.[4]

As Malcolm X and Martin Luther King were gaining more international attention, a young activist group of Black college students started the Student Nonviolent Coordinating Committee (SNCC) in support of Civil Rights in 1960. They started as an integrated group helping Blacks register to vote in the south.[5] SNCC worked closely with Martin Luther King's Southern Christian Leadership Coalition in its first several years.

Around 1964, Malcolm X also spent many hours aiding SNCC leaders he crossed paths with in Africa. His influence and the growing U.S. Intelligence's murderous repression, typified by the Schwerner, Goodman, Cheney murders, eventually changed the group's stance. Several years after Malcolm's death and murders of its members, SNCC leaders Stokely Charmichael (name later changed to Kwame Toure) and H. Rap Brown (later Imam Jamil Al-Amin) decided to change the "Nonviolent" part of its name to "National," and then decided to exclude whites from their membership.[6]

SNCC leaders first used the symbol of the black panther. They started an Alabama political party that used a black panther logo on a flag in 1965. Herman Ferguson and Maxwell Stanford, Jr. (Muhammad Ahmad) also organized the Revolutionary Action Movement (RAM) that year. RAM was a semi-clandestine, Black nationalist and Marxist group that elected Robert Williams its International Chairman and Malcolm X its International Spokesman. Williams had led a local NAACP chapter in the South, wrote the book *Negroes with Guns*, and

4 "The Shakurs...chapter." On Abbah Shakur as well as the Shakurs and Odinga in the OAAU, see several sources. Personal interview with former Black Panther and Shakur family friend, Watani Tyehimba, 5/10/00. Also, Lumumba Shakur et al., *Look for Me In the Whirlwind: A Collective Autobiography of the New York 21* (New York: Vintage) pp.241-2, 264-5. On Abbah Shakur as a former Garvey follower, Jasmine Guy, *Afeni Shakur: Evolution of a Revolutionary* (New York: Atria, 2004), p.70. On Mutulu, Committee to End the Marion Lockdown, *Can't Jail the Spirit: Political Prisoners in the U.S.* (Chicago: CEML, 2002), pp.147-50.

5 Howard Zinn, "Student Nonviolent Coordinating Committee," in Eds. Mari Jo Buhle, Paul Buhle, and Dan Georgakas, *Encyclopedia of the American Left* (Chicago, IL: University of Illinois Press, 1992), pp.75-6.

6 Ward Churchill and Jim Vander Wall, The COINTELPRO Papers: *Documents from the FBI's Secret Wars Against Dissent in the United States* (Boston: South End Press, 1990), p.105. These authors cite H. Rap Brown, *Die Nigger Die!* (NY:The Dial Press, 1969) as their key reference for this information. Shaila Dewan, "Widow Recalls Ghosts of '64 At Rights Trial," *The New York Times*, 6/17/05, p.A1.

organized armed units to protect civil rights workers before his exile in Cuba. Also inspired by SNCC leader Stokely Charmichael's use of the black panther, Stanford helped start RAM's Black Panther Party in Philadelphia and New York, while other chapters included California by mid-1966.[7]

In 1966, Bobby Seale, a 29 year-old graduate student in engineering, had attended RAM meetings while studying at Merritt College in Oakland, California. Huey Newton, a 24 year-old law student, was also studying at Merritt when he met Seale at an Afro-American Association meeting. They both disagreed with some of RAM's and the Afro-American's discreet tactics. Newton and Seale reportedly believed that these two groups relied on an underground status that didn't include enough of a militant self-defense in response to the rampant police brutality the two activists had personally experienced. So, in October of 1966, Seale and Newton started their own group in Oakland that they called The Black Panther Party for Self Defense.[8]

They decided that Seale should have the title Chairman and Newton Minister of Defense. As it was legal to openly carry guns in public at this time, Seale and Newton believed that Black Panther Party members should keep themselves armed and defend themselves against unwarranted police attacks. Newton instructed Panthers on their legal rights early in their membership. He also led them in countering incidents of police brutality in their Oakland neighborhood. *In cases of police brutality*, Newton had his Panthers surround the police with guns pointed while he recited the police brutality victim's legal rights.[9]

Huey Newton and Bobby Seale officially registered their group as a political organization in 1966. Their main activities involved starting

7 "SNCC…mid-1966." Muhammad Ahmad (Maxwell Stanford, Jr.) *We Will Return in the Whirlwind: Black Radical Organizations 1960-1975* (Chicago, IL: Charles H. Kerr Publishers, 2007), pp.120-124. Churchill and Vander Wall, *Agents of Repression*, pp.44-6. M. Newton, *Bitter Grain: Huey Newton and the Black Panther Party* (Los Angeles: Holloway House, 1980), p.15. On RAM and Williams, see Dan Geogakas, "Armed Struggle—1960s and 1970s," *Encylcopledia of the American Left*, p.57. Included in Georgakas' references is Robert Williams, *Negroes with Guns* (NY: Marzani & Munsell, 1962).

8 "Later in…for Self Defense." See Michael Newton, *Bitter Grain: Huey Newton and the Black Panther Party*, pp.12-14 (no known relation to Huey Newton). Ward Churchill and Jim Vander Wall, *The COINTELPRO Papers: Documents from the FBI's Secret Wars Against Dissent in the United States* (Boston: South End Press, 1990), pp112, 123 and Churchill and Vander Wall, *Agents of Repression: The FBI's Secret War Against the Black Panther Party and the American Indian Movement* (Boston: South End Press, 1991), pp.45, 52, 63. More information comes from former Panther Lee Lew Lee's documentary *All Power to the People* (1996) and information from former Panthers such as George Edwards, personal interview, 8/10/00. Note that in writing the history while in prison, ex-Panther Sundiata Acoli said Herman Ferguson and Max *Stamford* started RAM. S. Acoli, "A Brief History of the New Afrikan People's Struggle," p.8 freedomarchives.org/. Also see Bobby Seale, *Seize the Time* (New York: Random House, 1970), p.34, and Afeni Shakur, "We Will Win," in ed. Phil Foner, *The Black Panthers Speak* (New York: Di Capo/Perseus, 1970), p.161.

9 "They decided…membership." See, for example, Seale, *Seize the Time*, pp.28-9.

programs to provide political education to their community and free services to poor Blacks. They provided political education classes that taught Black history and the plight of the Black man in the Western world. They also talked to their membership about changing society to change their situation. They based their teachings on books by writers such as Black liberation theorist Franz Fanon, Chinese revolutionary communist leader Mao Tse Tung and Cuba's socialist revolutionary Che Guevera, along with speeches by Malcolm X. Newton, Seale and later Panther leaders required much reading when Panthers first joined the group.[10]

Seale and Newton created free community services as part of a Ten-Point Program. This program listed the Black Panther Party's aims and desires for their community. The first five points included self-determination, full employment, a form of reparations for the "robbery" by the capitalists in their community, decent housing and education that included Black history. The second five points included military service exemption, an end to police brutality and murder, freedom for Blacks incarcerated by the racist judicial system, trial by juries of Black peers and for basic needs to be met. To address the last point they started "survival" programs, such as free children's breakfast programs and free health clinics. They also addressed specific community issues, such as the need for a traffic light on a corner where kids were regularly getting hit by cars. They further created a newspaper that helped other Black Panther Party chapters duplicate these programs. It had a circulation of 125,000 copies a week by 1970.[11]

U.S. Intelligence targeted both the RAM-based and Seale/Newton-based Black Panther organizations from their inceptions. Some Americans only came to know about this targeting when anti-war activists burglarized an FBI office in 1971 and uncovered proof of the targeting. The activist burglars confiscated thousands of documents, and then copied them for politicians, reporters, and scholars. These

---

10 "Huey Newton...group." Ex-Panther Lee Lew-Lee's *All Power to the People* (documentary, 1996). On political organization and philosophy, see Huey Newton, *War Against the Panthers: A Study of Repression* (New York/London: Writers and Readers Publishing,1981/96), pp.28-35. Also see, Seale, *Seize the Time*, p. 82 and Afeni Shakur, "We Will Will," in ed. Phil Foner, *The Black Panthers Speak* (New York: Di Capo/Perseus, 1970), p.161.

11 "Seale and Newton...1970." Huey Newton, *To Die for the People: Selected Writings and Speeches*, ed. Toni Morrison, (New York: Writers and Readers Publishers, 1972, 1999), pp.3-6. Also see Michael Newton, *Bitter Grain: Huey Newton and the Black Panther Party.* Churchill and Vander Wall, *Agents of Repression* and *The COINTELPRO Papers*. Also, Lumumba Shakur et al. *Look for Me in the Whirlwind.*. On Panther newspaper circulation, see Seale, *Seize the Time*, p.179.

documents from the Counter Intelligence Program files provided the first proof of such operations and the first notion that such a program had an official name. Still, the media and politicians continued to cover up many details of Cointelpro.[12]

On the second anniversary of Malcolm X's assassination in February of 1967, the RAM-based Panthers invited Malcolm's widow, Betty Shabazz, to speak at a memorial event. Newton and Seale's Panthers joined as Shabazz's security, armed with shotguns and pistols while wearing their standard black attire of berets and leather jackets. Best-selling author Eldridge Cleaver covered the event as an editor at San Francisco-based *Ramparts* magazine. Cleaver saw Huey Newton stand down police and counter their racial epithets by using words such as "pigs" rather than curse words that, because of obscenity laws, could have brought on his arrest at that time. This event inspired the *Ramparts* editor to join the Panthers as their Minister of Information.[13]

The Black Panther Party for Self Defense's national leadership gained publicity in mainstream news that helped them build new chapters in the eastern states. For example, the Oakland Panthers entered the California state legislature wearing their black berets, leather jackets and holding rifles. Television news programs, radio programs, and newspapers covered this nationwide.

Later in '67, Bobby Seale and Huey Newton made Student National Coordinating Committee (SNCC) leaders Stokely Charmichael and H. Rap Brown honorary Panther leaders on the East Coast. Other SNCC members also began starting Panther chapters in Chicago and eastern cities.[14]

In the spring, Oakland police broke into the home of Newton's neighbor and destroyed his property near the Black Panther Party for Self-Defense's office. Newton went to the house, asked the police if they had a search warrant, and they placed Newton under arrest.[15] This was the first of several specious arrests. When Seale went to bail

12 "U.S. Intelligence...Cointelpro." Peter Zimroth, *Perversions of Justice*, pp.73-4. Churchill and Vander Wall, *Agents of Repression*, pp.39-40, and *The COINTELPRO Papers*, p.xi.
13 "On the second...of Information." Cleaver's detailed description in Newton, *Bitter Grain*, p.24.
14 "U.S. Intelligence...cities." Newton, *Bitter Grain*, p.38, 173. Churchill and Vander Wall, *The COINTELPRO Papers*, p.126. *Agents of Repression*, p.64, Newton, *Bitter Grain*, p.38
15 "For...arrest." Seale, *Seize the Time*, pp.106-7.

Newton out on one such charge, police arrested Seale on an antiquated law barring guns near a jail.[16]

Police failed to keep Newton and Seale imprisoned for long, but attacks continued upon their release. On October 27, 1967, the last night of Huey Newton's probation for a 1964 conflict, one of a long line of bizarre shootings involving Panthers occurred. An Oakland police officer pulled over the car Newton drove, accompanied by two passengers. At a later trial it was revealed that the officer had a list of Black Panther license plates on him and another police car following him. While accounts differ on the details of what happened, a shoot-out ensued that left one officer dead. Another officer and Newton were wounded. Newton left the scene for a hospital where police soon found, beat and jailed him.[17]

After over four years of legal battles, the state dismissed all the charges against Huey Newton. This supports Newton's claim that he didn't have a gun on him when police shot him. In those four years, a "Free Huey" movement gained international stature while Panther chapters rose in many cities nationwide. Newton later attained his CIA file that said he was on a U.S. Intelligence "hit list." This supported the theory that the October of '67 shooting was a police intelligence murder attempt.[18]

16 M. Newton, *Bitter Grain*, pp.31, 35-6.

17 "On October...him" For details, see Michael Newton, *Bitter Grain: Huey Newton and the Black Panther Party*, pp.29-31, 42-65.. For lesser details, see Ward Churchill and Jim Vander Wall, *Agents of Repression* (Boston: South End Press, 1990) and their *The Cointelpro Papers*.

18 "After over...attempt." On CIA file and 'hit list,' see "National Security, Civil Liberties and the Collection of Intelligence: A Report on the Huston Plan," reported in *U.S. Congress, Senate, Book III. Final Report of the Select Committee to Study Government Operations with Respect to Intelligence Activities*, 94th Cong. 2d sess., 1976, pp.936-960. Cited in Huey Newton, *War Against the Panthers* (New York: Harlem River Press/Writers and Readers, 1991), pp.43, 93n. On charges dismissed see, Newton, Bitter Grain, p.65.

5

U.S. INTELLIGENCE BEGINS MURDEROUS TARGETING & HARASSMENT OF PANTHERS

"Rulers perceive the greatest threat to be the national liberation movements around the world, particularly in Asia, Africa, and Latin America. In order for them to wage wars of suppression against these national liberation movements abroad, they must have peace and stability and unanimity of purpose at home. But...[American Blacks] too, demand liberation."

—Eldridge Cleaver, *The Black Panther* newspaper, 1969.

"The systematic attempt to liquidate the leadership of the Black Panther Party starting with the bullet fired into Huey P. Newton in October is but the most advanced stage of a national conspiracy in the mother country against Black people in the colony... The assassination of Dr. King was a move on a national scale similar to the attempted assassination of Eldridge Cleaver on a local scale; both attacks were against the politics of coalition. [Both King and Cleaver joined diverse groups] into a single movement against poverty and racism."

—Kathleen Cleaver, *The Black Panther*, 1968.[1]

Black Panther leaders strongly suspected that U.S. Intelligence orchestrated Martin Luther King's assassination. They also strongly suspected that police particularly targeted their own members for arrest and murder. Later revealed FBI documents detailed the U.S. Intelligence's "harassment arrest" strategy, which will be explored below. Other documents, mentioned previously, showed that they had a hit list of Black leaders and that Huey Newton was on that list.[2]

Several pages of FBI documents described how they instructed local police intelligence units to employ a "harassment arrest" strategy against the Revolutionary Action Movement and other Black activist

1 These and other Panther Quotes from Ed. Philip Foner, *The Black Panthers Speak* (New York: De Capo Press, 1995), pp.100, 146. Eldridge excerpt from "'The Black Man's Stake in Vietnam," *The Black Panther*, 3/23/69. Kathleen excerpted from "Liberation and Political Assassination," *The Black Panther*, 5/18/68.
2 "After over...in '67." On CIA file and 'hit list,' see "National Security, Civil Liberties and the Collection of Intelligence: A Report on the Huston Plan," reported in *U.S. Congress, Senate, Book III. Final Report of the Select Committee to Study Government Operations with Respect to Intelligence Activities*, 94th Cong. 2d sess., 1976, pp.936-960. Cited in Huey Newton, *War Against the Panthers* (New York: Harlem River Press/Writers and Readers, 1991), pp.43, 93n. On charges dismissed see, Newton, *Bitter Grain*, p.65.

groups in 1967. The pages detailed their strategy of draining Black activists of their time, money, and freedom. These FBI documents detailed how the FBI worked with Oakland police in using this strategy against the Panthers there, and how police worked with the FBI against other Black activist groups nationwide thereafter.[3]

U.S. Intelligence increased the violent nature of their attacks in direct proportion to the perceived threat of the Black Panthers' expansion and success of their programs. After police wounded and jailed Panther co-founder Huey Newton in October of 1967, U.S. Intelligence next focused on the remaining Panther leaders. By the end of '67, Bobby Seale and Eldridge Cleaver made alliances with white radicals to form the Peace and Freedom Party presidential ticket. The group made Cleaver their U.S. presidential candidate and Students for a Democratic Society co-founder Tom Hayden their vice-presidential candidate.

In the first two months of 1968, police raided and ransacked Eldridge Cleaver and his wife Kathleen's Oakland, California home. Kathleen Cleaver was the Communications Secretary for the Panthers, holding press conferences on behalf of the Panthers in their earliest years. A month later, police would arrest 25 Panthers in the area, including Seale and Panther Office Chief David Hilliard.[4]

When Martin Luther King's assassination occurred on April 4, 1968, Eldridge Cleaver worried that, with Seale and Newton in jail, police would use any excuse to kill him and any remaining Panther leaders. Just after the assassination, Blacks responded by rioting in over 100 cities, setting various sections of most major urban areas in flames. For example, In Washington D.C, SNCC leader Stokely Carmichael addressed crowds that spontaneously gathered and asked the mostly white-owned stores to close out of respect to MLK. When the stores didn't close, the crowds erupted in anger. They smashed windows and

---

3 "The documents...thereafter." See the text of a memorandum report on this strategy dated 8/30/67, Philadelphia FBI office Special Agent in Charge (SAC), to the FBI Director, Ward Churchill and Jim Vander Wall, *Agents of Repression* (Boston: South End Press,1990), pp.44-46. Also see a copy of an FBI document from 8/25/67, headed SAC Albany, Director, FBI on COUNTERINTELLIGENCE PROGRAM, BLACK NATIONALIST-HATE GROUPS, INTERNAL SECURITY. It was routed to over 20 listed city offices including Oakland area's San Francisco office and discussed strategies for "disrupting" and "neutralizing" Black activist organization's activities. These "hate" organizations included Martin Luther King's Southern Christian Leadership Conference. In Churchill and Vander Wall, *The COINTELPRO Papers*, pp.92-3.
4 "U.S. Intelligence...Hilliard." On Peace and Freedom Party, Churchill and Vander Wall, *The COINTELPRO Papers*, p.128. On raid of Cleaver's home and arresting 25 other Panthers, Newton, *Bitter Grain*, pp.68-9.

then set fire to many stores in their Black neighborhoods who they felt were connected to the white establishment.[5]

Despite having the largest per capita Black population, Oakland remained calm. The Black Panthers had spread the word that police would use the excuse of a riot to kill their membership and carry out assassinations in the name of "peace."[6]

Police took matters into their own hands. On April 6, they shot at Cleaver and several other original Panthers. Police reported a gunman in the neighborhood as the reason to fire over 1,000 rounds of ammunition for 90 minutes at a house in whose basement cowered Cleaver and 18 year-old fellow Panther Bobby Hutton. Another 20 minutes of tear gas shells caused a fire, and one hit Cleaver in the chest. While also suffering a gunshot wound in the foot, Cleaver told Hutton they needed to come out naked with their hands up to save themselves. He said that if they didn't, police could use the excuse that they were concealing any weapons, justifying further gunfire. Naked, Cleaver survived and was arrested, but the more modest Hutton came out behind him only shirtless with his arms raised and was fatally shot.[7]

With Hutton's murder, the FBI and California police intelligence had begun their murderous decimation of the Northern California Black Panthers. Several undercover agents ended up revealing how they set up Panther Field Marshall, George Jackson, in the San Francisco Bay area's San Quentin Prison. Jackson's books (written from his prison cell) *Soledad Brothers* and *Blood in My Eye*, inspired many, likely making him a target for intelligence agencies. Professor Angela Davis taught at UCLA when she headed Jackson's defense committee, before the university's dismissal of her for participating in such radical work.

5 FRANKLIN, BEN A. (April 6, 1968). "Army Troops in Capital as Negroes Rio." *The New York Times*. WILLS, Denise kersten (April 1, 2008). "People Were Out of Control: Remembering the 1968 Riots". *Washingtonian*. Brimelow, Ben (April 4, 2018). "Photos show present-day Washington, DC compared with the explosive 1968 riots that followed Martin Luther King Jr.'s death 50 years ago today". *Business Insider*. Brown, DeNeen L. (March 26, 2018). "A black bank witnessed devastation after the 1968 riots. Now 'the future is bright.'" *The Washington Post*.
6 "After Martin…their membership." On riots in over 100 cities, see *BBC News*, "On This Day: '1968: Martin Luther King Shot Dead.'" http://news.bbc.co.uk/onthisday/hi/dates/stories/april/4/newsid_2453000/2453987.stm
. Panthers keeping Oakland Blacks from rioting, see M. Newton, *Bitter Grain*, pp.71-2. Newton said the Panthers saw how 1967 riots in Detroit and Newark led to murderous police responses.
7 "Police took matters…shot." Mostly from Newton, Bitter Grain, pp.74-78. Also see Robert Scheer, "Introduction," in *Eldridge Cleaver, Post-Prison Writings and Speeches* (New York: Rampart/Vintage books, 1969), p.xix. Cited in Churchill and Vander Wall, *The COINTELPRO Papers*, p.128-9. Hutton's early membership appeared to increase his risk since police murderously targeted at least half of the original Panthers by the 90s. Bobby Seale in Lee Lew Lee's *All Power to the People* (documentary, 1996).

Attacks on Jackson culminated with his eventual murder in prison in 1971.[8]

FBI and police began focusing on other chapter leaders to follow through on FBI Director J. Edgar Hoover's orders to "destroy" and "eradicate" Panther chapters' programs in 27 cities.[9] Various sources estimated that the New York Black Panther membership ranged from 400 to well over 800 members months after its April of 1968 inception. New York Panther leaders claimed a much higher membership, saying they signed up 800 new members in a single month. This brought immediate attention to the New York Panthers by the FBI, as it quickly became the largest Panther chapter in the country.

The New York Police Department had a special intelligence unit working against leftist political groups called the Bureau Of Special Services (BOSS). Government officials assigned Lieutenant Angelo Galante to supervise a new BOSS unit focusing on the New York Panthers. Galante's background underscores U.S. Intelligence's concerns about the New York Black Panther chapters. Galante previously worked for the Office of Strategic Services (OSS) and the agency the OSS evolved into—the CIA. He specialized in fighting against revolutionary guerilla forces behind enemy lines.[10]

BOSS first mass-arrested members of a SNCC-based midtown Manhattan Panther chapter. When those Panthers went to trial, a mob of "off-duty" police beat them with clubs and Blackjacks *inside* the courthouse hallway. Undercover agents also helped entrap the Brooklyn Panthers on numerous occasions. The Brooklyn Panther chapter included Afeni Shakur's lifetime friend, Thomas McCreary (Tupac mentioned him in his song "Wordz of Wisdom").[11]

8 "With Hutton's…1971." See Tackwood, *Glass House Tapes*, and note that Tackwood also passed a polygraph about his account, as cited in Churchill and Vander Wall, *Agents of Repression*, p.95 note 205. This source also cites former FBI agent M. Wesley Swearingen's deposition taken in Honolulu, Hawaii, October 1980, p.2 in his discussions with FBI undercover agent Darthard Perry, a.k.a. Othello.

9 AIRTEL, dated 5/15/69, from Director, FBI to 27 SACs (names deleted; locations deleted other than Chicago, Albany, captioned BLACK PANTHER PARTY (BREAKFAST FOR CHILDREN PROGRAM), cited in Churchill and Vander Wall, *Agents of Repression*, pp.68, 399n.

10 "The leadership…lines." Murray Kempton, *The Briar Patch: The People of the State of New York v. Lumumba Shakur et al.* (New York, Dell, 1973) p.57. This book was a National Book Award winner. Also see, M Newton, *Bitter Grain: Huey Newton and the Black Panther Party* (Los Angeles: Holloway House, 1991), p.176.

11 "With membership…Wisdom')." On Panther New York estimates and courthouse beating, M. Newton, *Bitter Grain*, p.174, 176. Newton also described Brooklyn entrapment, but the best source for that is Paul Chevigny, *Cops and Rebels: A Study in Provocation* (New York: Curtis/Pantheon, 1972). Tupac mentions McCreary as his "Uncle Thomas" along with Pratt and Odinga in "Words of Wisdom" on *2Pacalypse Now* (1991). He mentions "Huey" in "Changes" *2Pac: Greatest Hits* (1997). He also mentions Pratt and Odinga in "White Manz World" on *Ma.k.a.veli:*

BOSS assigned at least six undercover agents to the Harlem and Bronx New York Black Panther chapters. Several of these agents even helped Lumumba Shakur and Sekou Odinga found these Panther chapters. At least one of the agents had originally joined Malcolm X's Organization of Afro-American Unity, where Lumumba Shakur and Sekou Odinga were previously involved in activism.[12]

In the 60s, these activists had shed what they called their "slave names"—the names of their ancestors' slave masters—for those of African independence leaders, such as the Congo's Patrice Lumumba and Guinea's Sékou Touré.[13] Lumumba's father Saludine "Abbah" Shakur (James Coston) had first taken the name Shakur, Arabic for "the Thankful," in the early '60s. Living in Harlem, Abbah Shakur joined Malcolm X's OAAU from its start, before Lumumba (born Anthony Coston) and Lumumba's teen friend Sekou Odinga (Nathaniel Williams) followed suit. Odinga started a Bronx Panther chapter and Lumumba started the Harlem Panther chapter. Abbah and his adopted son Mutulu Shakur (Jeral Williams) joined the Revolutionary Action Movement (RAM) and Abbah initiated a RAM-based Panther chapter.[14]

Police duplicated the Newton/Seale scenario of arresting one leader who came to bail out another when the Harlem and the Bronx chapters showed the most growth in '68.[15] By November of 1968, police arrested Harlem Panther leader Lumumba Shakur when he came to bail out Bronx Panther leader Sekou Odinga. Police had charged Odinga

Don Kiluminati, the 7 day theory (1996). The Panther membership estimates are likely well below actual numbers as the New York Panthers reported gaining 800 new members in a single month. On New York as largest chapter, see Gene Marine, _The Black Panthers_ (June, 1969), cited in Peter Zimroth, _Perversions of Justice: The Prosecution and Acquittal of the Panther 21_ (New York: Viking, 1974), p.46

12 "BOSS...activism." Zimroth, _Perversions of Justice_, pp.16, 48.

13 For example, Lumumba chose his first name in tribute to an important African leader whose rise and fall typified African history. Patrice Lumumba had won election to the presidency of the Congo and vowed to liberate it from Europe's Belgium. Belgium conquered the Congo with advanced weaponry developed during the European industrial revolution. While Belgium followed many European countries that invaded, colonized, and divided up virtually the whole of the African continent, Belgium's King Leopold's particular brand of brutality included chopping off the hands of any Africans caught stealing. Lumumba's independence from Western—European or American—control lead to his assassination, by former CIA agent accounts, through Western covert operations. John Stockwell, _In Search of Enemies_ (New York: Norton, 1978), p.172. Cited in Noam Chomsky and Edward Herman, _The Washington Connection and Third World Fascim_ (Boston: South End Press, 1979), p.50. Sekou Odinga came out and adopted his first name from the son of a poor farmer who became a labor movement activist and then the Marxist president of the African nation Guinea in 1958. Ed.s William Harris and Judith Levey, _The New Columbia Encyclopedia_ (New York: Columbia University Press, 1975), p.2768.

14 "The Shakurs...chapter." On Abbah Shakur as well as the Shakurs and Odinga in the OAAU, see several sources. Personal interview with former Black Panther and Shakur family friend, Watani Tyehimba, 5/10/00. Also, Lumumba Shakur et al., _Look for Me In the Whirlwind: A Collective Autobiography of the New York 21_ (New York: Vintage) pp.241-2, 264-5. On Abbah Shakur as a former Garvey follower, Jasmine Guy, _Afeni Shakur: Evolution of a Revolutionary_ (New York: Atria, 2004), p.70. On Mutulu, Committee to End the Marion Lockdown, _Can't Jail the Spirit: Political Prisoners in the U.S._ (Chicago: CEML, 2002), pp.147-50.

15 Peter Zimroth, _Perversions of Justice: The Prosecution and Acquittal of the Panther 21_ (New York: Viking, 1974), p.46

55

with driving a stolen car and planning a bank robbery in Stamford, Connecticut because he was armed, as most Panthers were, reportedly for self-defense. Police dropped the bank robbery charge but kept the car theft charge. Lumumba went to bail Odinga out, traveling with two women, three kids, and a gun. Police placed Lumumba in jail and charged him, too, with planning a bank robbery. Apparently, none of these charges led to convictions.[16]

Tupac Shakur's mother, Afeni Shakur (born Alice Williams), said in her autobiography that she couldn't believe these arrests. Afeni had first been emboldened by the American Indians fight against the Ku Klux Klan in her hometown of Lumberton, North Carolina. She moved to New York as a 13-year-old in 1960 and joined the Panthers in '68. With a precocious intellect, Afeni wrote an article that won her a citywide journalism award that year. Afeni soon married Lumumba and changed her name. Afeni saw Sekou Odinga as her mentor and said that he was such a beautiful, pure person that she couldn't believe it when police arrested him and Lumumba on incomprehensible charges.[17]

---

16 "By November...convictions." M. Newton, *Bitter Grain*, pp.180-1.
17 "'Tupac...charges." Lumumba Shakur, Afeni Shakur et al, *Look for Me in the Whirlwind: The Collective Autobiography of the New York 21* (New York: Vintage, 1971) p.292. Note that Lumumba Shakur and Sekou Odinga adopted their names from African nationalist leaders, Patrice Lumumba of the Congo, and Sekou Toure of Guinea. Frivolous arrest, see Newton, *Bitter Grain*, pp.180-1. Afeni's birth name was Alice Williams. On journalism award, see above and Peter Zimroth, *Perversions of Justice: The Prosecution and Acquittal of the Panther 21* (New York: Viking, 1974), p.12. Journalism award in Zimroth, p.13.

6

MURDERS IN LA AND THE NEW YORK 21

"[Racist policemen] must withdraw immediately from the black community, cease the wanton murder and brutality of black people, or suffer the wrath of the armed people. [Huey Newton] was free enough to realize this and free enough to express this."

—Alprentice "Bunchy" Carter, *The Black Panther*, 1969.[1]

The Los Angeles Black Panther chapter formed soon after the Oakland chapter. The LA Panthers, however, had to deal with a new FBI strategy. M. Wes Swearingen, who worked in the FBI's LA Counter Intelligence Program (Cointelpro) unit, described his unit's murderous machinations. He said the FBI paid informant members of the United Slaves Organization, a Black cultural nationalist group, to murder LA Panther leaders Alprentice Bunchy Carter and Jon Huggins. These United Slaves murderers, first reported as George and Larry Stiner, shot them on the UCLA campus in January of 1969 (note that the FBI commonly calls these undercover agents "informants"—a cover-up name that hides both their employment by the FBI and the insidious nature of their murderous actions).[2]

Other whistleblowers elaborated on this. LA police intelligence agent Louis Tackwood revealed the regular money, guns, drugs, and orders he gave to United Slaves leader and founder Ron Karenga to attack the Panthers.[3] Tackwood testified to this in court and before a Senate Intelligence committee. He further passed a polygraph test supporting his statements.

Karenga was considered by many to be a cultural revolutionary and social leader. However, a *Wall Street Journal* article detailed Karenga's ownership of multiple gas stations, portraying him as a wealthy business man rather than a grassroots activist. The *Journal* further noted Karenga's ties to the LA mayor and the Rockefellers,

1 Fred Hampton speech, originally printed in The Movement, January, 1970. Collected in ed. Philip Foner, *The Black Panthers Speak* (New York: Da Capo Press, 1970,95), pp.138-44.
2 "The second…1969." M. Wes Swearingen, *FBI Secrets: An Agent's Expose* (Boston: South End Press, 1995), pp.82-4.
3 This work with Karenga came from undercover police Louis Tackwood & Citizens Research-Intelligence Committee, *The Glass House Tapes: The Story of an Agent Provocateur and the New Police-Intelligence Complex* (New York: Avon Books,1973). Cited in *Agents of Repression*, p63. The "drugs" provided by Tackwood were reported in M. Newton, *Bitter Grain*, p. 97. Author's note: the irony of the United Slaves abbreviation as US is apparent.

along with his secret meetings with the police chief following MLK's assassination.[4]

While *The Wall Street Journal* article may have been a false smear of Karenga, later events suggest otherwise. After the Carter and Huggins murders, the FBI's United Slaves informants murdered four more Black Panthers.[5] Furthermore, Swearingen verified D'Arthard Perry's claims that the FBI then engineered the prison break of several United Slaves murderers.[6] And finally, New Haven Panther George Edwards stated that he attained a U.S. Intelligence document reporting Karenga's meetings with Governor Reagan, funding by the Rockefellers, and the Stiner's work with U.S. Intelligence.[7] It is important to note that there is still some debate as to whether the United Slaves (US) was a legitimate Black Nationalist cultural group or an FBI front.

Before John Huggins and Bunchy Carter were killed, they left a tape with the instructions that if anything happened to them, they wanted Panther Elmer "Geronimo" Pratt to take over, and Pratt took over as the LA Panther leader.[8] Years later, Geronimo Pratt said that US, as a group, shouldn't be held accountable for the FBI agent infiltrators who carried out these murders of Panthers. Geronimo, who later changed his last name to Ji Jaga, said that an undercover agent in the Panthers started the conflict that led to Carter and Huggins' murders when that agent slapped a United Slaves member.[9]

Geronimo gave a more detailed description of this undercover agent in an email that Kathleen Cleaver would help distribute. Geronimo said that in 1968, as he helped Bunchy Carter with security when Eldridge Cleaver was giving a speech at UCLA, a young woman named Elaine Brown ran up to the security gate crying and begging to meet Cleaver. After discussion with Cleaver, Carter allowed it. Pratt claimed that Brown then had sex with Cleaver and, at a later date, had

4 "'Tackwood testified…assassination." M. Newton, *Bitter Grain*, p.95-97.

5 Swearingen, *FBI Secrets*, pp.82-4.

6 From two affidavits, one given to attorney Fred Hiestand and the other to Charles Garry, filed in *Black Panther Party v. Levi*, No. 76-2205 and interview with Fred Hiestand, 1/9/80. Also cited in information given to Ernest Volkman, Penthouse magazine, April, 1980. All cited in Huey P. Newton, *War Against the Panthers* (New York: Harlem River/Writers and Readers, 1996) pp.81,101n. FBI undercover agents George and Larry Stiner were tried and convicted of the murders. They did four years in prison before escaping and not being heard from again. Hubert was never apprehended. *War Against the Panthers*, p.81. And Swearingen, *FBI Secrets: An Agent's Expose*, p.84.

7 Personal Interview with George Edwards, 7/24/07.

8 Churchill and Vander Wall, *Agents of Repression*, p.79.

9 "Years later…member." *Human Rights in the United States: The Unfinished Story, Current Political Prisoners—Victims of Cointelpro*, Issue Forum, U.S. Congressional Hearing, 9/14/00, 1:25 p.m. Rayburn House Office Building, Washington, D.C. Room 2000. ratical.org/co-globalize/CynthiaMcKinney/news/if000914HR.htm Also, Personal interview, Michael Warren, attorney for Tupac Shakur and Mutulu Shakur in New York, 9/2/03.

sex with LA leader John Huggins, whose wife, Erika, was pregnant at the time. Pratt became increasingly suspicious of Brown with each of these incidents.

Pratt further said that the murders of January of 1969 were carefully pre-arranged. He claimed that Elaine Brown slapped a United Slaves member with whom she had also been having sex. She then immediately ran from the US member to Huggins, saying that the US member was attacking her. Huggins took out his gun and shot at the purported attacker. The US member proceeded to shoot and kill Huggins and Carter. Elaine Brown would testify in court and accuse United Slave members George and Larry Stiner. Pratt accused Brown of working as an undercover federal agent and wreaking further havoc amongst the Panthers thereafter, and he would try to get her expelled from all Panther chapters, as will be explored later in this book.[10]

Other credible witnesses hold Geronimo in high regard while still giving a different view. For example, FBI whistleblower M. Wes Swearingen worked in the Los Angeles Cointelpro unit at the time. He said the Stiners were "informers" (getting paid by the FBI) and an FBI agent named Eric Galt arranged the Stiners' murder of Carter and Huggins. Swearingen further said that "Darthard Perry, a self-admitted and publicly acclaimed informer for the FBI, filed an affidavit in a Black Panther Party lawsuit against the government charging that he knew the United Slaves members who were responsible for the murders of the Panthers were FBI informers."[11]

New Haven Panther George Edwards, who also has great respect for Pratt, says he trusts Pratt's statements about the Carter and Huggins shooting. Edwards said that he only disagrees with Pratt's account about the Stiners. The Stiners went to jail in 1969 but would later escape. Perry claimed the FBI engineered their prison break from San Quentin in 1974, after which they never saw jail again.[12]

Thus, most of my sources agree that U.S. Intelligence orchestrated the murders of LA Panther leaders Carter and Huggins. The disagreement only lies in which particular individuals or groups remain responsible. Many people support that the FBI at least ran their

10 "Pratt gave a...chapters." http://whosemedia.com/drums/2007/05/09/was-elaine-brown-an-agent/
11 "All credible...informers'" M. Wesley Swearingen, *FBI Secrets: An Agent's Expose* (Boston, MA: South End Press,1995) pp.82-4.
12 Perry's claim, Swearingen, *FBI Secrets*, p.83. George Edwards, personal interview, 6/12/07.

murderous operations inside the United Slaves through undercover infiltrators. This mirrors U.S. Intelligence targeting of the Nation of Islam's Elijah Muhammad, while also infiltrating both the Nation of Islam and Malcolm X's group to predominantly target Malcolm X.[13] During Pratt's LA Panther leadership, it would appear as though the FBI agents, purportedly in the United Slaves, continued murdering Panthers with little-to-no retaliation (Pratt apparently didn't want to buy into the FBI's "divide and conquer" strategy, having Blacks kill each other).[14]

Whether the FBI set up the Los Angeles-based United Slaves as a front for intelligence operations or had agents infiltrate an already established group, evidence supports that U.S. Intelligence later ran a similar operation in Los Angeles during the '90s. A police whistleblower found that undercover police agents in Los Angeles-based Death Row Records were involved in similar activities against Tupac Shakur and the rap community nationwide. Other evidence supports that U.S. Intelligence supervised these agents involved in some of Death Row's illicit operations.[15]

Several disclosures and findings support that the FBI used undercover agents in the United Slaves to target the New York Panthers at the same time they were targeting the LA Panther chapter. FBI informant D'Arthard Perry stated that the FBI used US infiltrator Claude Hubert to kill several LA Panthers and then transferred him to New York City.[16]

Furthermore, on January 17, 1969, the day that LA leaders Carter and Huggins were murdered, police shot at Bronx Panther leader Sekou Odinga and two other Panthers while they were parked near the Harlem river. Odinga and Panther Kuwasi Balagoon escaped.

---

13 See Malcolm X speech in American Experience: "Malcolm X: Make It Plain." PBS and The Autobiography of Malcolm X cited in Assassination, p.411. Also note that Swearingen testified on behalf of Pratt, Perry testified on behalf of other Panthers, and Tackwood made sweeping disclosures.

14 Swearingen, FBI Secrets, pp.82-4.

15 "A police… " Randall Sullivan, LAbyrinth: A Detective Investigates the Murders of Tupac Shakur and Notorious B.I.G. the Implications of Death Row Records' Suge Knight and the Origins of the Los Angeles Police Scandal (New York: Atlantic Monthly Press, 2002). Nick Broomfield, Biggie and Tupac, film documentary, 2002. Also see FBI agent whistleblower Kevin Hackie's statements in this book and film, as well as Gary Webb, Dark Alliance (New York: Seven Stories, 1998), on Death Row silent partner Michael Harris. All elaborated more on below.

16 "Several…City." From two affidavits, one given to attorney Fred Hiestand and the other to Charles Garry, filed in Black Panther Party v. Levi, No. 76-2205 and interview with Fred Hiestand, 1/9/80. Also cited in information given to Ernest Volkman, Penthouse magazine, April, 1980. All cited in Huey P. Newton, War Against the Panthers (New York: Harlem River/Writers and Readers, 1996) pp.81,101n. FBI undercover agents George and Larry Stiner were tried and convicted of the murders. They did four years in prison before escaping and not being heard from again. Hubert was never apprehended. War Against the Panthers, p.81.

Police arrested 19 year-old Panther Joan Bird who they found cowering in the shot up car. They then beat her in the precinct.[17] (Also, undercover police agent Ralph White shot a gun in the Black Panther office when Harlem leader Lumumba Shakur was there around this same date, possibly suggesting a nationally coordinated plan to kill off Black Panther leaders in a unified strike.[18])

These mid-January attacks appeared to be the culmination of a bi-coastal operation using various FBI undercover agents in the United Slaves and the Panthers to frame and kill the Black Panther leadership in Los Angeles and New York. The police officers' shooting at Odinga, Balagoon, and Bird can be seen as a part of an elaborate FBI and BOSS plot against the New York Panthers. Police made the specious claim that they thwarted the three Panthers' attempt to shoot police coming out of a precinct, despite the fact that the precinct was 560 yards away (5 ½ football fields) and the Panthers' rifle did not have a telescopic sight.

New York police officers Roland McKenzie and Louis Scorzello told of coming upon Sekou Odinga, Kuwasi Balagoon, and Joan Bird while the three were involved in suspicious activity. McKenzie and Scorzello reported that they had a shootout with Odinga and Balagoon. However, while reportedly six feet away from the officers, only McKenzie's summons book pouch was hit by a Panther's bullet. Odinga and Balagoon escaped after the officers "immunized" their car with gunfire. After shooting up the car, the officers found 19 year-old Joan Bird huddled under the dashboard. When they took her to the nearest police precinct the admitting officer asked McKenzie, "Did you work her over?" in reference to her black eye and bruises.[19]

Furthermore, police said they only accidentally came upon Odinga and the other Panthers who were supposedly there to shoot at a police precinct. Evidence suggests this was a complete fabrication and the confrontation had been planned in advance. United Slave leader Ron Karenga was scheduled to speak as an honorary chair of

17 "Furthermore…precinct." Kempton, *Briar Patch*, p.77-8. Zimroth, *Perversions of Justice*, p.179-83. M. Newton, *Bitter Grain*, p.182.

18 An attempt by the FBI to murder Lumumba that day is uncertain but possible. BOSS undercover agent Ralph White admitted shooting his gun *inside* the Harlem office with Lumumba there, though he said it was several days before the 17th. White said Lumumba warned him to never do that again, but White made the false claim Shakur said this due to his storing dynamite in the office Zimroth, *Perversions…*, p.187

19 "These mid-January…visit." M. Newton, *Bitter Grain*, pp.181-5. Kempton, *The Briar Patch*, p.75-8. Zimroth, *Perversions of Justice*, pp.179-83.

a Harlem cultural festival the day that cops shot at Odinga—January 17th. U.S. Intelligence used his speaking engagement as part of their excuse for attacking the New York Panthers. Police claimed that Sekou Odinga, Harlem Panther leader Lumumba Shakur and 19 other leading Panthers had planned to bomb and shoot at police precincts to upstage Ron Karenga's visit.[20] New Haven Black Panther George Edwards attended that event and reported Karenga's security harassing him and his fellow Panthers. He also heard Karenga make verbal attacks against the Panthers at that event.[21]

Leading up to the incident, undercover BOSS agent Ralph White attained work in Lumumba Shakur's office at the Elsmere Tenants Council, a Bronx antipoverty agency. Then, several days before police shot at Odinga, FBI agent Roland Hayes finalized his work with Ralph White and his fellow BOSS undercover agent, Eugene Roberts, to plant dynamite at Lumuba's Elsmere Tenants Council office as a frame-up. Attorneys pressured Agent Ralph White to admit in court that he fired a gun in the back room of Shakur's office around this time. Was White trying to set up an "accidental" shooting of Lumumba on the day of the shootings at Odinga, Carter, and Huggins?[22] It would appear as though the FBI tried to assassinate the leaders of the two largest chapters in the country on the same day.

Failing to murder the New York leaders that day, FBI and police then used these January incidents to launch a mass arrest of the New York Black Panther leadership, over two months later. On April 2, 1969, police led a 5 a.m. mass arrest of Sekou Odinga, Lumumba and Afeni Shakur, along with others identified as the top 21 NYC Panther leaders, dubbed the New York Panther 21. They were charged with hundreds of counts relating to the alleged police precinct-shooting plans and for planning to bomb public places around New York City.

Only Sekou Odinga evaded the April 2 police sweep by climbing out of his third story window and escaping to Algeria. Once there he

20 "It appears…visit." M. Newton, *Bitter Grain*, pp.181-5. Kempton, *The Briar Patch*, p.75-8. Zimroth, *Perversions of Justice*, pp.179-83. Note that it's specifically Kempton, in his National Book Award-winning account, who said that the Panthers wanted to upstage Karenga, which he implied was the U.S. governement's claim for why the Panthers set up bombings and shootings of police that day. Of course, a jury found that it was only U.S. Intelligence that set up bombings and shootings the day of Karenga's speech.
21 Personal interview with George Edwards, 1/17/06.
22 "The FBI…Huggins?" Zimroth, *Perversions of Justice: The Prosecution and Acquittal of the Panther 21*, pp.3-5., 17, 187-8, 193. Kempton, *The Briar Patch: The People of the State of New York v. Lumumba Shakur Et Al*, pp.2-12, 73, 199, and M. Newton, Bitter Grain, 185.

joined Eldridge and Kathleen Cleaver, who had formed a Panthers-in-exile group. Police had earlier charged Eldridge with firing back at the cops after they had fired a fusillade of bullets at him, just before they murdered Panther Bobby Hutton. Eldridge jumped bail and Kathleen went with him to the African country that granted them asylum.[23]

The Panther 21 would await what was called the longest trial in New York history.

---

23 "FBI agent...asylum." Odinga was said to jump 35 feet down to the ground to make his escape. Kempton, *The Briar Patch: The People of the State of New York v. Lumumba Shakur Et Al*, pp.2-12, and M. Newton, Bitter Grain, 185. Also see Zimroth, *Perversions of Justice: The Prosecution and Acquittal of the Panther 21*, pp.3-5. Lumumba Shakur, Afeni Shakur et al, *Look For Me In the Whirlwind: the Collective Autobiography of the New York 21*.

THE MURDER OF FRED HAMPTON AND ATTEMPT ON GERONIMO PRATT

"You can jail a revolutionary, but you can't jail the revolution. You can run a freedom fighter around the country but you can't run freedom fighting around the country. You can murder a liberator, but you can't murder liberation."

—Fred Hampton, 1970, speech excerpt from *The Black Panthers Speak*.

The FBI's Counterintelligence Program (Cointelpro) continued coordinating their attacks in several of the largest cities' chapters. On April 2, 1969, as police intelligence were arresting New York Panther 21 en masse, the FBI had a key agent initiate an assault on the Chicago Panthers. On that day, an undercover FBI agent in the Chicago Panthers, William O'Neal, started an armed clash between the Chicago Panthers and Chicago's largest gang, the Blackstone Rangers (later changed to El Rukn). O'Neal's purposeful "provocation" coincided with a pay raise and successfully put an end to the Chicago Panthers' progress at politicizing the Blackstone Rangers and merging with them.[1]

Chicago's charismatic Black Panther leader, Fred Hampton, was the orchestrator of this doomed merger. Hampton proved dangerous in the FBI's perspective for several reasons. He rallied the people with persuasive speeches and built alliances with various radical groups.[2]

But the FBI appeared most concerned with Hampton's ability to make connections with and politicize the leaders of Chicago's huge, well-armed gangs. Hampton convinced Chicago's 3,000 member Blackstone Rangers gang to make the conversion to a radical political force as a new Black Panther chapter.[3] This would have effectively

1 "The FBI's…them." Senate Select Committee staff interview with Panther Deputy Minister of Defense Bobby Rush on 11/26/75; reported at p.198 of *The FBI's Covert Action to Destroy The Black Panther Party*. In the U.S. Senate Select Committee to Study Governmental Operations, Final Report, Book III: *Supplementary Detailed Staff Reports on Intelligence Activities and the Rights of Americans*, Books, , 94th Congress, 2nd Session, (U.S. Government Printing Office, Washington DC., 1976}. Referenced in Churchill and Vander Wall, Agents of Repression, p.66, note 18. On promotion, see p.66 note 19: See documents and evidence in the case of *Iberia Hampton, et. al. Plaintiffs-Appellants v. Edward V. Hanrahan, et al., Defendants-Appellees*, Transcript at 21741-62 and 21807-18. (Later referred to as *Appeal* or *Transcript*). Appeal PL #306 showing that the pay increase was sought by [FBI Special Agent Roy] Mitchell, with [FBI supervisor Marlin] Johnson's endorsement, in late February, and approved by FBI headquarters on March 11; Appeal, PL WON #3 shows the raise was to $450/month plus $125 monthly expenses.
2 "Chicago's …groups." Fred Hampton, "You Can Murder a Liberator, but You Can't Murder Liberation." In Philip Foner ed. *The Black Panthers Speak* (New York: Da Capo Press, 1970) , pp.146-50.
3 See documents and evidence in the case of *Iberia Hampton, et. al. Plaintiffs-Appellants v. Edward V. Hanrahan, et al., Defendants-Appellees*, Transcript at 21741-62 and 21807-18. (Later referred to as *Appeal* or *Transcript*). Churchill and Vander Wall, *Agents of Repression*, pp.64-5, .notes 5, 8.

doubled the national size of the Black Panther Party, which had an estimated 2,000-5,000 members in 40 chapters by the end of 1968.[4] The merge got far enough that the gang changed its name to The Black P. Stone Nation.[5]

After Panther infiltrator William O'Neal reported the pending merge in December of '68, the FBI quickly began taking steps to thwart it. It has been alleged that they sent fake letters to many people involved in the merge claiming the Stone Rangers leader planned to kill Hampton, and O'Neal may have also initiated an armed conflict between the two groups. O'Neal further destroyed merger negotiations with two other Chicago gangs, the Vice Lords and the Mau Maus, using similar tactics.[6]

O'Neal would also set out to damage Panther work with other radical political groups. He sent racially prejudiced messages to the white radicals in the national Students for a Democratic Society (SDS) office in Chicago. SDS had grown into the largest anti-war group by late 1968 (estimated between 80,000-100,000).[7] The FBI also helped O'Neal end discussions of a collaborative rainbow coalition between the Panthers, SDS, the Young Lords (a Latino group modeled after the Panthers who supported Puerto Rican independence), and another white group, The Young Patriots.[8]

The FBI had the same motives and used similar tactics for targeting the Chicago Panthers as they would with Tupac Shakur years later. The FBI worked with police gang intelligence units against the Chicago Panthers and recruited undercover Panther infiltrator William O'Neal by letting him off of several criminal charges. As we will see later, evidence supports that U.S. Intelligence similarly let record producer Suge Knight off of criminal charges and had him work with police gang intelligence units against Tupac.[9]

4 Over 40 chapters estimated by 'law enforcement experts' to Peter Zimroth in his *Perversions of Justice: The Prosecution and Acquittal of the Panther 21* (New York: Viking Press, 1974) p.39. That account reported 2,000 members by the end of '68 while historians and Panther sympathizers Ward Churchill and Jim Vander Wall reported 5,000 members in over a dozen cities that year. By most accounts, these numbers increased significantly up to 1970.

5 FBI Memorandum, SAC Chicago to Director, FBI, 12/20/68, COUNTERINTELLIGENCE PROGRAM, BLACK NATIONALST—HATE GROUPS, RACIAL INTELLIGENCE MATTER (BLACK PANTHER PARTY). In Churchill and Vander Wall, *Agents of Repression*, p.65 note11.

6 "After…Maus." *Appeal*, PL #16-17 and *Transcript* at 4113-4. Churchill and Vander Wall, *Agents of Repression*, p.66, .notes 15, 16.

7 "O'Neal…1969." Kirkpatrick Sale, *SDS* (New York: Vintage, 1973), p.664. Churchill and Vander Wall, *Agents of Repression*, p.66, note 21.

8 *Appeal*, #26-30 and WON 5. Also see *Transcript* at 6579 and 8907. Churchill and Vander Wall, *Agents of Repression*, p.66, .notes 22-3..

9 "The FBI had…Tupac." On Panthers, see, *Appeal*, PL WON #3 showed that FBI Chicago SAC Mitchell personally posted bond on one of O'Neal's charges and neither of his charges were prosecuted. On FBI collaboration with

Researchers rarely mention how much the Panthers' potential to politicize gangs likely concerned the FBI and US Intelligence agencies. Reportedly, Bunchy Carter had previously headed the several thousand strong Slauson street gang of LA. This may have motivated his early murder by the FBI—one of the first Panther murders.[10] Motives to heavily focus on New York Panther leaders Lumumba Shakur and Sekou Odinga likely included their former New York leadership in gangs estimated as many as 10,000 strong. It is believed that Afeni Shakur also led a female gang affiliated with one of the male gangs.[11]

It's of further interest to note Lumumba's belief regarding the U.S. Intelligence's perspective on gangs. He said that when he was active in gangs, U.S. Intelligence encouraged non-political gang violence for a "bad-nigger-kill-bad-nigger" population control of young Blacks. Lumumba said the Navy aided this by offering unlimited weapons for easy pilfering from the Brooklyn Navy Yard when he was a gang leader.[12]

By December of '69, the 21 year-old Chicago leader Fred Hampton had risen to the top of the national ranks of the Black Panther Party. Newton, Seale, and the New York Panther leadership were in jail. Eldridge and Kathleen Cleaver were in Algeria. Oakland's David Hilliard led the Panthers National Office and assigned Hampton as the national spokesman, with LA Panther leader Geronimo Pratt next in line. Groups such as the UCLA Law Students Association invited Hampton and other Panthers to give talks nationwide.[13]

On December 3, 1969, FBI and police conducted the most brutal of all their armed attacks on Panther locales. Ex-FBI agent Wes Swearingen said that his former partner, Chicago FBI supervisor Gregg York, told him how his unit convinced Chicago police to make a twilight raid on the Panthers, assassinate Fred Hampton in particular,

gang intelligence, see Appeal, PL #413 and Transcript at 26909. Churchill and Vander Wall, Agents of Repression, pp.64-6, .endnotes 5, 24. On Tupac, personal interview with his ex-Panther business manager, Watani Tyehimba, on gang radicalization plan. On Suge Knight let off charges and worked with gang police unit against Tupac, see Randall Sullivan, LAbyrinth (New York: Atlantic Monthly Press, 2002) and Nick Broomfield, Biggie and Tupac (BBC, 2002). Tupac info elaborated on later.

10 Elaine Brown, A Taste of Power: A Black Woman's Story (New York: Anchor/Doubleday,1992), picture caption on p.216. While Brown's book is problematic in many ways, this fact doesn't appear politically motivated as her false accounts of Huey Newton do.

11 "Heavy…teen." Lumumba Shakur et al., Look for Me In the Whirlwind: A Collective Autobiography of the New York 21 (New York: Vintage) pp.139-40, 148-150. Lumumba Shakur said that his Brooklyn and Queens-based Chaplains gang, for example, had about 10,000 members and was as well armed as some countries.

12 "It's…gangs." Kempton, The Briar Patch, p. 72.

13 "By December…talks nationwide." Transcript at 28911-15, 29037-8 and 29183-4. Agents of Repression, page69 endnotes, 59, 60.

and attempt to murder many other Panthers.[14] Trial transcripts and evidence supported this admission. After the FBI made up a claim that the Panthers killed a cop, police raided Hampton's home with artillery that included a machine gun. They wounded many Panther members in their sleep. They also killed Hampton, who remained asleep in his bed after an undercover agent in the Panthers supposedly drugged the punch he had with dinner. In that raid, police also murdered a visiting southern Illinois Panther captain, Mark Clark.[15]

A future FBI assistant director came in for the cover-up while his son led attacks in Los Angeles. High level FBI supervisor Richard G. Held came in as the new Chicago chief while his son, Richard W. Held, supervised the LA FBI Cointelpro unit. Only after many years did a federal judge rule that the operation was an FBI conspiracy and awarded the survivors close to $2 million.[16]

Richard W. Held orchestrated the attempted murder of LA Panther leader Geronimo Pratt with a raid of the LA Panther office only a few days after the Chicago raid. The FBI likely had added concern about Pratt because he was a highly decorated Vietnam War veteran. Police marksmen shot up Pratt's bed through his window. Pratt luckily slept on the floor that night due to back injuries from the war and remained unharmed, though police arrested him for possibly harboring a fugitive.[17] Held's targets later included environmentalist Judi Bari, Huey Newton, and possibly even Tupac.

14 Wes Swearingen, *FBI Secrets: An Agent's Expose*, pp.88-9.

15 "Trial...Clark." Documents introduced as evidence in case of *Ibera Hampton, et al., Plaintiffs-Appellants v. Edward Hanrahan, et al., Defendants-Appellees* (Nos. 77-1968, 77-1210 and 77-1370) Transcript at 33716. In *Agents of Repression*, pp.73, 403n. On FBI falsely telling police that the Panthers killed a cop and O'Neal drugging his punch, see *Me and My Shadow: Investigation of the political left by the United States government*, Executive Producer Tarabu Betserai, Pacifica Radio Archives, track 4. Hampton's drugging also comes from Hampton's mother's testimony that Hampton was talking on the phone with her and fell asleep mid-sentence, and from an FBI agent's trial admission.

16 "A future...million." Levin, S.K., "Black Panthers Get Bittersweet Revenge," *Colorado Daily*, November 10, 1982. Also see *Plaintiffs Motion for Sanctions Against Certain Defendants and Lawyers for Violations of the Rules, Abuse of Privilege, Bad Faith and Obstruction of Justice*, Nos. 70-C-3026, 70-C-1384, Northern District of Illinois, United States District Court, 1982 (inclusive). Cited in *Agents of Repression*, p.77, endnote 128.

17 "Richard...war." A Los Angeles FBI agent and a police intelligence agent both detailed aspects of these attacks on Pratt. Intelligence agent Louis Tackwood cites the attempted execution of Pratt and his unit's FBI supervision in Louis Tackwood & Citizens Research-Intelligence Committee, *The Glass House Tapes: The Story of an Agent Provocateur and the New Police-Intelligence Complex* (New York: Avon Books,1973) pp.104, 237-8. Cited in Churchill and Vander Wall, *Agents of Repression*, pp.79, 80-1,84, 213-4n.also see, Churchill and Vander Wall, *Cointelpro Papers*, p.225. For other attacks on Pratt, see M. Wesley Swearingen, *FBI Secrets: An Agent's Expose* (Boston: South End Press, 1995), pp.82-3. Swearingen worked in the LA FBI Cointelpro unit and said the FBI selected Pratt to be "neutralized," p.87.

8

FBI RAIDS AND THE MANUFACTURE OF THE EAST/WEST PANTHER FEUD IN NYC

U .S. Intelligence appeared to take advantage of their April mass-arrest of the New York Panther 21 leaders to set up a "fugitive operation." Researchers have found evidence that U.S. Intelligence planned to have a Panther commit murder and then visit the Chicago, LA, and other Panther chapters, so that police could then raid those chapters under the guise of pursuing him. Just weeks after the April of '69 NY Panther 21 arrest, George Sams came to the New York Panthers alleging that the National Black Panther office in Oakland had sent him. Sams, who had a long criminal record and some history of mental illness, had been officially expelled from the Panthers prior to this.[1] But police attacks, arrests of Panthers around the country, as well as undercover agent infiltrators at many offices, hurt the Panthers' ability to verify Sams' statements. Sams' actions, evidence, and later government admissions support the assertion that Sams worked undercover for the FBI.

In mid-May of '69, George Sams led a young New York Panther, Alex Rackley, to take a two-hour drive with him to "inspect" the New Haven, Connecticut, Panther office. Erika Huggins, the wife of slain LA Panther leader John Huggins, had started a Black Panther chapter there. Panther cofounder Bobby Seale had visited the New Haven office just days before as he was giving a speech at nearby Yale University. When Sams and Rackley arrived at the office, Sams put a gun to Rackley's head, and held a gun to New Haven Panther George Edwards. He ordered other New Haven Panthers to tie them up, claiming they were undercover FBI agent infiltrators. Edwards, an Air Force veteran and highly committed Panther, told his fellow New Haven Panthers that Sams better shoot him now or let him go. Edwards saved himself but Rackley ended up fatally shot.[2]

In a press conference, Huey Newton said that George Sams was an FBI agent that the FBI apparently then cut from employment.[3] Several aspects of events following the murder of Rackley support his statement. First, George Sams proceeded to travel to many Panther

---

1 "In…this." M.Newton, *Bitter Grain*, p.164.
2 "George Sams…shot." Edwards told this author this and the fact that he was in the 8th Air Force Strategic Air Command during the Cold War from 1955-1961, repairing bombing and navigation systems on B-4 bombers. Personal Interview, George Edwards, 7/8/00. Also see, M. Newton, *Bitter Grain*, p.165. Raided other chapters after visits, Donald Freed, *Agony in New Haven: The Trial of Bobby Seale, Erika Huggins and the Black Panther Party* (New York: Simon and Schuster, 1973), p.25, cited in Churchill and Vander Wall, *The COINTELPRO Papers*, p.25.
3 Huey Newton, *To Die for the People*, p.224.

offices, allegedly on the run from the FBI and police. Police and FBI then used the excuse of trying to apprehend Sams to go on murderous raids at over eight Panther offices around the country, such as those in Chicago and Los Angeles that would leave Hampton dead and Pratt's bed shot up.[4] All of these raids came just *after* visits by Sams. Professor and playwright Donald Freed's published account stated that an armed Sams actually walked right through the police and FBI line in Chicago. Police used the charge of harboring the "fugitive" Sams as a reason for jailing Panthers in all the offices they raided. Legal expenses would bankrupt most of these chapters.[5]

When police finally took Sams in custody, they charged Bobby Seale and eleven of the top New Haven Panthers with the murder of Alex Rackley. Similar to how New York kept the Panther 21 in jail awaiting trial for up to two years, New Haven kept Seale and New Haven chapter founder Erika Huggins in jail for 18 months awaiting trial. One report said that Sams was the only first-hand witness called into the courtroom. That the prosecution reported basing their charges on material provided by "a trusted ten-year informant" provides strong evidence that this was Sams.[6] However, the judge dismissed the charges against Seale and Huggins. New Haven Panther Captain Lonnie McLucas was acquitted of murder and other charges but convicted of conspiracy to murder and received 12 years in jail. Ultimately, Sams ended up in prison for pulling the trigger. Newton said it was because the FBI abandoned him.[7] Sams received a life sentence but was granted parole after only four years.[8]

The FBI had also used various tactics to pit Black Panther leaders against each other. Jailing various leaders aided the FBI in these strategies. It similarly helped them with developing divisive strategies they would later use on Tupac in the '90s. While Huey Newton was in jail, the FBI first created conflicts between him and his honorary East

4 "Several aspects…up." See Donald Freed, *Agony in New Haven: The Trial of Bobby Seale, Erika Huggins and the Black Panther Party* (New York: Simon and Schuster, 1973), p.25, cited in Churchill and Vander Wall, *The COINTELPRO Papers*, p.25.

5 "Several aspects…chapters." Donald Freed, *Agony in New Haven: The Trial of Bobby Seale, Erika Huggins and the Black Panther Party* (New York: Simon and Schuster, 1973), p.25, cited in Mumia Abu-Jamal, *We Want Freedom: A Life in the Black Panther Party* (Boston: South End Press, 2004), p.140. Sams traveling around the country with seemingly limitless money and setting up Panther chapters for raids is detailed in Churchill and Vander Wall, *The COINTELPRO Papers*, p.360, note114.

6 "Also, when…Sams." Churchill and Vander Wall, *COINTELPRO Papers*, p.360, notes 113, 114.

7 "The judge…him." Chucrhill and Vander Wall, *COINTELPRO Papers*, p.360 note 118.

8 Mumia Abu-Jamal, *We Want Freedom* (Boston: South End Press,2004), p.151.

Coast Panther leaders who also led SNCC, Stokely Carmichael and H. Rap Brown. The FBI divided Newton from the SNCC leaders with the use of undercover agents and a "bad-jacketing" strategy. This strategy involved creating a fake "CIA Informant Report" list and putting it in the car of Newton and other Panther leaders.[9]

But a key "divide and conquer" strategy they used against the Panthers evolved into what would become the East Coast versus West Coast feud, pitting the New York Panther 21 against the Oakland National office. It is believed that the FBI first set up this feud by distributing fake letters to turn Huey Newton against Minister of Information Eldridge Cleaver in Algeria. Mainstream media aided them in this effort.[10] The FBI also created fake letters and used undercover agents to divide Newton's Oakland office from Afeni's imprisoned New York 21. The FBI's media collaborators then helped this become the East versus West war—a strategy that would later be used against Tupac Shakur and other rap figures.[11]

Murders of important Panthers on both coasts began. Someone killed Black Panther newspaper editor Sam Napier, and the other Panther faction was blamed. Undercover agents reportedly influenced West Coast based Newton to believe that Geronimo Pratt and his wife, Sandra, sided with Cleaver and the New York 21. Researchers Ward Churchill and Jim Vander Wall said a statement of expulsion of Pratt and most of the New York 21 in *The Black Panther* newspaper "was apparently proposed and prepared by Elaine Brown, widely suspected among former party members of having been a police agent."[12]

Years later, Pratt said that Newton told him how Elaine Brown manipulated him, particularly before a key televised debate with Eldridge Cleaver. Newton only realized it after the expulsions, at which

---

9 "The FBI…sources." See, for example, published copies of FBI documents on this strategy against the Panthers and SNCC in Churchill and Vander Wall, *The COINTELPRO Papers*, pp.126-8, including FBI memorandums dated 10/10/68 and 7/1068. Also see FBI memorandums from SAC, Chicago to Director, 1/10/1969, 3/24/69, 4/8/69 in *Agents of Repression*, pp.43-4, 49, 66. And, 10/10/68 memorandum. *COINTELPRO Papers*, pp118-19,127.

10 "But a…effort." See text of FBI COINTELPRO memorandum from G.C. Moore to W.C. Sullivan, dated 5/14/70, copied in Churchill and Vander Wall, *The Cointelpro Papers*, p149.

11 "The FBI…figures." See copies of FBI memorandums dated 2/2/71 sent to about 30 offices that attempts to split Newton and Cleaver as well as an Airtel memo that attempts to split Newton and Afeni Shakur's New York Panther 21, Churchill and Vander Wall, *The COINTELPRO Papers*, pp.160-1. M. Newton told how this was turned into an East vs. West Panther war, *Bitter Grain*, p.203. For FBI manipulation of the media in this regard, see copy of FBI memorandums dated 7/768 and 8/5/68 in which Albany, NY comments on Miami's success with a television station's Panther coverage that was sent to approximately 40 other cities' offices. Also see 10/10/68 memorandum. *COINTELPRO Papers*, pp118-19,127.

12 "Murders of important Panthers…East/West war's murders." See *COINTELPRO Papers*, pp 148-50, 362 notes 129-131. Kathleen Cleaver, Personal interview, 11/10/02.

time he tried to expel Brown, but her backers convinced him otherwise.[13] While Pratt hid from California police just after his expulsion, his pregnant wife Sandra was murdered. Panther Communications leader Kathleen Cleaver said that when she came back to the U.S. from Algeria she barely evaded her own murder in the East versus West war. Later evidence would suggest that undercover agents perpetrated most of these East/West war's murders.[14]

Lumumba Shakur's brother, New York Panther Zayd Shakur, led the New York Panthers while Lumumba, Afeni, and Sekou Odinga were in jail. Zayd worked hard to quell the East versus West feud but when he found his fellow New York Panthers murdered for unknown reasons and police were arresting Panthers without substantiation, he went underground.[15] As the New York Panther 21 went to trial by 1971, the FBI had achieved their goal of neutralizing much of the Black Panther leadership across the country through the use of harassment arrests, imprisonment, murder, and undercover agent influence.[16]

---

13 Pratt description which was delivered through an email of Kathleen Cleaver's. http://whosemedia.com/drums/2007/05/09/was-elaine-brown-an-agent/

14 "While Pratt…murders." See *COINTELPRO Papers*, pp 148-50, 362 notes 129-131. On Kathleen Cleaver, Personal interview, 11/10/02.

15 "Lumumba…underground." Assata Shakur, *Assata* (New York: Lawrence Hill, 1987), p.231.

16 One of the last Oakland Panther National Chairs, David Hilliard, also went to trial in '71. Police charged David Hilliard with the attempted murder of officers as part of their allegation that he and fellow Panthers, Eldridge Cleaver and Bobby Hutton, had a "shootout" with them. As stated above, sources described it as a police onslaught without resistance. Nonetheless, Hilliard faced the prosecuting Assistant District Attorney (ADA) Frank Vukota in court three years later. Covering the trial, the *San Francisco Chronicle* said that Vukota introduced no evidence of Hilliard ever having a gun. They also commented on ADA Vukota consistently pointing his finger a number of times at Hilliard. *The Chronicle* detailed one of several farcical moments in that trial when they reported particular interactions between ADA Vukota, David Hilliard and his defense attorney Vincent Hallihan. First, Hilliard had to sit through Hallihan describing him and his fellow Panthers as dim-witted when addressing the jury: "we have to think how these rather simple people felt at the time (of the shootout)." *The Chronicle* then said that when Hilliard was sitting on the witness stand, ADA Vukota "went over near Hilliard, and pointing his finger once again, said, 'he has hatreds.' Hilliard, cool and restrained during most of the trial, leaned forward and said to the prosecutor, 'you've got hatreds.'" While Vukota admitted that Hilliard may not have had a gun, Hilliard received a several year jail sentence as a result of that trial. Donovan Bess, "Case Goes to Jury: Hilliard Trial's Bitter End," *The San Francisco Chronicle*, 6/11/71, p.5. On sentence, see M. Newton, *Bitter Grain*, pp.78, 210.

THE PANTHER
21 TRAGICOMIC
TRIAL

"Black Panther historians argue themselves over the beginning at the spirit of the Black Panther Party. Some say it had its beginnings around 400 years ago when you first decided we were not human beings. Others attribute it to the 100 million or so that you killed on slave ships. Others to Gabriel Prosser, Denmark Vesey, Nat Turner and of course [military general and Haitian slave rebellion leader] Toussaint L'Ouverture. Some even say it began at the time of the fugitive slave act and the Dred Scott decision. But...all agree on the modern adaptation of it—that Franz Fanon put it on paper, that Malcolm X put it into words, and that Huey P. Newton put it into action."

—Afeni Shakur, *Rat*, 1970. *The Black Panthers Speak*.[1]

Individuals from racially diverse revolutionary groups soon crowded the underground due to the FBI's Cointelpro repression. The Weather Underground (a.k.a. Weathermen) led a "cadre" organization of mostly white revolutionary anti-war and anti-racism groups nationwide. Other Panther-aligned groups modeled their programs after the Panther programs and experienced similar, though less brutal, repression. These included the aforementioned Puerto Rican Young Lords, The White Panthers in Detroit, and the American Indian Movement (AIM), as well as socialist, communist, and anarchist groups throughout the country.[2]

While space precludes extensive details, the U.S. Intelligence attacks on AIM were particularly brutal. Besides the typical assassinations, U.S. Intelligence used other tactics against AIM in a brutal reign of terror starting in the early '70s. For example, when the last national AIM leader, John Trudell, protested on the U.S. Capitol steps and burned an American flag, his house was burned down within hours. His pregnant wife, mother-in-law, and three young children died in the blaze (see notes).[3]

1 Afeni Shakur, "We Will Win: A Letter from Prison," originally in *Rat*, January 7-20, 1970, collected in ed. Philip Foner, *The Black Panthers Speak* (New York: Da Capo Press, 1970,95), p.161
2 "Individuals from...groups." See Churchill and Vander Wall, *Agents of Repression: The FBI's Secret War Against the Black Panther Party and the American Indian Movement*. Also see their, *The COINTELPRO Papers: Documents from the FBI's Secret Wars Against Dissent in the United States*. American Indian Movement (AIM) representatives as well as Young Lords representatives had said they modeled some of their programs on the Panther survival programs. Lee Lew Lee, *All Power to the People* (documentary film, 1996).
3 "While space...inside (see notes)." Of the many brutal assaults on the American Indian Movement, the story of John Trudell, AIM's last national leader is particularly heart-wrenching. This FBI-targeted AIM leader had been warned in the late '70s that if he didn't stop his Indian rights work that his family would be killed. Trudell protested on the Washington DC Capitol steps and someone burned down his house within hours. His wife, Tina, his mother-in-law Leah Hicks-Manning, and his three young children were all killed in that incident. *Agents of Repression*,

Another infamous U.S. Intelligence attack on AIM gained international attention partly through actor/producer Robert Redford's documentary, *Incident at Oglala*. In that 1975 South Dakota incident, an FBI force attacked an AIM house on the Pine Ridge Reservation. Two FBI agents and an AIM member were killed. AIM member Leonard Peltier languishes in jail despite a federal prosecutor admitting that the government "doesn't know who shot the agents." Numerous international groups, leaders, and celebrities have since attempted to gain Peltiers' release with FBI documents to help prove his innocence, to no avail.[4]

The fear of being drafted into possible slaughter during the Vietnam War radicalized much of white America. After its 1960 inception, the predominantly white Students for a Democratic Society (SDS) had gone from being a group that organized around civil rights and economic issues to the largest antiwar organization in the country with an estimated membership between 80-100,000 at its peak by the end of 1968. In its final year, 1969, the SDS leadership split due to a disagreement on tactics, though it is believed undercover FBI infiltrators helped magnify these divisions. At least half of the SDS leaders formed a new group they called The Weathermen (later Weather Underground for feminist reasons), which would embrace militant tactics.[5]

Other civil rights and anti-war activists also became disillusioned by the seemingly small effect of their peaceful protests, while violent attacks on leftist groups went unprosecuted. Racists and reactionaries, either working for U.S. Intelligence or unprosecuted by U.S. courts, conducted hundreds of bombings and murders. These included bombings of Black churches and buildings as well as murders of Blacks and their white activist supporters.[6] Blacks reacted partly by

pp.362-3. When he finally got out of mourning, Trudell went on to become a musician. His albums include *Graffiti Man*. On other horrors in American indian history, see *Agents of Repression*, and for example, see .pbs.org/wghb/aia/part4/4h1567.html . For other info, see Howard Zinn, *A People's History of the United States*.

4 Jon Lurie, "The Wiping of the Tears: 25 Years after the era of A.I.M. Militancy on Pine Ridge, " reprinted from *The Circle*, 8/1/00, oocities.org/crazyoglala/WipingTears_Lurie.html. On FBI documents supporting frame up of Peltier, see, for example, Churchill and Vander Wall, The COINTELPRO Papers, copy of document in the book, p.272.

5 "The fear...reasons)." The most comprehensive source for information on SDS is Kirkpatrick Sale, *SDS* (New York: Vintage, 1974), p.664. On membership numbers see p.664. Also see, former SDS president Todd *Gitlin's The Sixties: Years of Hope, Days of Rage* (New York: Bantam, 1989). On see, for example, their *Prairie Fire: The Politics of Revolutionary Anti-Imperialism; Political Statement of the Weather Underground*, (Communications Co., 1974), published in hiding.

6 "Other civil...supporters." While Black radicals bore the brunt of FBI tactics, the FBI used violence against white radicals, too. For example, an FBI-sponsored group, The Secret Army Organization, shot up the house of a white radical, San Diego State economics professor Peter Bohmer. The Secret Army Organization leader, FBI infiltrator Howard Godfrey, was in the car from where the shots were fired. A grand jury in Chicago found that the FBI and Army Intelligence had cooperated in funding and directing a right wing terrorist organization against left wing activists throughout that city. Zoccino, Nanda, "Ex-FBI Informer Describes Terrorist Role," *Los Angeles Times*, January 26, 1976. Also see Parenti, Michael, *Democracy for the Few*, (New York: St. Martin's Press, 1980), p.24. Cited in Churchill and Vander Wall, *Agents of Repression*, p.203, 377

rioting, which some leading sociologists claimed was the key to getting civil rights legislation passed.[7] At least several groups of activists began retaliating by planting their own time bombs in buildings of companies connected to Vietnam War atrocities. These activists would call to get the bomb sites evacuated in order to spare innocent people from physical harm.[8]

The Weather Underground would most notably use this bomb planting tactic. In response to Fred Hampton and Mark Clark's murders, for example, they blew up Chicago police cars and a Haymarket Square police statue. They also claimed to always evacuate people from the area of bombings and proceeded to carry out at least 20 more bombings in the early '70s. These were a small percentage of an estimated several thousand student-linked political bombing incidents, in a two year period alone, to protest the Vietnam war and racist government actions.[9] They also used a myriad of other tactics that included newspaper and book publishing in response to the U.S. military and police assaults on Black and third world people.

The Weather Underground, the Panthers, and other revolutionary groups survived for a number of years because of above ground support. Various celebrities, politicians, and activists aided them in their mission. These included actors such as Donald Southerland, Jane Fonda, Marlon Brando, and Jean Seberg (who was particularly targeted amongst actors), politicians Tom Hayden and Shirley Chisolm, and musicians such as John Lennon, Jimi Hendrix, and composer Leonard Bernstein. Bernstein even held fundraisers for the New York Panthers and helped accumulate money towards their exorbitant bail.[10]

The New York Panther 21 gained huge international publicity. Several books exclusively covered them and, because of this massive

7 Frances Fox Piven and Richard A. Cloward, *Poor People's Movements: Why They Succeed, How They Fail* (New York: Vintage, 1977).

8 "At least...harm." Jane Alpert, *Growing Up Underground* (New York: Citadel, 1989).

9 "The Weather Underground...time." On their list of bombings, see *Prairie Fire: The Politics of Revolutionary Anti-Imperialism*, (CommunicationsCo., 1974) p.16. This book was published by the Weather Underground leadership in hiding. This was part of an estimated 2,800 student-linked political bombing incidents in a 15 month period at this time to fight racism and stop the Vietnam War, according to Kirkpatrick Sale, *SDS* (New York: Vintage, 1974), p.632. Sale used figures drawn from an Alcohol, Tobacco and Firearms of the Dept. of Treasury survey to come up with these figures.

10 "The Weather...bail." See for example, Hayden and Fonda in M. Wesley Swearingen, *FBI Secrets*; Chisolm and Bernstein, Zimroth, *Perversions of Justice*; Hendrix in "Jimi Hendrix, Black Power and Money," *Teenset*, January, 1969; and, Constantine, *Covert War Against Rock*, p.61. Douglas Pringle, *The Jimi Hendrix Companion* (New York: Simon & Schuster, MacMillan, 1996), p.63. Brando in Lee Lew-Lee, *All Power to the People* (documentary, 1995). Southerland, Robert Sam Anson, "To Die Like a Gangsta," *Vanity Fair*, March 1997. Lennon in Fenton Bresler, *Who Killed John Lennon?* (New York: St. Martins, 1989). Regarding Bernstein's support, it's interesting to note that an FBI memorandum dated 5/21/70 was directed at Bernstein, who was Jewish, for his Panther support. It discussed manufacturing anti-Semitic literature that would be attributed to the Panthers and sent to Bernstein. Another FBI memo discussed success with this tactic in setting the Jewish Defense League against the Panthers. See *COINTELPRO Papers*, pp162-3.This was another strategy duplicated later against Tupac in the '90s.

support leading up to the trial, the 21 Panther defendants dwindled down to about 13. Some were held on charges elsewhere while others, such as Dharuba (born Richard Moore) and Cetewayo (born Michael Tabor) gained release on bail and escaped to join Odinga and the Cleaver faction in Algeria. The indictment counts also dwindled down from 30 counts charged to each defendant, to 12 for each.[11]

Afeni Shakur rose to stardom as a leader, acting as her own trial lawyer during this time. The New York 21 had chosen Afeni for first release on the raised bail and they made her their spokesperson and Harlem leader as they awaited trial for close to two years. It is during this release that Afeni became pregnant with Tupac. Most media reports claim New Jersey Panther Billy Garland was Tupac's father. Lumumba, still jailed, divorced her upon hearing the news of her pregnancy.

After several months the judge then revoked all bail and Afeni was back in prison. Afeni fought to keep her pregnancy while studying to defend herself in court as her own attorney. She petitioned for a daily glass of milk and egg to keep her fetus healthy as she studied law books in prison. She had plenty of time, however, as a major publisher said the Panther 21 trial was the longest trial in the history of the state and, possibly, the longest trial in the history of the U.S. [12]

Afeni was up against a lot. The Assistant District Attorney (ADA) prosecuting the case, Joseph Phillips, introduced six undercover agents as witnesses. The judge showed his continual bias throughout the trial, from setting each Panther's bail at an absurd $100,000 to prompting ADA Phillips about what to say. A former Justice Department lawyer also complained that the judge and prosecutor met nightly to confer on how to gain a guilty verdict. (Regarding the bail, when Phillips showed a film in the court, *The Battle of Algiers*, as evidence the Panthers used this movie to learn bombing tactics, several Panthers with obstructed views responded, "We paid $100,000 for a ticket and can't see the movie."). [13]

Early in the New York trial, defense attorney Gerald Lefourt asked Eugene Roberts, "Isn't it a fact that you helped murder Malcolm X?"

"YES!" Afeni exclaimed from her chair.

11 "'The New York...each." Zimroth, *Perversions of Justice*, pp.9-12, 297-9. Jasmine Guy, *Afeni Shakur: Evolution of a Revolutionary*, pp.107-110. Kempton, *Briar Patch*, and Lumumba Shakur, Afeni Shakur et al: *Look for Me in the Whirlwind.*.

12 "After several...U.S." Note from publisher of autobio, *Look For Me In the Whirlwind*, p363. Also see Jasmine Guy, *Afeni Shakur: Evolution of a Revolutionary* (New York: Atria, 2004), pp.110-11.

13 "Afeni was up...movie.')." Zimroth, *Perversions of Justice: The Prosecution and Acquittal of the Panther 21,*, pp.160, 289-92.

Even the Panther 21 trial Judge John Murtagh, who had been so antagonistic to the Panthers, said "Yes, we would all like to know the truth about the assassination."[14] Among the undercover police agents infiltrating the New York Black Panthers, Eugene (Gene) Roberts and two others were there from its inception. Bureau Of Special Services (BOSS) agent Roberts had formerly infiltrated Malcolm X's Muslim Mosque Number One. Undercover agent Roberts had joined Malcolm's security detail and said he was the first to arrive at Malcolm's body and he "proceeded to give Malcolm X mouth-to-mouth resuscitation." As noted earlier, evidence supports that he was there to make sure U.S. Intelligence succeeded in the assassination of Malcolm.[15]

At the 1969 trial, Afeni's legal study paid off, as did her brilliant court performance. When the judge denied most every legal motion set forward by Afeni, she showed the jury how he had completely stopped listening to what she was saying. The judge had denied many objections by Afeni to the district attorney's lies and illegal tactics. For example, Afeni said, "May I state for the record that, whether you are demanding that I refrain from making objections or not, Mr. Murtagh, what you are in effect doing is denying me my right to defend myself. If you are going to demand that I not make objections, then I ask you to demand that the district attorney stop standing up in open court and telling continuous lies."

"Request denied," replied the judge.

So, after a query by the other lawyer about how court rules allow objections, and Judge Murtagh stating that Afeni was acting "disorderly," Afeni finally asked, "May we ask the district attorney to cooperate in having a just trial?"

"Request denied," said the judge, causing Panther-supporting courtroom spectators to erupt with laughter.

Jurors later said they took particular note of this response by the judge. They also would note being "thrilled" when 23 year-old Afeni, only 5'4" and 5-8 months pregnant with Tupac during the trial, told the rotund, white ADA Phillips to sit down during the trial.[16] Books documented these and other moments where various Panthers

14 Kempton, The Briar Patch: The People of the State of New York V. Lumumba Shakur Et Al, p200.

15 Kempton, pp.200-201. "What appeared to be twenty minutes later," Roberts finished "police finally got there and took him over to the medical center." This disclosure contradicts police officer Henry's attempt to call backup officers and Police Inspector Taylor's claim of 20 police officers at the Ballroom.

16 "But Afeni's legal...trial." With Judge Murtagh. Kempton, The Briar Patch, 246-8. This and jurors comments this remark, Peter Zimroth, Perversions of Justice, pp.288, 368, 376-7.

entertained their courtroom supporters by mocking the prosecutors (see footnote).[17]

Many revolutionary anti-war Panther supporters watched the New York 21 trial closely in the courtroom and on the news. But one group took action against the judge's particular show of bias. Early in the trial someone set off a bomb at the judge's home. Two reports cited the Weather Underground as planting this bomb.[18]

The jury went out to decide their verdict for about two hours. When they came back, the court clerk repeated each of the 12 counts individually for all 13 defendants, saying, "How do you find, sir?" In the end, half of the drained and embattled Panther defendants finally found freedom after 2 years of incarceration.

To each count of every defendant, 156 total, the foreman of the jury responded, "Not guilty." Afeni Shakur sobbed quietly, as did Panther defense attorney Gerald Lefcourt and several jurors. Spectators called out, "Right on!" and "Power to the people!" Many jurors and writers credited Afeni's trial work for getting all of the Panther 21 off.

---

17 Afeni said that she and the other Panthers were upset about Dharuba Moore and Cetewayo Tabor failing to help raise more bail for the others. The Panthers then worried that the two skipping bail for Algeria would hurt their case. Jasmine Guy, *Afeni Shakur: Evolution of a Revolutionary*, pp.107-110. But they weren't so upset that they couldn't get some entertainment from Tabor and Eldridge Cleaver during the trial. Just before closing his case, ADA Joseph Phillips brought up the issue of Dharuba Moore and Cetewayo Tabor in Algeria. ADA Phillips presented a taped phone call he had of Tabor. He introduced the tape stating, "He threatens to kill me. You know what he must have thought, 'To hell with the other defendants. I'm clear. I can say anything I want.' " With his back to the defendants, Phillips played the tape, which began with, "Mr. Tabor, this is ADA Phillips in New York County, and we have a number of problems that you have created as a result of your leaving New York."

Tabor responded, "Hello, motherfucker, who is this?...*the* Phillips?" "Yes the Phillips, the one you refer to as 'pig Phillips.'" "Yes, pig Phillips, yeah. Right on." "How do you like Algiers, Mr. Tabor? [Pause ten seconds.] Mr. Tabor, hello, hello, Mr. Tabor." "Joe? Joe Blow." "Who is this?" asked Phillips. "This is Eldridge Cleaver, who is this?" "ADA Phillips...we have to advise him of his rights." "Are you recording this?" asked Cleaver. "Yes, I am," said Phillips. "So are we," said Cleaver, "and I want to inform you of the charges against you." Phillips laughed, "I don't want to be informed of any charges. I've got enough problems with my own case without getting any additional cases today, Mr. Cleaver." Cleaver continued, "You are wanted for crimes against the people." "Now wait a minute, I, uh, uh [laugh]. If you say so," Phillips responded. "We plan to see to it that you die for your crimes...Joe Blow," said Cleaver. "May I speak with Mr. Moore?" asked Phillips. "Take that shit off your fucking calendar because we're through with your fuckin' courts. We're through with you from now on. It's war. Do you understand that?" Cleaver asked rhetorically. "Mr. Cleaver, do you believe a man of your, uh, of your purported intellect and writing ability has to degenerate to that type of argument or vilification?" "You're no good...death to all fascist pigs and that includes you," Cleaver concluded and passed the phone over to Ceteweyo [Tabor]. "What did you say, Joe?" "I thought you might be able to give us some assistance in finding Mr. Moore," said Phillips. "You know I wouldn't give you any assistance of any kind, Joe." "My opinion, Mr. Tabor, is that in talking to me and authorizing us to tell the court...you have rendered considerable assistance to us."

"I'll be seeing you soon, Joe, and, uh, what has to be done is just something that has been decreed by the masses of the people. You see, you know and I know that you are guilty...and give Murtagh my regards too...and tell him we'll get back; I'll be knocking at your door one night... 'Power to the People' and death to the fascist pig."

"Uh, Mr. Tabor, uh, I'm surprised that after all that we have gone through you can still utter threats to kill people. It's rather remarkable; you think you would have learned that, uh, killing people is not the solution to any problem. [Five second pause.] Are you still there, Mr. Tabor? [Seven second pause.] Hello. Hello."

Phillips concluded that this tape had proven his point and nailed the Panthers on trial. He expected shock and worry from the defendants he had his back to. But when he turned in triumph to look upon them, the thirteen Panthers were laughing. Kempton, *The Briar Patch*, pp.189-94.

18 "Many revolutionary ...bomb." M. Newton, *Bitter Grain*, p.191. Also on Weather Underground bombing judge's home, see Zimroth, *Perversions of Justice*, p52. The Weather Underground's leadership didn't list this among their bombings cited in a later book, *Prairie Fire*, which they published in 1974.

Lumumba Shakur and five others remained in jail, as the state had lodged warrants against them for other crimes.[19]

---

19 "In the end...crimes." On courtroom scene, jury time of deliberations, etc. see quoted trial transcript and spectator Zimroth in Zimroth, *Perversions of Justice*, pp.308-9. On jury and writer's opinions crediting Afeni with winning case for Panthers, see Zimroth's interviews, pp.310 on, particularly pp.367-8, 377 and Connie Bruck "The Takedown of Tupac," *The New Yorker*, 7/7/97, p. 47. On Lumumba and others' stay in jail after verdict, Zimroth, *Perversions of Justice*, p.310.

10

LABELLED TERRORISTS

"Chemical warfare began to change the shape and attitude of the brothers and sisters who participated in, what we called then, the revolution. Whether it be the civil rights aspect of integrating into or assimilating into America, or the revolutionary nationalist fight for self-determination and/or liberation by nationhood. ...[Our] ability to fight chemical warfare was a significant contribution. ...So the Lincoln Detox became not only recognized by the community as a political formation but its work in developing and saving men and women...we began to move around the country and educated other communities around acupuncture drug withdrawal."

—Mutulu Shakur[1]

Arguably one of the single most important historical factors aiding the New York Panther 21 and other embattled Black Panthers was the continuing shift in the general perception of Black revolutionaries. The activist burglary of an FBI office had a huge effect on changing this climate. In March of 1971, two months before the Panther 21 trial ended, activists broke into a Media, Pennsylvania FBI office. They removed a thousand documents and exposed the FBI Counter Intelligence Program, a vast program against law-abiding citizens protesting against the Vietnam War and for civil rights and economic justice.

The documents also showed the FBI's sophisticated tactics and collaborative work with local police and many mainstream media outlets nationwide. The activists' distribution of these documents influenced Congress and mainstream media outlets to at least acknowledge some of these brutal FBI agents employed byCointelpro. More independent publishers released books based on these documents. Independent magazines also published articles revealing the FBI's illegal and murderous targeting of leftists groups.[2]

For public relations' sake, the FBI officially ended Cointelpro in 1971. However, agents and later events support that the program

---

1 "Interview from Lompoc Federal Prison with Tyehimba Jess of WHBK Radio in Chicago,"10/30/92, http://mutulushakur.com/site/1992/10/interview-on-acupuncture/.

2 "Arguably...Cointelpro." On Media break-in, Churchill and Vander Wall, *The COINTELPRO Papers*, pp.xi, 332. See for example, *The FBI's Covert Program to Destroy the Black Panther Party*, 94th Congress, 2nd Session, U.S. Government Printing Office, Washington, D.C., 1976. Seymour Hersh, "CIA Reportedly Recruited Blacks for Surveillance of Panther Party," *New York Times*, March 17, 1978, p. A1, A16. quoted in Huey P. Newton, *War Against the Panthers* (New York: Harlem River Press/Writers and Readers Publishing, 1996), p.90.

continued. For example, former Cointelpro agent M. Wesley Swearingen said that the FBI actually continued the program under different names[3] Various judges later agreed that an FBI/police Cointelpro continued against Black activists.[4]

More and more U.S. Intelligence agents ended their careers and risked their lives to reveal how their groups initiated the terrorism against leftists. In 1973, Louis Tackwood, the agent working in Los Angeles' version of BOSS, the Criminal Conspiracy Section (CCS), described how the FBI had a liaison agent in CCS and vice versa. Tackwood gave hours of description that became the book, *The Glass House Tapes*. CIA agents such as Phil Agee and Victor Marchetti also published exposés on the Central Intelligence Agency. Marchetti's book came out only after court-enforced CIA deletions. Agee circumvented CIA censorship by first publishing his book in England.[5]

Afeni Shakur kept up her activism after giving birth to Tupac Amaru Shakur on June 16, 1971, a month after her release from prison following her trial acquittal. She immediately set him on a revolutionary course. Calling him her "Black prince of the revolution," she named him after the last Incan leader to die trying to fight off the Spanish invaders. She also named her close friend, LA Panther leader Geronimo Pratt, Tupac's godfather (some sources say Afeni further named her close friend Assata Shakur as Tupac's godmother).[6]

By that time, police began new attacks on Geronimo Pratt. Wes Swearingen and other agents testified that LA FBI informants set Pratt up on a murder frame-up. In his memoir, former FBI agent Swearingen said he looked into the FBI's file on Pratt and saw that they had on audiotape that Pratt was hundreds of miles away in Oakland just before and after the murder.[7] An FBI-paid lawyer had infiltrated Pratt's defense counsel, according to the California Attorney-General's office in a declaration filed in court, and the FBI paid another person on

3 Deposition of former FBI agent M. Wesley Swearingen, taken in October 1980, in Honolulu, Hawaii, p.2, in Churchill and Vander Wall, *Agents of Repression*, p.62

4 *Handschu, et al vs. Special Services Division a/k/a Bureau of Special Services*, U.S. District Court, S.D.N.Y., 71 Civ. 2203 (CSH) Memorandum Opinion and Order, Mar. 7, 1985, p.26. Ibid, Memorandum Opinion and Order, May 24, 1979, p.3. Connie Bruck, "The Takedown of Tupac," *The New Yorker*, 7/7/97, p.54.

5 "More and more…England." Citizens Research and Investigation Committee and Louis Tackwood, *The Glass House Tapes: The Story of an Agent Provocateur and the New Police-Intelligence Complex* (New York: Avon Books, 1973). Phil Agee, *Inside the Company* (New York: Bantam, 1975). Victor Marchetti and John Marks, *The CIA and the Cult of Intelligence* (New York: Dell,1974).

6 "Afeni…godmother)." Connie Bruck, "The Takedown of Tupac," *The New Yorker*, 7/7/97, p.47. On Assata Shakur, see editorial, "Thoughts and Notes on Tupac," *The Amsterdam News*, 12/17/94, p.24.

7 Wes Swearingen, *FBI Secrets: An Agent's Expose* (Boston: South End Press, 1995), p.86.

Pratt's defense team. This led to Pratt's conviction and imprisonment for over 25 years.[8]

Afeni regularly traveled to the West Coast to help with Pratt's legal defense team of activist lawyers who helped Pratt for years. While they initially failed to acquit Pratt, the lawyers did uncover the various forces teamed up against him and eventually exonerated him. A judge finally ruled in his favor (Geronimo dropped his birth name and changed his last name to ji Jaga by that time). Pratt's lawyers found that the CIA had joined forces with the FBI in their attacks on Pratt. *New York Times* journalist Seymour Hersh found that the CIA went against its charter (to not work against Americans inside U.S. borders) by spying on many American leftists inside the U.S. The U.S. ended up awarding Pratt several million dollars for false imprisonment.[9]

Afeni continued her activism and accepted invitations to speak at Harvard, Yale, and many other colleges nationwide. With the assistance of Lumumba's adopted brother, Mutulu Shakur, she would begin work on an historic lawsuit against the New York police. This suit would bring about the broadest restriction on any city's police intelligence activities.[10]

By 1973 Afeni moved in with Mutulu, a cofounder of the Republic of New Afrika (RNA).[11] The RNA was politically aligned with the Panthers, had similar goals, and experienced similar police repression. The RNA formed in 1968 when 500 grassroots activists had met in Detroit to declare independence for the Black nation inside the U.S. The following year, police attacked the RNA convention at Rev. C.L. Franklin's ("Queen of Soul" Aretha's father) New Bethel Church in Detroit. Police fired 800 rounds in the church and then held 150

8 "An FBI-paid…years." Amnesty International, *Proposal for a commision of inquiry into the effect of domestic intelligence activities on criminal trial in the United States of America* (Amnesty International: New York,1980), p.25. Cited in Churchill and Vander Wall, *Agents of Repression*, p.91.

9 "Afeni regularly…U.S." On Pratt's legal settlement, Todd Purdum, "Ex Black Panther Wins Long Legal Battle," *The New York Times*, April 27,2000, p.A18. On CIA joining forces with FBI against Pratt, with CHAOS against Pratt, see Alex Constantine, *The Covert War Against Rock* (Venice, CA: Feral House, 2000), pp.15,18; and Angus McKenzie, *Secrets: The CIA's War at Home* (Berkeley: University of California Press, 1999), p.69. CIA spying on Americans, Seymour Hersh, "Huge C.I.A. Operation Reported in U.S. Against Antiwar Forces, Other Dissidents in Nixon Years," *New York Times*, 12/22/74, p.A1.

10 "Afeni…activities." Speaking at colleges, Connie Bruck, *The New Yorker*, p.47. *Handschu, et al vs. Special Services Division a/k/a Bureau of Special Services*, U.S. District Court, S.D.N.Y., 71 Civ. 2203 (CSH) Memorandum Opinion and Order, December 16, 1981, p.6. Benjamin Weiser, "Threats and Responses: Law Enforcement" *New York Times*, 2/12/03, p.17. Also, Associated Press, "Judge Backs Expanded Police Surveillance," *New York Times*, 3/22/03, p.2.

11 Personal interview, Watani Tyehimba, 5/10/00. Former Panther Teyhimba has been a friend of Afeni since that time. Also see, *Can't Jail the Spirit: Political Prisoner in the U.S.* (Chicago: Committee to End the Marion Lockdown, 2002), p.65.

people incommunicado before a judge set up court in the police station and got most of them released.[12]

Lumumba and Mutulu's brother, NYC Panther Zayd Shakur, started a new militant self-defense group. Zayd, who had gone underground after having his life threatened trying to mend the East/West Panther rift, worked with Panther Sekou Odinga to form the Black Liberation Army (BLA). The BLA reportedly protected activist leaders from armed police assault by regularly positioning snipers in various rooftop locations.[13]

Afeni and Zayd's close NYC Panther friend Assata Shakur (born Joanne Chesimard) had quit the Panthers because of the East/West feud. However, the respect Assata attained amongst other Panthers due to her vast political knowledge and her speaking abilities led to continued targeting despite her exit from the group. She continued finding white detectives following her around in her Harlem neighborhood. One day in 1970, she saw her picture on the front page of the *Daily News* saying police wanted her for questioning regarding a cop's murder. In fear, she joined her close friend Zayd in his underground hiding. Tupac knew Assata as his aunt.[14]

The FBI started a propaganda campaign against Assata Shakur, calling her "the revolutionary mother hen" of the Black Liberation Army. They accused the BLA of murdering a number of New York City police officers (most of these accusations came with little evidence and few valid convictions). The FBI conducted a nationwide manhunt for Assata in 1972.[15] Posters with her face appeared in police precincts and banks that cited her involvement in serious criminal activities, putting her on the FBI's most wanted list, and to all levels of police she became a shoot-to-kill target.[16]

12 "The RNA...released." On RNA alignment with Panthers, see Huey Newton, "To the Republic of New Afrika: September 13, 1969," *To Die for the People* (New York: Writers and Readers Publishing, 1972,99), pp.96-101. On RNA founding, Chokwe Lumumba, "20ᵗʰ Anniversary Commemoration of the Historic New Bethel Incident," *By Any Means Necessary!* Vol.5, No.2, 1989, NAPO, Box 31762, Jackson, MS 39286, p.11. On New Bethel Attack, Dan Georga.k.a.s and Marvin Surkin, *Detroit: I Do Mind Dying* (New York: St. Martin's Press, 1975), pp.664-8. Both of these last two sources and their information was obtained in the essay "A Brief History of the New Afrikan Prison Struggle," by Sundiata Acoli, p.10-11. Acoli is an imprisoned former New York Panther 21 member who was attacked in a car with Zayd and Assata Shakur. This essay can be found at freedomarchives.org/. His bio and contact info can be found in *Can't Jail the Spirit: Political Prisoner in the U.S.* (Chicago: Committee to End the Marion Lockdown, 2002), p.65.
13 On Zayd Shakur and Sekou Odinga as founding the BLA, see Churchill and Vander Wall, *The COINTELPRO Papers*, pp. 306-7. On snipers, Lee Lew Lee, *All Power to the People*.
14 "Afeni and Zayd's...his aunt." Assata Shakur, *Assata*, pp.231-4. On Tupac's aunt Assata, Cathy Scott, *The Killing of Tupac Shakur* (Las Vegas: Huntington Press, 1997), p.65
15 "Afeni would...Assata in 1972." *The COINTELPRO Papers*, p.308
16 Lennox Hinds, on behalf of the National Conference of Black Lawyers, in a petition to the United Nations Commision on Human Rights. 12/11/78. "The Injustice of the Trial." In *Covert Action Quarterly*, #65, Fall 1998, p.43.

In May of 1973, New Jersey police pulled over Zayd and Assata Shakur's car. Police fatally shot Zayd, while wounding Assata and former Panther 21 member Sundiata Acoli. Shots from one of the three killed a police officer. Assata said that police proceeded to beat her at the scene and torture her in a hospital. She said that in the hospital, she was only saved from more torture when a white nurse intervened. But, she said, prison officials used torturous tactics on her thereafter.[17]

New Jersey police charged Assata with killing the police officer. The case didn't reach trial for four years because prosecutors brought Assata to trial six times for alleged involvement in a half dozen other major criminal actions spanning from 1971 to 1973. They failed to gain a conviction at any of those hearings.[18]

By 1976, Assata's lead trial lawyer, Stanley Cohen, reported several breakthroughs in her case. He was found dead soon after with all his papers stolen.[19] At the trial, Assata's other lawyers presented tests and medical experts to prove her innocence in court. For example, Assata's fingers tested negative for gun residue when police conducted it. Furthermore, doctors' findings supported that police shot Assata while she was in a seated position with her hands raised and that the bullet immediately severed a median nerve that wouldn't have allowed her to pull a gun trigger. Nonetheless, prosecutors won a conviction against her for killing the police officer during that '73 stop. [20]

Afeni Shakur worked with Mutulu Shakur on his Cointelpro Litigation and Research activities, the success of which was supposed to stop the Counter Intelligence Program (Cointelpro). Mutulu Shakur's life-long activism put him under constant FBI surveillance. His work with the Revolutionary Action Movement and leadership of the Republic of New Afrika likely brought on this surveillance. Mutulu's FBI file revealed that agents' reports on him were delivered to the FBI Director every 3 months since he was 19 years old. Mutulu Shakur also cofounded and directed the National Task Force for Cointelpro Litigation and Research.[21]

While traveling to Los Angeles to aid in Geronimo Pratt's defense, Afeni also advocated for the Panther platform as she worked

---

17 "In May...thereafter." On torture, see Assata Shakur, *Assata* , pp.3-11, 82-3. On mass of evidence supporting her innocence, see Lennox Hinds, on behalf of the National Conference of Black Lawyers, in a petition to the United Nations Commision on Human Rights. 12/11/78. "The Injustice of the Trial," In *Covert Action Quarterly*, #65, Fall 1998, p.43. Also, *The COINTELPRO Papers*, p.308. Assata Shakur, *Assata*, pp.3,5, 9-10, 82-3.
18 See chart of trial charges and outcomes in Assata Shakur, *Assata*, p.xiv.
19 Assata Shakur, *Assata*, p.247.
20 "At...stop." Lennox Hinds, "The Injustice of the Trial." *Covert Action Quarterly*, Fall 1998, #65, p.43.
21 "Mutulu Shakur's...Chicago." Committee to End the Marion Lockdown, *Can't Jail the Spirit: Political Prisoners in the U.S.* (Chicago: CEML, 2002), pp.147-50.

on an historic New York lawsuit brought on by a wide-array of anti-war activists, such as Abbie Hoffman.[22] Similar to a lawsuit taking place in Chicago after Fred Hampton's murder, the New York lawsuit accused the New York police department of violating the legal rights of New York activists with everything from illegal spying to perpetrating violence against activists. After close to a decade, a judge agreed with most of the lawsuit's charges and the suit's lead lawyer, Barbara Handschu, helped the group gain the most restrictions on police intelligence of any city nationwide. This forced the NYPD to "officially" end it's police Cointelpro activities.[23] In the '80s, the judge for that case found that the NYPD had continued its Cointelpro activities with a police unit targeting Blacks called The Black Desk.[24]

Mutulu Shakur made his living by using a Canadian degree in acupuncture to combat the heroin epidemic. According to a PBS Frontline investigation, the CIA contributed to this epidemic by admitting in their documents that they were trafficking heroin out of the Vietnam area during the war.[25] Mutulu helped direct the Bronx's Lincoln Detox, where he and other activists also politically educated clients. These activists were linked to Black nationalism, the Latino community's Young Lords, and the white SDS/Weather Underground. They said that they were fighting the "chemical warfare" being waged on their communities. Despite its reported success, New York City defunded Lincoln Detox. Mutulu continued his work anyway, founding a national acupuncture group. He was invited to China to further his work with acupuncture. The Zimbabwe Afrikan National Union also invited Mutulu to visit their country in 1980, because of his continued political leadership.[26]

---

22 "Afeni was the first…settlement as it affects Black activists.'" Handschu, et al vs. Special Services Division a/k/a Bureau of Special Services, U.S. District Court, S.D.N.Y., 71 Civ. 2203 (CSH) Memorandum Opinion and Order, December 16, 1981, p.6.

23 Ibid, Memorandum Opinion and Order, May 24, 1979, p.3. Also see, Handschu, et al vs. Special Services Division a/k/a Bureau of Special Services, U.S. District Court, S.D.N.Y., 71 Civ. 2203 (CSH) Memorandum Opinion and Order, Mar. 7, 1985, p.26. And on widest restrictions, New York Sun, 12/5/02, and Benjamin Weiser, "Threats and Responses: Law Enforcement" New York Times, 2/12/03, p.17. Also, Associated Press, "Judge Backs Expanded Police Surveillance," New York Times, 3/22/03, p.2.

24 Barbara Handschu et al, plaintiffs, Rev. Calvin Butts, Sonny Carson, C. Vernon Mason, Michael Warren, Intervenors v. Special Services Division a/k/a Bureau of Special Services et al, Memorandum Opinion and Order, Judge Charles Haight, U.S. District Court, Southern District of New York. 71 Civ.2203-CSH, p.34.

25 See, Can't Jail the Spirit: Political Prisoners in the U.S. (Chicago: CEML, 2002), pp.147-50. And, for example, Alfred McCoy, The Politics of Heroin: CIA Complicity in the Global Drug Trade (New York: Lawrence Hill, 1972,1991).

26 On Lincoln Detox success, it was reportedly "recognized as the largest and most effective of its kind by the National Institute of Drug Abuse [NIDA], National Acupuncture Research Society, and the World Academic Society of Acupuncture." This and Zimbabwe travels, CMEL, Can't Jail the Spirit, pp.147-8. Mutulu Shakur noted that SDS/Weather Underground leader Bernardine Dohrn's sister, Jennifer, worked with him at Lincoln Detox. "On the History of the Use of Acupuncture by Revolutionary Health Workers to Treat Drug Addiction, and US Government Attacks Under the Cover of the Counterintelligence Program (COINTELPRO), 10/30/92, http://mutulushakur.com/site/1992/10/interview-on-acupuncture/.

The FBI claimed that Mutulu founded the Revolutionary Armed Task Force (RATF)—a rainbow coalition of activists from the BLA and Weather Underground, as well as an Italian revolutionary and the Young Lords (on others, see notes).[27] Reports said some RATF worked at Lincoln Detox and took extreme measures when the city tried to close it. The government charged the group with robbing banks to support Lincoln Detox when the city barred its funding.

The FBI also accused RATF (one activist said this was the BLA's Multinational Task Force) of breaking Assata Shakur from jail and helping her gain exile status in Cuba. A judge then convicted members of RATF on a failed bank truck robbery that killed a police officer and a guard. Police went after Mutulu, not for any involvement in that actual crime, but for being a "co-conspirator."[28]

It's likely not a coincidence that by 1980, U.S. Intelligence started using the label "terrorist" to justify assault on radical leftists. New York closed its Bureau Of Special Services Cointelpro unit, but they created several new ones that appeared to carry out similar duties. One New York unit that had started in 1971, the year BOSS disbanded, was the similarly undercover Street Crime Unit. Another unit created in 1980 was the Joint Terrorist Task Force, which New York and U.S. Intelligence started in response to the RATF and BLA. California had started a similar ad hoc unit out of Los Angeles. The FBI utilized these Task Forces as more openly-formed amalgams of national, state, and city police agent units that were formerly run covertly. Echoing the more universal erosion of constitutional rights to come after 9/11, California and New York labeled Mutulu Shakur and other activists "terrorists" to justify the work that violated their constitutional rights.[29]

---

27 "Reports...activists." Churchill and Vander Wall, *The Cointelpro Papers*, pp.309, 410-11, note 24. *Agents of Repression*, p.364. Assata Shakur, "Assata Shakur: The life of a revolutionary," *Covert Action Quarterly* #65, Fall 1998, p36. Some reportedly linked to RATF and serving long political prisoner sentences include white Weather Underground radicals Kathy Boudin, Dave Gilbert, Sara Evans, Susan Rosenberg, Marilyn Buch and Judy Clark. A doctor who aided some of the wounded RATF members, Allan Berkman, MD, was jailed. This was the first time a doctor was jailed for such a charge since the doctor who aided John Wilkes Booth after he shot Abraham Lincoln. Italian activist Silvia Baraldini was arrested as linked to RATF, as were Black activists (mostly former Panthers) Sekou Odinga, Chui Ferguson, Edward Joseph Anthony Laborde, Bilal Sunni-Ali, Iliana Robinson and Kuwasi Balagoon. The Puerto Rican independistas who formed the Movimiento de Liberación Nacional (MLN) were Ricardo Romero, Maria Cueto, Steven Guerra, Julio Rosado and Andres Rosado. All from *COINTELPRO Papers*, pp. 310-11, 322, 411-12. CMEL, *Can't Jail the Spirit*, pp.147-8.
28 "The FBI said... 'co-conspirator.'" Churchill and Vander Wall, *The COINTELPRO Papers*, p.309. On BLA Multinational Task Force, see Sundiata Acoli, "A Brief History of the New Afrikan Prison Struggle," 2/19/92, freedomarchives.org/.
29 "It's likely...rights." On Street Crime Unit, see *New York Times*, 2/15/99, in Frank Morales, 'The Militarization of the Police," *Covert Action Quarterly*, Fall/Summer, 1999, p.46. On Joint Terrorist Task Force, Churchill and Vander Wall, *The COINTELPRO Papers*, pp. 309-11.

CIA-LINKED DEALERS HOOK AFENI AND NEWTON

"Even though you were a crack fiend, I always knew you were a Black queen," —Tupac Shakur, "Dear Mamma," *Me Against the World,* 1995.

"Couldn't survive in this capitalistic government
'Cause it was meant to hold us back with ignorance
Drugs and sneak attacks in my community, They killed our unity
But when I charged them they cried immunity."
—Tupac Shakur, "Panther Power"(1989) *Tupac Shakur: The Lost Tapes,* 1998.

I n 1981, the charges against Mutulu Shakur sent him into hiding and onto the FBI's Most Wanted list. The FBI visited a young Tupac at school to question him about his stepfather Mutulu's whereabouts. Mutulu later said that Tupac became politically precocious at this time when he began attending political meetings with him. Tupac would also begin to radicalize after experiencing the deaths of his parents' revolutionary friends and the imprisonment of his aunt Assata. In '81, Rev. Herbert Daughtry asked 10 year-old Tupac what he wanted to be when he grew up. Tupac responded, "a revolutionary." Daughtry saw this as reflecting his mother's revolutionary view of the world in "wanting to make a complete change for the better."[1]

During this time, the FBI continued targeting Afeni Shakur. They reportedly visited her job sites for many years and intimidated employers into firing her or refusing to hire her. The beleaguered Shakurs moved dozens of times, but Afeni managed to stay politically active, even writing a chapter of a book, *Human Rights for Everybody,* co-written by other activists including her ex-husband Lumumba Shakur, Howard Zinn, Noam Chomsky, Grace Paley, and Juan Jose Pena.[2]

By 1982, a drug dealer named Kenneth "Legs" Saunders (a.k.a. Legs McNeil) entered Afeni's life. After moving through dozens

1 "By 1981...better"' On Mutulu underground on the FBI's Most Wanted list and FBI queries of Tupac, see Cathy Scott, *The Killing of Tupac Shakur,* p.65. On Tupac attending political meetings with Mutulu and experiencing the death of his parents' friends, see Mutulu Shaku's interview discussing Tupac's Post-traumatic Stress from that time, *Tupac: Resurrection* (DVD, Paramount, 2004). On Rev. Daughtry's quotes, see transcript of his 1996 memorial speech, Armond White, *Rebel for the Hell of It: The Life of Tupac Shakur* (New York: Thunder's Mouth Press, 1997), p.2.
2 "The FBI...Pena." On FBI keeping Afeni unemployed, see Testimony of Tupac Shakur's attorney, Michael Warren, former Black Liberation Movement leader, New York vs. Tupac Shakur, sentencing hearing transcript, pp. 46-50. The use of this FBI tactic is backed by Michael Swearingen, *FBI Secrets: An agent's expose* (Boston, MA:South End Press,1995), p. 116. On Afeni moving dozens of times, see Scott, *The Killing of Tupac Shakur,* p.66. On Afeni writing chapter of book with Chomsky et al, see Marilyn Vogt, "Letter: Re: *Human Rights for Everybody,*" New York Review of Books, Volume 24, Number 21 & 22, January 26, 1978. Other authors included poet Allan Ginsburg Latino activists Armando Gutierrez and Juan Jose Pena, as well as feminist activist Kate Millet .

of homes and homeless shelters, Afèni moved into Legs' home.[3] Legs eased Afeni's poverty while she tried to raise Tupac and his younger sister Sekyiwa, Afeni's daughter by Mutulu. Afeni said Legs introduced her to crack, "That was our way of socializing. He would come home late at night and stick a pipe in my mouth."[4]

Much research supports that U.S. Intelligence inserted Legs into the struggling Afeni's life. Radio reporter Richard Boyle, who covered the trial of Vietnam Veterans Against the War leaders in the '70s, said that an undercover female government agent moved in with the anti-war group's leader. He claimed that this practice wasn't uncommon and that U.S. Intelligence "often uses women, or men, to get in personal relationships with their targets."[5]

Legs' connections support that this was his role in '82. He was an associate of New York drug lord Nicky Barnes.[6] Barnes assisted the first national "Black drug kingpin," Frank Matthews, who worked untouched for years. The Justice Department indicted Matthews' entire network in '73, but dropped charges on nine of them due to their CIA ties. Matthews left the U.S. with millions of dollars and Barnes took his place from '73 into the late 80s. Barnes' ability to remain jail-free suggests that he was either one of the nine with CIA ties or that he had similar support from U.S. Intelligence groups. Professor Clarence Lusane of American University said that Barnes won so many "acquittals on gun, narcotics, bribery, and murder charges," that the *New York Times* called him "Mr. Untouchable."[7]

Afeni Shakur's relationship with Barnes' associate, Legs, only ended when she made her move to Baltimore. She reported that after several years with Legs, when she moved to Baltimore, he apparently went to jail for credit card fraud. When she called the prison to speak with him, prison officials claimed he died of a crack-induced heart attack.[8]

3 Cathy Scott, *The Killing of Tupac Shakur* (Las Vegas, NV: Huntington Press, 1997), p.66. On Legs Saunders, the major motion picture release, *Tupac: Resurrection* (Paramount/MTV Films, 2003).

4 Ronin Ro, *Have Gun Will Travel: The Spectacular Rise and Violent Fall of Death Row Records* (New York: Doubleday, 1998), p.139.

5 KSAN radio reporter Richard Boyle, on the CD, *Me and My Shadow: Investigation of the political left by the United States Government*, producers Tarabu Betserai and Adi Gevins from "The Pacifica Radio Archives." Track 3.

6 Robert Sam Anson, "To Die Like A Gangsta," *Vanity Fair*, March 1997, p.248. Also, Cathy Scott, *The Killing of Tupac Shakur* (Las Vegas, Nevada: Huntington Press, 1997), p.66.

7 "Mutulu Shakur…'Mr. Untouchable.'" According to a 1976 "Top Secret" Justice Department report. Jefferson Morley, "The Kid Who Sold Crack to the President," *The City Paper*, 12/15/89, p.31. On Barnes acquittals and *New York Times* label, see Hank Messick, *Of Grass and Snow* (Englewood, CA: Prentice-Hall, 1979), p.148. Both cited in Clarence Lusane, *Pipe Dream Blues: Racism and the War on Drugs* (Boston, MA: South End Press, 1991), pp.41-42, notes 76 and 79. Mutulu Shakur also alluded to Nicky Barnes as a "rat," suggesting that he, too, thought Barnes worked for the government. See the momentary display of Mutulu's Thug Life Code in *Tupac:Resurrection* DVD at the Mutulu Shakur interview.

8 "Afeni…attack." Cathy Scott, *The Killing of Tupac Shakur*,.p.66.

At around the same time that Nicky Barnes and Legs were dealing cocaine, the CIA was in the midst of running a California-based cocaine trafficking operation with a similar network. As supported by a CIA Inspector General's findings, during the mid-80s, U.S. Intelligence supplied the nation's top West Coast-based drug trafficker, "Freeway" Ricky Ross.[9] A longtime probation officer for Ross stated that drug lord Michael Harris was one of two major dealers learning the trade and buying from Ross. Harris would later provide seed money for the Death Row Records music label that produced Tupac's last two CDs.[10]

The tactic of inserting undercover agents into activists' lives can be seen repeatedly throughout the Civil Rights Movement. *The New York Times* described how an FBI "informant" (paid FBI employee) became the boyfriend of Malcolm X's daughter, Qubilah Shabazz, and then ensnared her in a plot to assassinate Nation Of Islam leader Louis Farrakhan. The boy convinced Shabazz that Farrakan was plotting against her mother, Betty Shabazz, who was believed to have blamed Farrakhan for some aspect of Malcolm X's death.[11]

U.S. Intelligence again employed these tactics against Huey Newton. Black Panther cofounders Newton and Bobby Seale had originally barred any Panthers' use of drugs. That attitude changed with the huge use of marijuana among youth, but no reports were found of Panthers receiving drug-dealing charges. Reports cited various undercover agents trying to get close to Newton after he was released from prison. One in particular, Earl Anthony, said he worked for the FBI and CIA as he dealt bulk weed to Newton.[12] Seale said Newton started selling cocaine at this time. Newton claimed he wasn't involved in heavy drugs and cited the FBI's failed attempts to arrest him for

9 "About...Ross." On CIA's California based trafficking, see Gary Webb, *Dark Alliance: The CIA, the Contras, and the Crack Cocaine Explosion* (New York: Seven Stories, 1998). The CIA's trafficking revealed by Webb was later disclosed in the CIA's Inspector General Report of 1998, cited in Dale Russakoff, "Shifting Within Party to Gain His Footing," *The Washington Post*, A1, A8, 7/26/04.
10 "A...CDs." On Harris learning from Ross, see Gary Webb, *Dark Alliance*, p.148. Webb detailed the CIA cocaine trafficking network, and a CIA Inspector General backed his findings in 1998. On Inspector General's findings, see Dale Russakoff, "Shifting Within Party to Gain His Footing," *The Washington Post*, A1, A8, 7/26/04. On Harris providing Death Row seed money, see Ronin Ro, *Have Gun Will Travel* (New York: Doubleday, 1998), p.78. The courts later acknowledged this by ordering Suge Knight to pay Harris's wife, Lydia, $107 million in 2005 for her and her husband, providing that seed money. Remmie Fresh, "Suge Ordered to Pay $107 Million," AllHipHop News, 3/30/05. allhiphop.com/news/.
11 "*The New York Times*...death." Mike Wilson, "For Malcolm X's Grandson, a Clouded Path," *New York Times*, p. A1.
12 "Of the many...Newton." Earl Anthony, *Spitting in the Wind: The true story behind the violent legacy of the Black Panther Party* (Malibu, CA: Roundtable, 1990), p122. Coming out in 1990, following Churchill and Vander Wall's extensively more revealing accounts, Anthony's book appears as part fact and part subterfuge. Among other undercover agents that got involved with the Oakland Black Panther office, LA Panther Melvin "Cotton" Smith eventually admitted he had been an undercover police intelligence agent. Smith travelled up to Oakland and worked in that Panther office before then traveling to the New York office where Assata Shakur worked. He continually tried to get Panthers to drink liquor with him. See Churchill and Vander Wall, *Agents of Repression*, pp.86, 404n. #130, and 408n, #166. Also Assata Shakur, *Assata: An Autobiography*, pp.228-230.

drugs.[13] Several sources claim that Black Panther Elaine Brown helped get Newton using cocaine. Geronimo ji Jaga (formerly Pratt) said Newton told him in 1988 that Brown "kept cocaine and sexy women on him everyday/night."[14]

As previously discussed, evidence supports many Panthers' belief that Elaine Brown, Huey Newton's lover around 1970, was an undercover agent. Panthers such as Communications Secretary Kathleen Cleaver and New Haven Panther George Edwards added to researchers' claims that Elaine Brown was "widely suspected among former [Black Panther] party members of having been a police agent."

Brown's history of negative actions against the Black Panthers nationally peaked when she became Newton's lover just after his prison release. That was when she reportedly influenced Newton in a variety of negative ways.[15] For example, evidence supported that Elaine Brown helped Earl Anthony influence Huey Newton's drug involvement. This includes her arrest for cocaine possession in 1976. Unlike other Panthers who often received heavy sentences for small charges, a judge only sentenced Brown to complete "a series of yoga lessons."[16]

Cleaver and Edwards believe Brown's spy work also led to murders of Panthers. Many Panthers more particularly believed that Brown influenced Newton to expel Geronimo and his wife, Nsondi (Sandra "Red" Pratt) from the Black Panther Party, after which pregnant Nsondi was found bullet-riddled and stuffed in a sleeping bag

13 "Seale…drugs." Stated by Bobby Seale at the first Black Panther Film Festival, New York, 1999. On Newton's claims, for example, see "Teletype from FBI San Francisco to director, 2/16/74. FBU "Informative Notes," 2/16/74, prepared for "J.L.B." FBI Memorandum from Supervisor Gary L. Penrith to SAC San Francisco, 4/13/73. Newton noted here that these documents said he might be "shaking down" drug dealers to donate money rather than buying or selling drugs with them. Huey Newton, *War Against the Panthers* (New York: Harlem River/Readers and Writers, 1991), pp48-9.

14 Newton quote from a description written by Geronimo Pratt and sent by Kathleen Cleaver's email http:// whosemedia.com/drums/2007/05/09/was-elaine-brown-an-agent/ Also see personal interview, Watani Tyehimba, 5/10/00. Tyehimba, a former LA RAM-based Black Panther who supported Pratt's defense, said he understood that Pratt helped Newton with withdrawal symptoms when they ended up in prison together. See more notes below on agents trying to get Newton using drugs.

15 "Evidence supports…release." Personal interviews with Kathleen Cleaver, 10/5/02 and George Edwards, 8/20/00. Cleaver also made a strong implication of Brown's spy work when directly asked about it by an audience member at the 2nd Black Panther Film Festival. Churchill and Vander Wall also stated that "Elaine Brown, widely suspected among former [Panther] party…" *COINTELPRO Papers*, p.153, 362 note 131. Note also the FBI memos on pp.151-2 that discuss the split in Panther factions that Brown was believed to have influenced between Newton's Oakland office versus the still united Cleaver faction in Algeria, Pratt in LA and the Shakur-led chapter in New York. This became known as the "East/West" split. These memos discussed trying to stop Kathleen Cleaver coming from Algeria to re-unify Huey Newton's national Oakland office with these other key chapters. "FBI Memo, 2/17/71, To: Director (100—448006) From: San Francisco (157-601) COINTELPRO—BLACK EXTREMISTS, RM.," *COINTELPRO Papers*, pp. 151-2. On Brown as Newton's one-time lover, she also apparently visited Newton in prison before that, see Elaine Brown, *A Taste of Power* (New York: Doubleday, 1992), pp.242, 246, 258. Much thanks to Kathleen Cleaver for her information and support. On Brown's cocaine conviction, see Xeroxed clipping of a California news article from April 24, 1976, supplied by ex-Panther George Edwards.

16 "Evidence…lessons." Xeroxed clipping of a California news article from April 24, 1976, supplied by ex-Panther George Edwards. Thanks to one of New Haven's former top Black Panthers, George Edwards, for his very compelling stack of evidence first compiled and reported in Lee Lew Lee's powerful Panther documentary *All Power to the People* (1995). Edwards then kindly donated his information, time, and insights to this author. Personal interview, George Edwards 8/22/00.

on a roadside. Reportedly there was no serious police investigation of her murder.[17]

Geronimo recalled Huey Newton telling him that it took many months for him to come out of his drug and sex euphoria and realize he was surrounded by agents. Newton said he first began to suspect when it came out during Geronimo's trial that Brown's name was on a receipt from a paint shop that changed the color of Geronimo's car. Newton said she also testified against the United Slaves members who weren't the ones who pulled the trigger on Bunchy Carter and John Huggins. Newton said he became convinced she was an FBI agent and put Brown in a "Panther jail," but his "advisors" eventually got her back involved in the Panthers against his wishes (Pratt also noted Brown receiving psychiatric treatment at UCLA which he called a "prerequisite for patsies of Elaine's type.")[18]

While Earl Anthony's book, *Spitting in the Wind,* appears part disclosure and part cover-up, it supports former Panthers' claims about Elaine Brown. Anthony represented Brown as a committed Panther who linked him with another "committed activist," Jay Richard Kennedy. He failed to mention, and his fact-checking editors failed to disclose, that a popular book, David Garrow's *Bearing the Cross: Martin Luther King, Jr. and the Southern Christian Leadership Conference,* named J.R. Kennedy as a top CIA informant four years prior to Anthony's publication. FOIA-released CIA documents back this claim, as does the King family lawyer, William Pepper, in his book *Orders to Kill.* Brown said that before Newton, Jay Kennedy had been her lover for two years. Anthony appeared to be trying to protect the covers of both Brown and Kennedy with this "committed activist" description.[19]

The CIA documents, Brown's incidental disclosures, and whistleblower reports further support Brown's likely U.S. Intelligence work. The CIA documents on Jay Kennedy verified that he was a CIA-

---

17 On Pratt and his wife's expulsion and murder see, Churchill and Vander Wall, *Agents of Repression,* pp.87-8; *COINTELPRO Papers,* p. 153, 362 note 131. Researchers also claim that Brown heavily aided the FBI's manufacture of the East/West war. Former Panther National Communications Director Kathleen Cleaver further cited belief in Brown's possible connection to the murder of two LA Panther leaders and Black revolutionary George Jackson. Personal interviews with Kathleen Cleaver, 10/5/02 and George Edwards 8/22/00.

18 "Geronimo reported...type.')" Newton quote from a description written by Geronimo Pratt and sent by Kathleen Cleaver's email http://whosemedia.com/drums/2007/05/09/was-elaine-brown-an-agent/.

19 "While Earl Anthony's...description." This writer's copies of CIA documents on Jay Kennedy, for example, were FOIA-obtained by ex-Panther turned filmmaker Lee Lew Lee and given to George Edwards and then this writer. See, for example, CIA internal memorandum in CIA file for Chief, Security Research Staff, from Allan Morse, one Jay R. Kennedy report. 6/9/65, p.7. On Jay Kennedy as Brown's ex-lovers, Elaine Brown, *A Taste of Power* (New York: Doubleday, 1992), pp.79-86. Earl Anthony, *Spitting in the Wind: The True Story Behind the Violent Legacy of the Black Panther Party* (Malibu, CA: Roundtable, 1990) pp.79, 151. Jay Kennedy as CIA's "Principal source," David Garrow, *Bearing the Cross: Martin Luther King, Jr. and the Southern Christian Leadership Conference* (NY: Quill, William Morrow, 1986), p285. William Pepper, *Orders to Kill: The Truth Behind the Murder of Martin Luther King, Jr.* (New York: Warner Books,1995) pp.82, 445.

supported writer who had infiltrated the civil rights movement by the start of the '60s. Kennedy got himself in a position as a manager for a longtime Martin Luther King supporter, entertainer Harry Belafonte, before Belafonte fired him.[20] Brown incidentally revealed evidence of her undercover work when she cited Jay Kennedy as a lifelong mentor whom she went to for guidance as late as the '90s, despite that the published reports on Jay Kennedy's CIA work started appearing in the mid-80s.[21] The surrounding of Newton with government agents fits with CIA whistleblower John Stockwell's statement that U.S. Intelligence used such agents in psychological warfare against Huey Newton until his death.[22]

Earl Anthony published several books that appeared to mix information with "disinformation," such as the notions described above. Elaine Brown continued lecturing and similarly writing both information and disinformation in books and for newspapers. Brown's negative reflections on Huey Newton in her *A Taste of Power: A Black Woman's Story* contradicts accounts by top women in the Panthers such as Afeni Shakur and Kathleen Cleaver (whose account holds particular validity given the Cointelpro-induced animosity provoked in Newton towards Eldridge Cleaver). Many other books on the Panthers also contradict Brown's accounts. [23]

Elaine Brown's later statements and activist work provide more contradictions on her real motives. In a 2003 lecture of Brown's, she rejected the idea of many undercover agents in the Panthers, despite that a number of agents openly testified against the Panthers in trials and that evidence supported the fact that many more agents were never

20 "The CIA...him" Memorandum from Howard Osborn, Director of Security to Deputy Director of Support. 3/27/68. Also see Pepper finding that Jay Kennedy was the CIA's "Informant A"-- William Pepper, *Orders To Kill: The Truth Behind the Murder of Martin Luther King, Jr.* (NY:Warner Books, 1995), p.82.

21 Rosemary Bray, "A Black Panther's Long Journey," *New York Times Magazine*, 1/31/93, p.68. J. R. Kennedy as "Principal source"-- David Garrow, *Bearing the Cross: Martin Luther King, Jr. and the Southern Christian Leadership Conference*, p.285. Brown's *Taste of Power* also mentions discussion with Jay Kennedy while she was a Panther, several times in the book, see, pp.175, 262.

22 Ex-CIA agent John Stockwell in Lee Lew-Lee, *All Power to the People* (Documentary, 1996).

23 "Earl Anthony...accounts." In *A Taste of Power*, Brown's 1992 published account, she said Newton physically abused her, which no other source collaborated as Newton having done to anyone. Newton wrote his doctoral thesis in 1980, based on his FBI and CIA file. His surviving wife published it in 1991 and one FBI document detailed the same kind of smear they would attempt on Newton as Brown carried out. In Brown's later memoir, she described Newton's early '70s, post-prison apartment as a "twenty-fifth-floor penthouse...[with] many balconies." An FBI document described how an FBI media collaborator Ed Montgomery helped the FBI smear Newton with a false report in a front page *San Francisco Chronicle* article as one of it's "counter-intelligence activities." The article characterized Newton's apartment as "luxurious," in contrast to "the ghetto-like BPP 'pads' and community centers." Other FBI memorandums detailed their intent to carry out this smear campaign. The FBI also created a fake letter from an anonymous Panther they sent from the Oakland Panther office to Panther offices nationwide complaining about Newton's alleged luxurious apartment. Elaine Brown, *A Taste of Power: A Black Woman's Story* (New York: Anchor/Doubleday, 1992), p.9. FBI memorandum from San Francisco to hqtrs., 11/24/70, and from SAC New Orleans to director, 12/11/71, in Newton, *War Against the Panthers*, p.61-2. Afeni Shakur in Jasmine Guy, *Afeni Shakur: Evolution of a Revolutionary* (New York: Atria, 2004), p.77, and Kathleen Cleaver, personal interview, 10/5/02. Many other books on the Panthers also contradict Brown's accounts.

revealed. Brown's defenders might say her work of heading the Oakland Panthers when Newton fled the country in the '70s, her work on behalf of prisoners, and her writing on behalf of Black activists support good intentions. While certainty is hard to come by in these assessments, evidence of Brown's past misdeeds undermine any purportedly good intentions with her later activist work.[24]

24 "Elaine Brown's later…question." This writer attended Brown's 2004 lecture in Washington D.C. Brown wrote an article and signed an advertisement on behalf of former honorary Black Panther, Imam Jamil Al-Amin (formerly H. Rap Brown, Elaine Brown, "Black Panther Party Long Victimized by Campaign of Lies," *Atlanta Journal-Constitution*, 3/25/00.

12

TUPAC, HUEY NEWTON, AND THE "ANNIVERSARY" MURDERS

"The United States was transformed at the hands of the ruling circle from a nation to an empire...The United States as an empire necessarily controls the whole world either directly or indirectly...The ruling reactionary circle, through the consequences of being imperialists, transformed the world...They laid siege upon all communities of the world, dominating the institutions to such an extent that the people were not served by the institutions in their own land. The Black Panther Party [wanted to] reverse that trend and lead people to...seize the means of production and distribute the wealth and the technology in an egalitarian way to the communities of the world."

> —Huey Newton, *To Die for the People: Writings and Speeches*, ed. Toni Morrison

"...they loved the sight
of your dimming and flickering starlight...
they wanted 2 c your lifeless corpse
This way u could not alter the course
Of ignorance that they have set
2 make my people forget...
I had loved u forever because of who u R
 And now I mourn our fallen star"

> —Tupac Shakur, excerpt of "Fallen Star (4 Huey P. Newton)," *The Rose That Grew From Concrete*, Tupac's Collected Poems.

In the mid-80s, Tupac Shakur had his acting debut at 13, while living in Harlem. In 1984, Tupac starred in a production of *A Raisin in the Sun* held at the Apollo Theater as a political benefit for Jesse Jackson's presidential run. Within another year, Afeni Shakur moved Tupac and his sister Sekyiwa to Baltimore. Afeni then successfully fought to get Tupac into the magnet public high school, The Baltimore School for the Arts, where Tupac studied acting, dance, Shakespeare, and writing for three years. Tupac also founded activist groups there that worked on anti-violence campaigns and AIDS prevention education. [1]

While living in Baltimore, Tupac Shakur attended meetings of the New Afrikan Panthers, a group that helped inspire his development of activist work in school. The New Afrikan Panthers included young Black activists ranging from their mid-teens to late-twenties that comprised the young adult section of the revolutionary group, the New Afrikan People's Organization (NAPO). Afeni's close friend, ex-Black Panther Watani Tyehimba, along with attorney Chokwe Lumumbawho served as its chairman, helped found NAPO and served as its security director. Tupac lived with Tyehimba for long stretches in 1985 and '86. The New Afrikan Panthers and NAPO would, at one point, had chapters in ten cities nationwide. [2]

In New York at this time, law officials spread a wide net over the activist community and jailed many who had any association with the Revolutionary Armed Task Force that they linked to the Brinks Bank truck robbery, Assata's escape, and Mutulu Shakur's Lincoln Detox. [3] In early 1986, a judge jailed Watani Tyehimba for not giving a grand jury information on the whereabouts of Mutulu Shakur. Tyehimba said that with no previous criminal record, "I was held in Civil Contempt of Court, which is less than a misdemeanor, but was still housed as though I was a convicted criminal for 14 months, including 23 hours a day lockdown for the first 40 days." [4]

Later in '86, five years after the Brinks robbery, government police finally caught Mutulu Shakur. Mutulu evaded the authorities longer than any of the other activists charged as being an RATF member. [5] Three days before Mutulu's capture, his brother, Lumumba Shakur, Afeni's ex-husband and the founding Harlem Panther leader, was found dead in Louisiana. Mutulu suspected that a police informant learned of Mutulu's whereabouts and decided to target both brothers. [6]

---

1 "In the mid-80s...education." On Harlem acting, see Michael Eric Dyson, *Holler If You Hear Me: Searching for Tupac Shakur* (New York: Basic Civitas, 2001), p.33. 17 year-old Tupac Shakur in video, *Tupac Shakur, Thug Angel, Life of an Outlaw*, QD3 Entertainment, 2002.

2 "While living...nationwide." Personal interview, Watani Tyehimba, 5/2/00. Personal interview with Chokwe Lumumba, 5/10/00. Teyhimba was a former Revolutionary Action Movement-based Los Angeles Black Panther who befriended Afeni Shakur working on Geronimo Pratt's case.

3 Churchill and Vander Wall, *The COINTELPRO Papers*, pp.309-315.

4 Personal Interview with Watani Tyehimba, 11/8/02.

5 Churchill and Vander Wall, *The Cointelpro Papers*, pp.411-12. Footnote 29.

6 "Three...hiding." "Lumumba Abdul Shakur—Afeni's First Husband," 2PacLegacy.net, 7/2/17, 2paclegacy.net/lumumba-abdul-shakur-afenis-first-husband/.

Despite the FBI claiming to have disbanded Cointelpro, a federal judge stated that the FBI violated Mutulu's rights through Cointelpro actions. However, the judge's acknowledgment of the FBI's Counterintelligence Program's continuance against Mutulu failed to keep the activist leader out of prison.[7] Mutulu began serving a sixty-year sentence in August of 1988 for merely "conspiracy" to commit armed robbery and murder. The court also found Mutulu guilty of aiding Assata Shakur's prison escape. Some claim this came without concrete evidence linking him to the actual undertaking.[8] A parole board repeatedly denied Mutulu parole in part because, like Geronimo Pratt, he refused to renounce his politics.[9]

In 1987, a Baltimore teen living near Tupac was murdered. Following the tragedy, Afeni decided to move the family to Marin City, near Oakland, and into the house of Geronimo Pratt's second wife, Linda Pratt. A few weeks after Tupac's move, gunmen shot two of Tupac's Baltimore activist friends in the head.[10] But Oakland would also prove to be dangerous for the Shakurs. Afeni didn't realize that residents had nicknamed the northern California city "Cokeland" in those days. Despite the troubled environment, while living with Pratt, Tupac excelled in school and read voraciously. He also directed and starred in Shakespeare plays that he rewrote with modern dialogue.

Tupac would clash with his mother due to her drug problem, but never lost sight of his goals. When Afeni's crack problem intensified, Tupac left home and dropped out of high school his senior year. He remained virtually homeless until taken in by Leila Steinberg, who would eventually become his first manager.

Tupac quickly impressed the similarly political Steinberg with his photographic memory and his precocious ability to plainly communicate a Marxist analysis of America's class system as well as other political issues. For example, in an interview while he was a little known teen in high school, Tupac explained that "for the upper class," George H.W. Bush was "a perfect president…that's how society is built. The upper class runs [society] while…the middle class and lower class, we talk about it." Tupac also read hundreds of graduate school level

7 Connie Bruck, "The Takedown of Tupac," *The New Yorker*, 7/7/97, p.54.
8 "Still…undertaking." Churchill and Vander Wall, *The COINTELPRO Papers*, p.309. On BLA Multinational Task Force, see Sundiata Acoli, "A Brief History of the New Afrikan Prison Struggle," 2/19/92, freedomarchives.org/.
9 Cathy Scott, *The Killing of Tupac Shakur* (Las Vegas, Nevada: Huntington Press, 1997) p.66.
10 Michael Eric Dyson, *Holler If You Hear Me* (New York: Basic Civitas Books, 2001), pp.84.

books as a teen, from socialist and anarchist classic texts, to philosophical treatises, poetry, Shakespeare, and cutting-edge contemporary books on alternative historical analyses, feminism, and psychology.[11]

Tupac further maintained his later renowned, packed schedule of productivity. He assisted Steinberg in her after-school activist art programs, wrote poetry, led several rap groups, and recorded his first album. He dedicated one of his poems to Huey Newton and titled one of his songs "Panther Power." Tupac coupled his art with his activism, attending New Afrikan Panther meetings. He was elected the youngest-ever national chairman at 17 along with Watani's eldest son, Yakhisizwe Tyehimba, who was elected as national security director of the group.[12] Tupac stayed in that leadership position for almost two years and he was NAPO's top newspaper distributor in California, helping to create their *Panther Power* mini-newspaper insert.[13]

During Tupac's leadership tenure in 1988, his idol Huey Newton was arrested on a minor charge that put him in prison with Geronimo Pratt (ji Jaga). Newton would endure two years in prison and then almost two decades of constant arrests on what would appear to be frame-ups and trumped up charges. Despite this, he still earned a doctorate, wrote several books, and started a Panther-inspired school for children in Oakland after he was released from prison. Huey Newton proved himself to be a great intellect in the books he wrote along with the books published of his conversations with renowned psychologist Erik Erikson and his speeches edited by future Nobel Prize for literature winner, Toni Morrison.[14]

In prison, Geronimo Pratt took Newton under his wing (reportedly Newton was going through drug withdrawal in prison) and the two compared their experiences with U.S. intelligence agencies. They commiserated about how the FBI and CIA pitted them against each other for the last 18 years. On August 22, 1988, the day officials

---

11 "Tupac…psychology." Michael Eric Dyson, *Holler If You Hear Me: Searching for Tupac Shakur* (New York: Basic Civitas, 2001). Dyson details the incredible library of books that Steinberg showed him as part of Tupac's mass of readings, pp.93-99. Also see some of Tupac's incredibly precocious and insightful political analyses in the preceding, pp.77-84.
12 Personal Interview with Tupac's business manager, former Panther Watani Tyehimba, 3/10/2003.
13 "Tupac further…insert." Personal interviews, W. Tyehimba, 5/10/00 and C. Lumumba, 5/5/00. On poetry see Tupac Shakur, *The Rose That Grew from Concrete* (New York: MTV Books, 1999), p.111. Tupac Shakur, *The Lost Tapes* (Herb N' Soul, 2001).
14 "During…Morrison." Huey Newton, *To Die for the People* (New York: Random House/Writers and Readers, 1972/95) ed. by Toni Morrison. Huey Newton, *Revolutionary Suicide* (New York: Harcourt Brace/Writers and Readers, 1973/95). Erik Erickson and Huey Newton, *In Search of Common Ground* (New York: W. W. Norton & Co., 1973).

were to release Newton from prison, he chose to remain incarcerated and announced a press conference for the following day. There, he said that he wouldn't leave prison until officials freed Pratt. Pratt, however, asked that Newton leave in order to help him from the outside. [15]

Once out, Huey Newton worked for Pratt's release and it is likely that he was consulting with and possibly gaining inspiration from Tupac. Newton worked with Geronimo's lawyer and made speeches for Pratt's release. It is around this time that most Black political prisoners started identifying themselves as "New Afrikans." New Afrikan Panther leader Tupac said he consulted with Geronimo as well as the "Panther Minister of Defense," Newton's official Panther position. In the summer of '89, Newton called East Coast Black Panthers who had restarted a Black Panther newspaper and said he wanted to reunite the Black Panthers, which, with Tupac's group, would have spanned two generations. [16]

U.S. Intelligence reportedly still had Newton under surveillance and these moves likely contributed to his untimely death. A minor conviction for gun possession led Newton to stay unarmed, while undercover police continued watching his every move and on August 22, 1989, exactly one year after Huey Newton refused prison release on Pratt's behalf, a gunman shot down Newton in Oakland. The assailant shot Newton three times, including twice in the head as he lay on the ground. [17]

In addition to its anniversary timing, many other aspects of Newton's murder suggest that it was a possible U.S. Intelligence assassination. The *San Francisco Examiner* found many discrepancies

15 "In prison…outside." *Last Man Standing*, new Pratt biography. Personal interviews with former Black Panthers Watani Tyehimba, and George Edwards. Torri Minton, "Huey Newton Gives In, Gets Out of Quentin," *San Francisco Chronicle*, August 27, 1988, A3. Torri Minton, "Prison Protest by Ex-Panther Newton," *San Francisco Chronicle*, August 24, 1988, B8. Paul Liberatore, "How Huey Newton Let a Panther Down," *San Francisco Chronicle*, September 16, 1988, p. A13. On the continued targeting of Newton with seeming frame-ups, see examples in M. Newton, *Bitter Grain*, pp.210-16. On doctorate, see his published doctoral thesis, War Against the Panthers, which gained him his doctorate at the University of California at Santa Cruz in the History of Conscience. On Panther school, Newton, *Bitter Grain*, p218..

16 "Once out…generations." On Black political prisoners starting to identify themselves as New Afrikans, see *Can't Jail the Spirit: Political Prisoners in the U.S.* a collection of biographies (Chicago: Committee to End the Marion Lockdown, 1st ed.1988, 5th ed.2002). Newton's work for Pratt, see Paul Liberatore, "How Huey Newton Let a Panther Down," *San Francisco Chronicle*, 9/16/88, p.A13. On Tupac's quote, see *Tupac Shakur, Thug Angel, Life of an Outlaw*, QD3 Entertainment, 2002. On Newton reuniting Panthers, personal interview, Billy X, *Black Panther* newspaper editor, 2nd International Black Panther Film Fest. Also, Newton attended African People's Socialist Party (a.k.a. Uhuru Movement) meetings. Personal interview of Watu of Afrikan People's Socialist Party, 10/28/03.

17 "On August 22…execution." On shooting details, Lori Olszewski and Rick DelVecchio, "Huey Newton Shot Dead On West Oakland Street," *San Francisco Chronicle*, Wednesday August 23, 1989, pp. A1, A14. Clarence Johnson and Lori Olszewski, "Friends Say Huey Newton Had Financial Problems." *San Francisco Chronicle*, 8/24/89. On "known military-style…" A Special Forces Group military commander described how after dropping the assassination victim with the first shot, he then puts two bullets in their head. Stephen Kinzer, "Commandos Left a Calling Card: Their Absence," *New York Times*, 9/26/01, p. B6.

in Oakland Police Lt. Mike Sims account of the murder. When Sims repeatedly said the police had "no suspects, no clues," the *Examiner* reported that police had been videotaped arresting three men near the scene within minutes of the murder. Sims then claimed that only two men were arrested, neither of whom were linked to Newton's murder. Oakland Police corrected Sims the following day, saying the two were suspects, though they only named and charged one. As detailed further below, it is also important to note that Richard Held, Special Agent-in-Charge of the Los Angeles FBI office, spoke with Lt. Sims at his press conference regarding Newton.[18]

The FBI and police claimed that the accused shooter, Tyrone Robinson, appeared to have acted in self-defense. Newton supposedly pulled a gun following an argument over money he owed Robinson for cocaine. However, this claim is contradicted by the earlier police statement that they didn't find a gun belonging to Newton at the scene nor why the shooter would put two additional bullets in Newton's head as he laid on the street. As a Special Forces commando described in an unrelated article, putting two extra bullets in the head is a signature move in a combat military execution (later attempted on Tupac, Ch.19).[19]

Furthermore, witness Michelle Johnson, who lived just across the street from where Newton was killed, gave a description of the murder that was consistent with a murder setup. Johnson heard a brief argument and recognized one of the two men as Huey Newton. The other man ordered Newton into a car. Newton protested, "Man, I ain't getting in your car." She next heard shots, peeked out her window and saw Newton slumped on the sidewalk. This first-hand account may imply that Newton was not killed over a dispute about drugs, but that Newton's assailants had plans of kidnapping and murder.[20]

Johnson's description, along with other aspects of the murder, supports the claims of Newton's brother and local activists that the FBI did in fact murder Newton.[21] That Newton was murdered exactly a year

18 "'Then, the *San Francisco*...charged one." Churchill and Vander Wall, *the COINTELPRO Papers* pp.320, 417, 418.
19 "He also was said to have...was found at the scene." Ward Churchill and Jim Vander Wall, The Cointelpro Papers (Boston, MA: South End Press, 1990), pp.320, 417, 418.
20 "Also, witness...plans.'" "Witness Michelle...Newton." Michelle Johnson directly quoted Clarence Johnson and Lori Olaszewski, "Friends Say Huey Newton Had Financial Problems," *San Francisco Chronicle*, 8/24/89, A1.
21 Newton's brother, Melvin Newton said this, as did Omali Yeshitela, a leader of the Uhuru House, a Black nationalist group in Oakland. Yeshitela dismissed the police version of Newton's murder as ludicrous. Omali believed that the government signed Newton's death certificate when they pressed the weapons charges, leaving

after refusing his prison release and calling a press conference on behalf of Pratt also deserves more scrutiny. Examples of such a "threat-timed" targeting tactic further support that U.S. Intelligence was involved in murdering Huey Newton. [22]

Several other Black leaders' assassinations came with similar anniversary timing as Newton's death. Martin Luther King's family lawyer, William Pepper, argued that U.S. Intelligence orchestrated Martin Luther King's assassination exactly one year after he officially announced his opposition to the Vietnam War.[23] A gunman assassinated Congo president Laurent Kabila on January 16, 2001, the fortieth anniversary of the assassination of Kabila's former comrade, and Congo's first independently elected president, Patrice Lumumba. Later investigations would suggest that Lumumba's assasinnation was facilitated by U.S. intelligence agencies and recently disclosed government documents detail their plan to poison the Congolese leader.[24] This apparent "anniversary murder" tactic engenders a conscious or subconscious warning to political activists and progressive leaders. U.S. Intelligence would also appear to use this intimidation tactic against Tupac Shakur.

him unarmed and defenseless. Both cited in Sharon McCormick, "Mourners Pay Respects to Huey Newton," *San Francisco Chronicle*, August 28, 1989, p. A3

22 Newton's friend Pat Wright, in Clarence Johnson and Lori Olszewski, "Friends Say Huey Newton Had Financial Problems." *San Francisco Chronicle*, August 27, 1989. CIA agent John Stockwell in Lee Lew-Lee, *All Power to the People* (Documentary, 1996).

23 William Pepper, *Orders to Kill*, p.5.

24 Antoine Roger Lokongo, "Hands Off the Democratic Republic of Congo, Now!" *The Burning Spear*, October 2003, p.17. Also heard on Pacifica's WBAI radio in New York. On CIA assassinating Lumumba, see, for example, Ed.s James DiEugenio and Lisa Pease, *The Assassinations* (Los Angeles, CA: Feral House, 2002), pp.162-3. Also see, Alexander Cockburn and Jeffrey St. Clair, *White Out: The CIA, Drugs and the Press* (New York: Verso), excerpted in Dave Greaves, "The CIA, Drugs and Big Media" *Our Times Press*, 9/98, p.8. On CIA attempting/aiding Patrice Lumumba assassination, see Mark Mazetti and Time Weiner, " Files on Illegal Spying Show CIA Skeletons from Cold War," *New York Times*, A1, 6/27/07.

13

FBI ORCHESTRATES ARMED ATTACKS

"I see no justice, all I see is niggas dying fast;
The sound of a gun blast, then watch the hearst
pass…
Just another day in the life 'G,' gotta step lightly 'cause
cops try to snipe me…
Fuck you to the Marin County Sheriff Department.
Fuck you to the FBI. Fuck you to the CIA. Fuck you
to the B-U-S-H.
Fuck you to all you racist, redneck mothafuckers!"
    —Tupac Shakur, *2Pacalypse Now*, "I Don't Give a Fuck"
    1991.

The other key figure quoted in the cover-up of Huey Newton's death, Richard W. Held, had the resume of a true killer. Son of an FBI Assistant Director, Held gained high leadership status at a young age. At 27 he headed the FBI Counter Intelligence Program unit in L.A. and directed the FBI-paid informants in the United Slaves who targeted members of the Black Panthers. It also appears as though Held framed Geronimo Pratt after a failed murder attempt of the LA Panther. I will also show how he may have then directed infiltration and murder within the American Indian Movement, and covered up FBI murders of Puerto Rican independence activists. [1]

The FBI originally sent Richard Held to head the San Francisco office as Special Agent in Charge (SAC/Director) in 1985 where his cover-up activities suggest that he continued his murderous Cointelpro work of the '60s and '70s. When Held came to the San Francisco area he took over his earlier duties of targeting Pratt. However, the recently martyred Huey Newton's support of Pratt posed a setback to Held's sabotage of the defense[2]

In 1989 Held made unfounded statements to the media blaming Newton's murder on a botched drug deal.[3] Police immediately followed up on Held's accusations and made statements that contradicted the strong evidence that the shooter only had Newton's murder in mind.[4]

1 "Another key figure…activists." Ward Churchill and Jim Vander Wall, *Agents of Repression*, p.84, and *The COINTELPRO Papers*, pp.320, 417, 418. Swearingen, *FBI Secrets: An Agent's Expose*, p.87. Swearingen worked in Held's LA Cointelpro unit.
2 "The FBI…'80s." Ward Churchill and Jim Vander Wall, *Agents of Repression*, p.84. Swearingen, *FBI Secrets: An Agent's Expose*, p.87.
3 Ward Churchill and Jim Vander Wall, *The COINTELPRO Papers*, pp.320, 417, 418.
4 Ward Churchill and Jim Vander Wall, *The COINTELPRO Papers*, pp.320, 417, 418. Eyewitness Michelle Johnson directly quoted Clarence Johnson and Lori Olaszewski, "Friends Say Huey Newton Had Financial Problems," *San Francisco Chronicle*, 8/24/89, A1.

The year after Newton was murdered, a bomb went off under the car seat of prominent environmental leader and head of the Earth First! environmental group's Redwood Summer campaign, Judi Bari. Later evidence and disclosures indicate that the FBI was likely behind the bombing. The car bomb exploded in Oakland, California in May of 1990, paralyzing Bari from the waist down. She and her passenger in the car, fellow activist, Darryl Cherney, launched a lawsuit against the FBI. While working on the suit, a reporter asked Bari about the FBI's search for the bomber. Proving her label as "queen of the quip" she responded, "I hope the FBI find their man. And when they do, I hope they fire him." [5]

The government eventually agreed to settle the suit for several million dollars. A judge noted how the FBI directed the Oakland police to accuse Bari of transporting the bomb to use against the logging industry she battled. Researchers have accumulated much evidence to support that Richard Held actually directed the 1990 operation to plant the bomb, which had a motion-detection trigger, under Bari's seat. This was the second attempt on her life. Months before the bombing, a logging truck had nearly killed her and her three young children when it ran them off a highway. Someone also nailed a picture of Bari to her door with crosshairs over her face and feces smeared on it. The crosshairs are reportedly a known FBI threat tactic.[6]

After the bombing, Judi Bari chronicled dozens of murderous Cointelpro-type tactics the FBI used against her and her chapter of Earth First! leading up to the car bomb incident.[7] This research supported Bari's lawsuit, which had gained enough Congressional support to take the area FBI supervisor, Richard Held, and his collaborator in the Oakland police, Lt. Mike Sims, to court. Held and Sims had extensively collaborated with the Newton murder cover-up a year earlier. Former colleagues and writers say the Bari suit sent Held into early retirement

5 "A year later…him.'" On the Bari quote, this writer heard it on tape of her played on WBAI radio, NYC, 3/3/00. On other information, see Ward Churchill, "The FBI Targets Judi Bari" Covert Action, Winter 1993-94, Number 47. Robert J. Lopez, "Bomb victims jailed," Oakland Tribune, May 26, 1990; and Dean Congblay, "Police Say Car Bomb in the Back Seat: How Earth First! victims became suspects," San Francisco Chronicle, May 28, 1990. Sgt. Michael Sitterud, Oakland Police Follow-Up Investigation Report (1) RD No. 90-57171, May 2, 1990, pp.1, 3.

6 "The government…tactic." n Churchill, CovertAction, p. 5. Darryl Cherney on "Better Living," with Gary Null, WPFK, Pacifica radio, 7/29/03. Bari vs. Sims, U.S. Court of Appeals for the Ninth Circuit, Case No. 97-17375, dated filed, 9/24/99, CV-91-01057-CW, Opinion of Judge Reinhardt, pp.5, 24. Circuit Judge Schroeder concurred, 12178. Bill Weinberg, "Victory in Judi Bari Case: FBI Agents & Oakland Police to Pay $4.4 million in California Terrorism Coverup," The Shadow #46, July-August 2002, p.11. Dennis Cunningham and Ben Rosenfeld, "Snatching Victory From the Jaws of Death," Covert Action Quarterly #75, Fall 2003. More information on the Judi Bari/Darryl Cherney case can be found at .judibari.org.

7 See her five-page printed speech, Judi Bari, "Community Under Siege," 5/8/91, in which she details Held's Cointelpro tactics against the Panthers, the American Indian Movement and then Earth First! She listed and described at least 8 key tactics against her and her group. theanarchistlibrary.org/library/judi-bari-community-under-siege.

in 1993, though not before three armed attacks were mounted on up and coming star Tupac Shakur in Held's Bay area.[8]

Many aspects of Tupac Shakur's time in the San Francisco Bay area indicate that Richard Held kept a close eye on the rapper. As discussed earlier, Held returned to Geronimo Pratt's area and continued the FBI cover-up work on Pratt's case. As Held led the FBI fight against Pratt's defense team, Tupac performed musical benefits to raise money for his defense and discussed legal strategy with his godfather, Pratt.[9]

Tupac Shakur only left the New Afrikan Panthers due to a break into the music world, but he didn't give up his activism. While he toured with the Grammy-nominated Digital Underground (DU) in 1990 and recorded with them on their world tour in 1991, Tupac also started a new activist project. Called The Underground Railroad at the time, the program worked to nurture young Black activist leaders.[10]

Suspiciously, as soon as Tupac's burgeoning stardom became apparent, police assaults against the musician began. By 1991 Tupac had landed a solo record deal for his album *2Pacalypse Now* and a top movie role in *Juice*. In October of that year, Oakland police stopped Tupac for jaywalking, beat his head against the pavement, and choked him until he was unconscious. Tupac sued for $10 million and received a $15,000 settlement several years later.[11]

A second armed attack occurred just after the release of *Juice*, a film that focuses on the struggles of young Black men in Harlem and the police brutality that they face. In January of 1992, unknown assailants conducted a drive-by shooting of Tupac's limousine following the debut of the film. The limousine was taking him from his San Francisco premiere to its after-party. Many suspect that the hit was orchestrated by Cointelpro-ace Richard Held. Luckily no one was hit. [12]

8 "Judi Bari's…area." Held's former colleague M. Wesley Swearingen called the Bari bombing another example of the FBI's continued COINTELPRO as "an effort by the FBI to neutralize Judi Bari." Swearingen, *FBI Secrets*, p.06. On Bari's lawsuit leading to Held's early retirement, see Swearingen quote in Ward Churchill, "The FBI Targets Judi Bari" *Covert Action*, Winter 1993-94, Number 47. On Richard Held later leading a top credit card company, see Covert Action Quarterly's founding co-publisher Louis Wolfe, *Human Rights in the United States: The Unfinished Story, Current Political Prisoners—Victims of Cointelpro*, Issue Forum, U.S. Congressional Hearing, 9/14/00, 1:25 p.m. Rayburn House Office Building, Washington, D.C. Room 2000. ratical.org/co-globalize/CynthiaMcKinney/news/if000914HR.htm Wolfe said his investigation led to him finding out that Held was CEO of a major credit card company in California. This underscores the revolving door between U.S. Intelligence and the wealthiest families in the United States, discussed in Ch.20.

9 "Many aspects…Pratt." On FBI/Held's work against Pratt and his legal team in 1985, see *Pratt V. D.J. McCarthy, et al.*, NO. CR. 81-3407-PAR (K), United States District Court, Central District of California, 1985; Vol.3[A], pp.452-53. Cited in Churchill and Vander Wall, *Agents of Repression*, p. 92 note 195. Also see Swearingen, *FBI Secrets*, p.167. On music benefits for Pratt, see Bruck, The Takedown of Tupac, *The New Yorker*, 7/7/97, p.49.

10 "Tupac Shakur…leaders." Bruck, *The New Yorker*, 7/7/97, p50, 52.

11 "As soon as…later." "Claim Against the city of Oakland, California, Claimant: Tupac Shakur" by John Burris, Esq. Photocopied for Ed.s Jacob Hoye and Karolyn Ali, *Tupac: Resurrection* (New York: Atria Books, 2003), pp78-9. Danyel Smith "Introduction," Vibe editors, *Tupac Shakur* (New York: Crown Publishing, 1997), p.17. Personal interview, Watani Tyehimba, December 11, 2002. Robert McFadden, "At Two Rallies, Protesters Accuse Police in Killings," *New York Times*, 8/3/03, p.32. Several other deaths in police custody have occurred via choking.

12 "The timing…hit." Drive-by shooting on a limousine described by Tupac's friend, Troy, who was in limousine, on video *Thug Immortal* (Video, Xenon Entertainment, 1997).

14

LA RIOTS AND FRED HAMPTON JR

"We cannot afford the luxury just to look at Hip Hop as some kind of abstract phenomena. We have an obligation similar to the way Harriet Tubman utilized negroe spirituals and the way the late, great Nat Turner utilized the church. We have a responsibility. There's too many of us in Sing Sing for us to be kept hold by Bling Bling. We know what Che Guevara said about the Cuban Revolution— 'The role of the propagandist is as important as the role of the guerilla.' So we're going to hold those cats accountable. We knew in the '60s it was The Movement, first, that had James Brown say 'I'm black and I'm proud.' You're going to see that same type of resistance, that same type of community from the streets, reinforcing some forces that at some point want to use Hip Hop as a tool, not just using Hip Hop as some abstract type of thing."

—Fred Hampton Jr. 2006 interview.[1]

Tupac Shakur provided the FBI with another reason to target him in 1992 when he started funding the New Afrikan People's Organization. When Tupac sued the Oakland police for brutality, he hired NAPO national chair Chokwe Lumumba. He kept him as his consulting lawyer from then on. Tupac then officially hired ex-Panther and NAPO security director, Watani Tyehimba as his business manager. Tupac also promoted the New Afrikan Panthers in his lyrics and often spoke at NAPO gatherings.[2]

While Tupac worked on his second film, John Singleton's *Poetic Justice,* in Los Angeles at the end of April of 1992, sections of the city were rioting in response to the acquittal of the four white cops caught on video beating motorist Rodney King. It was the largest riot since the '60s and sparked smaller riots across the country.[3]

1 See youtube.com: type in Fred Hampton Jr. on Hip Hop.
2 "Tupac Shakur gave…gatherings." Personal interview, Watani Tyehimba, 5/20/03 and also see added features of Sarah Lazin, *Tupac: Resurrection* (MTV, 2003)
3 "While Tupac…cities." John Singleton and Veronica Chambers, *The Making of Poetic Justice* (New York: Delta, 1993). Alexander Cockburn, "Beat the Devil," *The Nation*, June 1, 1992, pp.738-9. On smaller riots in several other cities, see Pacifica Radio's *Democracy Now!* DemocracyNow.org "From COINTELPRO to the Shadow Government: As Fred Hampton, Jr. Is Released from 9 Years of Prison, a Look Back at the Assassination of Fred Hampton," 3/5/02.

Historically, U.S. Intelligence has put huge resources into targeting the forces playing a part in riots. In the '60s, U.S. Intelligence documents revealed research into which prominent activist figures most inspired the rioters. When their results pointed to Martin Luther King, U.S. Intelligence focused even more resources into the targeting of the civil rights leader.[4] Mike Davis, author of the best-selling book, *City of Quartz*, wrote how U.S. Intelligence used the 1992 LA riots as an opportunity to wage full scale war on communities of color, particularly chapters of two LA gangs that had declared peace and were becoming radicalized by former Black Panthers. [5]

After the 1992 riots, which raged for several days, evidence supports that U.S. Intelligence also targeted particular activists whose parents were Panther leaders, including Chicago's Fred Hampton Jr. and Tupac Shakur. The slain Chicago Black Panther leader's son, Fred Hampton, Jr., held a rally to protest the Rodney King police acquittal. Hampton, Jr. was Chicago's 22 year-old National People's Democratic Uhuru Movement leader. Hours after the rally, police and FBI agents picked Hampton up as he was walking with his three year-old daughter. They arrested him on several charges and Hampton claimed that the police officer leading FBI agents in arresting him, Joseph Grubesette, had also arrested his Panther leader father years earlier.[6]

Police accused Hampton of "firebombing" a store along with lesser charges. Police reportedly based their claims solely on a bottle filled with gasoline found intact at the store. Police didn't present fingerprints, eyewitnesses, or any other physical evidence at the trial. The trial judge asked how police could charge Hampton with arson

4 "Historically, U.S. Intelligence…him." Regarding '60s investigation on who influenced rioters, see William Pepper, *Order to Kill* (New York: Time Warner, 1998), p.446. On riots as one of the few disruptive mobilizations tactics that helped get national legislation passed for the poor, see Frances Fox Piven and Richard A. Cloward, *Poor Peoples' Movements* (New York: Vintage, 1979).

5 "Mike Davis…Panthers." On attack of gang truce leaders see, for example, Gang truce leader Dewayne Holmes received a 7 year prison sentence for allegedly stealing $10 at a gang unity dance. Mike Davis, "Who Killed Los Angeles? Part Two: The verdict is given," *New Left Review* 199/1993, p.34-5. Operation Hammer work to break up legal gang peace summit meetings also discussed by LA activist on WBAI Radio, 4/15/02. FBI work with LAPD in Operation Hammer in Megan Garvey & Rich Winton, "City Declares War on Gangs," *Los Angeles Times*, 12/4/02. Kody Scott (a.k.a. Sanyika Shakur), Monster: The Autobiography of an L.A. Gang Member (New York: Penguin, 1994), pp.vii-viii, 347-9. Tupac planned activist projects with Scott, Vibe ed.s, *Tupac*, '97, p.51. Mitchell Landsberg & John Mutchell, "In Gang's Territory, a Weary Hope," The Los Angeles Times, 12/5/02, p.A.1. "Rival Gangs Extend Reach to Small Cities," Houston Chronicle, 9/20/94, p.20. Reuters New Service, "Gangs Found in Military, Magazine Says," *St. Louis Post –Dispatch*, 7/17/95, p4A. Mike Davis, "Who Killed LA? A Political Autopsy," *New Left Review*, 197, 1993, p.7.

6 "After the…father." Personal interview, Fred Hampton, Jr. at Third Black Panther Film Festival, New York, 8/1/03. Fred Hampton Jr, as told to Heru, "Assassination Attempt on Fred Hampton,. Jr." 10/2/02, Davey D's Hip-Hop Corner: the New Source for the Hip-Hop Generation, daveyd.com/FullArticles/articleN1274.asp On walking with daughter, Heru, "Fred Hampton, Jr. Interview," AWOL Magazine 2002.

at a store when they couldn't even show that a fire ever occurred there. Nonetheless, the government's claim that Hampton had a "predisposition" to commit the crime led to a conviction and an 18-year sentence for "aggravated arson," of which he served nine.

During his time in prison, Fred Hampton Jr. reported what he believed were government orchestrated murder attempts behind bars. Hampton also believed that a New York attorney who worked to defend him from continued police attacks was herself murdered and all of her legal papers on his case were stolen. As noted previously, Assata Shakur also claimed that the FBI had a part to play in the murder of her lawyer, whose wife found him dead in their home and all of Assata's trial papers missing. The striking similarities in these two cases lends credence to Hampton's belief that a latter-day FBI Cointelpro orchestrated both of these attacks, or, at the very least, were commited by the same perpetrators.

Owing to Tupac's widespread fame by 1992, they couldn't have targeted him as brazenly as they did Hampton. But U.S. Intelligence had a particular longtime concern about political musicians and had developed more sophisticated strategies for attacking them. An exposed intelligence document reviewed by a 1976 Congressional committee examining the FBI's Counterintelligence Program detailed the many tactics developed to be used against political musicians. It instructed agents to:

> "Show them as scurrilous and depraved. Call attention to their habits and living conditions, explore every possible embarrassment. Send in women and sex, break up marriages. Have members arrested on marijuana charges. Investigate personal conflicts or animosities between them. Send articles to the newspapers showing their depravity. Use narcotics and free sex to entrap. Use misinformation to confuse and disrupt. Get records of their bank accounts. Obtain specimens of their handwriting. Provoke target groups into rivalries that may result in death." [7]

---

7 "U.S. Intelligence also…death.'" As noted above, one intelligence document a Senate committee found included strategies for use against political musicians such as "Intelligence Activities and Rights of Americans," Book II, April 26, 1976, *Senate Committee with Respect to Intelligence Report*. Excerpted in Alex Constantine, *The Covert War Against*

Evidence supports that U.S. Intelligence used most of these tactics against Tupac. Intelligence-linked conservatives such as Pat Buchanan blamed rappers for the LA riots and U.S. Intelligence particularly targeted those singing about the Rodney King incident.[8] Tupac emerged as a public figure, agitator, and critic in 1992. His solo debut, *2Pacalypse Now,* released in November of '91, was quickly becoming a gold record. It included song lyrics with militant responses to police brutality, such as "I remember Rodney King and I blast on his [the cop's] punk ass." [9] Critical acclaim for his role in *Juice* and starring in Academy Award-winner Singleton's next film, *Poetic Justice,* showed him to be a rising star in the film as well as the music industry.

In one of their issues, *Rolling Stone* magazine gave Tupac and several other rappers the opportunity to comment on the King verdict and the riots. Tupac said

> "The difference between 1992 and the Watts riots twenty-seven years ago is AK-47s, crack, unemployment. Those people wanted to see tomorrow—now people really don't care. It was like getting slashed with a knife. The Latisha Harlins decision [in which a Korean grocer got five years probation in the fatal shooting of a fifteen-year-old black girl] came, and we took that. When they gave the grocer probation and then sent a black man to jail for shooting a dog, we took that shit. When we went to the Rodney King trial every day and saw them call us gorillas, we took that. But this verdict was like Marie Antoinette saying, 'Let them eat cake.' America's got to feel what it is to live in the ghetto for three days. We get looted, we get beat down, we get grabbed out of trucks every day. It's hypocritical to be sensitive to white victims but not to us. I feel for the Koreans who lost their businesses and for the people who got hurt, but I feel more for my people." [10]

Rock (Los Angeles: Feral House, 2001), p.9. U.S. Senate Select Committee to Study Government Operations, *The FBI's Covert Program to Destroy the Black Panther Party,* U.S. Government Printing Office, Washington. D.C. 1976.
8 "Buchanan Call For Winning Back 'Soul of America'" *Los Angeles Times,* 5/28/92, p.A5.
9 Tupac Shakur, "Souljah's Revenge," *2Pacalypse Now* (Interscope, 1991).
10 "*Rolling Stone*…cake.'" Allan Light, "L.A. Rappers Speak Out," *Rolling Stone,* June 25, 1992, p.15.

With Tupac's fame, any new attack on him would require more covert police actions. Evidence suggests that U.S. Intelligence used sophisticated tactics in a bizarre attack on Tupac at the Marin Fest in August of 1992. As discussed earlier, research indicates that U.S. Intelligence used an anniversary threat-timing tactic in their assassination of Martin Luther King as well as in Huey Newton's assassination in 1989. Thus, the Marin Fest coordinators' scheduling of the event on August 22, the anniversary of Newton's murder, was the first indication that U.S. Intelligence may have been planning a third attempt on Tupac's life.

A documentary, *Thug Immortal*, provided a detailed account of the Marin Fest and showed other aspects of the event that suggest involvement by U.S. Intelligence. This video, along with *Tupac: Resurrection*, shows Tupac performing at a previous outdoor concert, singing his radical slogan, "Panther Power," which railed against America's "capitalistic" system, rapping it's "time to change the government now, Panther Power!"[11] In '92, Marin invited Tupac to the festival as an honorary guest.

The producers of *Thug Immortal* also present an eyewitness, Marku Reynolds, who gives a detailed account of the attack. Reynolds said Charles "Man-Man" Fuller and Mutulu Shakur's son, Maurice "Mopreme" Harding, were body-guarding Tupac. An old Marin neighborhood friend of Tupac's, Reynolds describes how he was joking with Tupac while the entertainer signed autographs when a threatening group of men approached them. He said one of them rushed at Tupac without provocation, but Fuller stopped him. Then another went around them and punched Tupac. Reynolds reenacts how Harding used a gun to try and ward them off, firing a warning shot straight up toward the sky. Seconds later, other gunshots sent Harding and Tupac running for their Jeep. Reynolds said he never saw a gun in Tupac's hands.[12] Tragically, one of the gunshots fatally hit a six-year-old boy a block away.[13]

---

11 "In the...government.'" *Thug Immortal* (Documentary, Xenon Entertainment, 1997). Also see lyrics for "Panther Power" Tupac Shakur, *The Lost Tapes*, (HerbNSoul, 1989/2000). This footage can also be seen in Laura Lazin and Karolyn Ali, *Tupac: Resurrection* (MTV, 2003).
12 "Marku Reynolds...Tupac's hands." Mostly Marku Reynolds in video, *Thug Immortal*,
13 Veronica Chambers, "Ain't Nothing Changed but the Weather," *Premiere*, August, 1993, p.84.

Reynolds goes on to say that right after the shots ended, a number of men ran after Tupac and Harding's Jeep, blaming them for the child's death. Reynolds states that one person, who apparently stopped Tupac from closing his car door, punched Tupac multiple times in front of police officers. Others tried to turn the Jeep over as Harding started driving away. A group of assailants, with an estimated 200 others following, attacked Tupac with bottles, bricks, and stones. Harding drove his Jeep through the crowd as the mob followed the car until he pulled up in front of a police precinct a few blocks away. There, many kept attacking Tupac while ignoring Harding, who had the gun.[14]

Marku Reynolds described how he saw police standing around Tupac's Jeep holding shotguns. Despite this armed police presence, the assailants continued attacking Tupac and destroying his Jeep in the process. Tupac then crawled under a parked police car and, after additional police units pulled up, police started dispersing the crowd. Police only arrested Tupac and Maurice Harding following the incident. They released Tupac after several hours and didn't charge him with a crime. Originally, they charged Harding with shooting the boy, until witnesses cleared him and he was released.[15]

Eyewitness accounts support that the person who punched Tupac did so to set up his murder. When Reynolds saw Harding's warning shot to the sky fail to scare off the attacker's group, he heard another round of shots that sent Harding and Tupac running. This supports that the group were in fact armed and fired at Tupac (A *Thug Immortal* technician or editor distinctly cut out an important part of Reynolds' account—what happened between Harding's shot and Harding running). Other eyewitnesses also supported that this group of attackers shot at Tupac. Witnesses approached the police and said that they saw the shooter of the 6-year-old boy. When police showed them a line-up with Harding, they said he wasn't the one who fired the fatal shot.[16]

---

14 "The assaillants then…gun." Marku Reynolds in video, Thug Immortal, Don't Back Down Productions, 1997. Also, Robert Sam Anson, "To Die Like A Gangsta," Vanity Fair, March 1997, p.248.Connie Bruck, "The Takedown of Tupac," The New Yorker, July 7, 1997, p.47.
15 "Reynolds saw…charge." Marku Reynolds in video, Thug Immortal, Don't Back Down Productions, 1997. Also, Robert Sam Anson, "To Die Like A Gangsta," Vanity Fair, March 1997, p.248.Connie Bruck, "The Takedown of Tupac," The New Yorker, July 7, 1997, p.47.
16 Veronica Chambers, "Ain't Nothing Changed but the Weather," Premiere, August, 1993, p.84. On Harding living in Marin, Attorney Michael Warren, personal interview, 4/10/00.

Furthermore, police actions suggest their link to an FBI-planned murder attempt. That police at the Marin Fest merely watched people punch Tupac and try to overturn his car without intervening suggests foreknowledge or, at the very least, complacency. Police standing around with shotguns when Harding reached the precinct may also suggest a stand down order. While they may have only been waiting for additional police units to arrive, the fact that they only arrested the victims and not any of the assailants—top suspects for the boy's murder—provides further support that certain police authorities had a part to play in the attack. Police and prosecutors dropped all charges against Harding and made no charges against anyone else at the scene. Was this to avoid details coming out during the trial? Prosecutors would similarly drop a case involving Tupac in Atlanta faster than expected.[17]

FBI Cointelpro veteran Richard Held's tactics and expertise can be seen mirrored in this event and may better explain these bizarre circumstances. As previously detailed, a slew of evidence implicated Held in the murderous attacks on Huey Newton and Judi Bari in the San Francisco Bay area within the last several years. Bari wrote detailed articles on how Held used similar Cointelpro tactics against the Black Panthers, the American Indian Movement, and her group. She cited these tactics as including intimidation, propaganda, and fake vigilantes (to create a "lynch-mob mentality"), as well as local police and government complicity.[18]

Upon closer scrutiny, it appears as though Richard Held may have used similar devious tactics during the Marin Fest event. For example, local government could have had Tupac come in as an honorary guest at the event, which was being held on the third anniversary of Huey Newton's murder. It may be coincidental that the cofounder of the Black Panthers and advisor to Tupac was murdered on the same day as this particular attempt on Tupac's life, but as has been shown, this is an often repeated occurrence throughout the civil rights movement. Within several years, two other key people in Tupac's life were murdered on similarly significant dates.

---

17 See also, Robert Sam Anson, "'To Die Like A Gangsta," *Vanity Fair*, March 1997, p.248.Connie Bruck, "The Takedown of Tupac," *The New Yorker*, July 7, 1997, p.47.
18 Reprinted from a Booneville, CA speech, Judi Bari, "Community Under Siege," 5/8/91. .things.org/~jym/ef/community-under-siege.html

Regarding Bari's mention of Richard Held's "propaganda in the media" Cointelpro tactic, other researchers and former coworkers of Held's attested to how he "specialized" in media manipulation and Held may have employed this manipulation in order to sway Marin's perception of Tupac.[19] Leading up to Marin Fest, Reynolds and others reported that people in Marin were accusing Tupac of making negative remarks about Marin residents to the media.

In *Thug Immortal*, the filmmakers implied that the people promoting these rumors were quoting a local paper's skewed reporting of a national magazine's interview with Tupac. In the magazine interview, Tupac openly discussed his teen homelessness in Marin City and his mother's drug dealers as, "shitty, dumb niggas who had women, rides, houses, and I ain't have shit. They used to dis me because I was at the bottom." Tupac said he got "love" from people in Marin City, "but it was the kind of love you give a dog or a neighborhood crack fiend."

The local Marin newspaper spun this interview, implying that Tupac denigrated Marin City residents as mostly dogs and crack fiends. Some people further hyped this newspaper's allegations and Tupac was threatened when he visited Marin in the weeks leading up to the festival.[20] These false rumor tactics are also referred to as "whisper" campaigns in political battles. The allegations provided the Marin Fest assailants a personal excuse for attacking Tupac, shielding the FBI from suspected orchestration.

The allegations may have further provided a "fallback" plan, in case the attackers failed to fatally shoot Tupac. Judi Bari claimed that Held's FBI Cointelpro employed tactics to cultivate a lynch mob mentality. This gained greater momentum when the Marin Fest crowd was led to believe Tupac, not the attackers, was to blame for the child's shooting. Marku Reynolds' bizarre account of the event lends further credibility to nefarious activity going on behind the scenes. Despite saying that he was a friend of Tupac's, that he never saw Tupac holding

19 See copied FBI memorandum of Held's in his LA FBI Cointelpro team member, M. Wesley Swearingen's memoir, *FBI Secrets: An Agent's Expose*, pp.118-127. Also see Churchill and Vander Wall, *Agents of Repression*, p.80. Sophisticated media work against LA Panther supporters, see FBI memorandum, "To: Director, FBI (100-448006), From: SAC, Los Angeles (157-4054) Date 4/27/70," against Jane Fonda and more damaging Held work against Jean Seberg, FBI memorandum dated 4/27/70. Memorandum copies published in Ward Churchill and Jim Vander Wall, The COINTELPRO Papers (Boston: South End Press, 1990). pp.212-216. "Specialized," p.214.

20 "Reynolds and at least…Marin Fest." Mostly Marku Reynolds in video, *Thug Immortal*, (Xenon/Don't Back Down Productions, 1997). Also, the interview quote from Robert Sam Anson, "To Die Like A Gangsta," Vanity Fair, March 1997, p.248.

a gun, and that he only saw Harding shoot a warning shot straight up, Reynolds joined the crowd in angrily going after Tupac. The assailants were the top suspects for influencing the crowd to develop this lynch-mob mentality.[21] The media would continue to blame Tupac for the boy's murder despite eyewitnesses saying Harding hadn't even fired the fatal shot.

21 "Reynolds saw...charge." Marku Reynolds in video, *Thug Immortal*, Don't Back Down Productions, 1997. Also, Robert Sam Anson, "To Die Like A Gangsta," *Vanity Fair*, March 1997, p.248.Connie Bruck, "The Takedown of Tupac," *The New Yorker*, July 7, 1997, p.47.

15

THE CODE OF
THUG LIFE

"They'll let you go as far as you want, but as soon as you start asking too many questions, boom, the block will come down...I don't think Bush is a bad president because for the upper class, he's a perfect president. And that's how society is built. The upper class runs [society] while...the middle class, we're just lost; we're going through the motions. We're the worker bees and they get to live like royalty."[1]

—Interview of Tupac when he was 17, before he decided on his gangsta persona.

I n 1992, U.S. Intelligence were given yet another motive to murder Tupac Shakur. The entertainer worked with his stepfather and political activist Mutulu Shakur in helping to politicize and radicalize the Bloods and Crips. In 1991, gang leaders finally took action regarding police execution-style shootings after witnesses told Crip leader Dewayne Holmes that police shot his unarmed cousin. Former Black Panthers and others helped organize a truce between the largest chapters of the Bloods and Crips by April of '92. At that truce meeting, a few days before the Rodney King riots, they vowed to fight racism instead of each other.[2] Black entertainers, politicians, and religious leaders such as Harry Belafonte, Jesse Jackson, and Louis Farrakhan helped to extend this gang peace truce through the majority of the LA gang chapters and then throughout the U.S.[3]

Tupac and Mutulu aided this peace truce in at least two ways. First, imprisoned Mutulu helped broker the Bloods/Crips peace truce between the gang members inside the federal prison system.[4] Then he

1 Micheal Eric Dyson, *Holler If You Hear Me*, pp.80-82.
2 "A little-known...each other." Mike Davis, "In L.A., Burning All Illusions," *The Nation*, 6/1/92, p.745. Mike Davis, "Who Killed LA? A Political Autopsy" *New Left Review*, 197/1993, p.7. Personal interview, Watani Tyehimba, 10/17/02. Jesse Katz, "Man Freed in Death of Gang Leader Courts: Rodney Compton is to get one year probation in the slaying of Tony Bogard, who helped reach a truce between the Crips and Bloods," *The Los Angeles Times*, 6/1/94, p.3. His cousin, Dewayne Holmes, worked with ex-Black Panther Michael Zinzun and local Shiite Muslim leader Mujahdid Abdul-Karim to rally Bloods and Crips factions against the LAPD instead of each other. Jesse Jackson and others helped the gangs increase the factions engaging in the peace truce and working against racist police attacks on their community. Mike Davis, "Who Killed LA: Part Two: the Verdict is Given," *New Left Review* 198, pp.34-5.
Sullivan, *LAbyrinth*, p.34 and photo.
Sulivan, *LAbrynth*, p.152.
Randall Sullivan, *LAbrynth*, pp.205-207, 225.
OJJDP Summary, August 2000—Youth Gang Programs and Strategies, "Suppression Programs" pp.21-26 ncjrs.gov/pdffiles1/ojjdp/171154.pdf
3 On Jackson, see Mike Davis, "Who Killed LA: Part Two: the Verdict is Given," *New Left Review* 198, pp.34-5. On Belafonte and other Black activists see, Joe Garofoli, "Singer Belafonte feels the beat of antiwar sentiment/ Keynote speaker at Oakland rally hears international criticism," *San Francisco Chronicle*, 4/5/03, pA.15.
4 Mutulu reportedly started organizing the truce in the Lompoc Penitentiary. hitemup.com/tupac/family.html . He was considered highly revered in the prison system as a political activist. Connie Bruck, "The Takedown of Tupac,"

developed a new hidden political plan with Tupac. They devised their "Thug Life Movement" as a plan with several goals. It included having Tupac take on a "gangsta" persona for the purpose of appealing to gang members and then politicizing them while also trying to influence gang members to abide by certain codes of conduct that decreased Black victimization. It further tried to persuade gang members to make legal money through making music, and politicizing other rappers. [5]

However, this creation of a negative image of Tupac both hurt his appeal to mainstream society and gave his detractors more reason to criticize him. Tupac's later increase in use of terms like "bitch" and "'ho," albeit regrettable, might be better understood as the regular street slang amongst much of his audience. Various negative forces would also come into his life to increase this lyrical tendency, but Black feminists such as bell hooks spoke out on Tupac's behalf, and Danyel Smith described Tupac's first three CD's lyrics about women as "uplifting, pro-choice and anti-abuse."

One defense lawyer, Iris Crews, stated having a hard time joining Tupac's case on one of the rapper's many low-level criminal charges until she could find out who he really was. She said, "Had he been this foul-mouthed, woman-hating kid, I wouldn't have done it." But instead she recalled how one day in a court recess, she saw Tupac with his extended family of children climbing all over him. Tupac said to her, "If I don't work, these kids don't eat." Crews said he'd been deprived of his own childhood and, "at twenty, he had twenty people to support."[6]

It was during this time that Tupac and Mutulu drew up a specific "Code of THUG LIFE" that consisted of 26 points for gang members. These included not endangering innocent people with their criminal activity and prohibiting gang members from ever working with the government. In 1992, at a "Truce Picnic" in California, Tupac

The New Yorker, 7/7/97, p.53.

5 "Then, he...class." Personal interviews with Tupac's business manager, ex-Black Panther and NAPO security director, Watani Tyehimba, 5/10/00. And Chokwe Lumumba, national chair of NAPO, 5/5/00. On other Thug Life goals, also see Bruck, *New Yorker*, p. 50 and Tupac Jacob Hoye and Karolyn Ali, eds, Afeni Shakur, concept, *Tupac: Resurrection* (New York: Atria, 2003), pp.116-17. A final note on the name came from an interview Mutulu Shakur gave to *AllHipHop.com*. He said that Tupac called himself a "thug." Tupac had said he did that because that's what all the adults called him and his friends. Mutulu said that the British called the young citizens of India, whom the British colonized, "thuggies." These Thuggies ended up accepting this name and organizing as a major factor that fought for India's independence from Britain. Sone excerpt "masses..." from Tupac Shakur, "Wordz of Wisdom," *2Pacalyspe Now*, 1991.

6 "One defense...support." Connie Bruck, "The Takedown of Tupac," *The New Yorker*, 7/7/97, p.56.

was reportedly instrumental in getting rival Bloods and Crips gang members to sign the Code of THUG LIFE.[7]

Mutulu and Tupac further inspired former Crip gang leader "Monster" Kody Scott to change his name to Sanyika Shakur as he joined the New Afrikan Movement (Tupac later said he planned an activist collaboration with Sanyika). Sanyika's book, *Monster*, detailed his and other gang members' embrace of Black nationalism and revolutionary socialism.[8] After the LA riots, Bloods and Crips including Sanyika Shakur (as Monster Kody Scott) first revealed gang community improvement plans in *The Nation* magazine. This included a written proposal from the Bloods and Crips truce leaders.[9]

Government officials were quick to respond to Sanyika Shakur's politicization. After Sanyika Shakur first made his political conversion in the late '80s, prison officials placed him in solitary confinement for years. And then in the mid-90s, they revoked his bail following the publication of his book.[10]

Gang peace summits and conversions to Panther-inspired radicalism spread eastward. Bloods and Crips called a gang peace truce in Atlanta. In New York, the Latin Kings acquired Panther-linked Young Lords consultants in their reported conversion to political activism. Later in New York, a Bloods leader rallied his group around Panther literature and espoused unity with Latinos.[11] Bloods and Crips gang leaders even traveled to England and spoke to a socialist Black group called Panther.[12]

U.S. Intelligence and conservative government forces had many reasons to find the movement of gang members converting to leftist political activism a major concern. The Bloods and Crips not only encompassed a large majority of the estimated 100,000 gang members

---

7 "Tupac and Mutulu...LIFE." From literature, "Code of THUG LIFE" by Tupac Shakur and Mutulu Shakur. Provided to this author by former New Haven Black Panther George Edwards.

8 "Writers...socialism." Kody Scott (a.k.a. Sanyika Shakur), *Monster: The Autobiography of an L.A. Gang Member* (New York: Penguin, 1994), pp.vii-viii, 347-9. Tupac planned activist projects with Scott, Vibe ed.s, *Tupac*, '97, p.51. Mutulu "revered," Bruck, *New Yorker*, p.53.

9 "After the...leaders." Alexander Cockburn, "Beat the Devil," *The Nation*, June 1, 1992, pp.738-9.

10 "Government...publication." See transcript of Sanyika Shakur's speech videotaped and presented at a 1995 forum where he was to speak at after his 1994 publication, when his parole was revoked and he was imprisoned again. -unix.oit.umass.edu/~kastor/fallprogram/fall-shakur.html

11 "Gang peace...Latinos." On Atlanta, personal interview with eyewitness Tony Parker, 7/7/03. On Latin Kings, see Jennifer Gonnerman, "Throne Behind Bars: The Latin King Leader on Love, Law Enforcement, and Landing Back in Jail," *Village Voice*, 4/7/98, p.61. Also, see video, *Black and Gold*, Big Noise Films, 1999. On New York Bloods, Chris Hedges, "Old Colors, New Battle Cry: Gang's Founder Calls for Focus on Community, Not Crimes," New York Times, 1/31/00, pp.B1, B6.

12 Tim King, "US street gang leaders to address London rally," *The Guardian*, 10/28/94.

in Los Angeles,[13] but reports acknowledged how the two gangs had spread to states across the U.S. from Texas to New York. Studies showed 1,100 individual Bloods and Crips gangs active in 115 cities nationally.[14] By 1995, the Bloods and Crips were even reportedly active in all four branches of the armed services and at more than 50 military bases around the U.S.[15]

U.S intelligence reacted to these gang activist conversions in several ways. The LAPD framed gang peace leaders and focused mass-arrests on gang unity meeting participants. U.S. Intelligence further used the LA riots as an opportunity to wage full-scale war. They started targeting the gangs that were declaring peace and becoming "radicalized" by former Panthers. The CIA director worked with the FBI director, who sent extra agents to work alongside police. They did this through anti-gang Operation Hammer as well as a post-riot program launched by President Bush called Weed and Seed. Watani Tyehimba said that a lecturing LA Black activist reported it was commonly believed that Weed and Seed stood for weeding undercover agents into the gangs to seed conflict and end the truce.[16]

Also, by a Presidential Executive Order, federal authorities formed Joint Task Force—Los Angeles (JTF-LA). This task force echoed the Joint Terrorist Task Force used in New York against Tupac's stepfather Mutulu Shakur. The JTF-LA used U.S. Army and Marine forces, as well as aid from the national guard, the FBI, and the Bureau of Alcohol, Tobacco and Firearms, in working with Los Angeles police. The California National Guard commander, Major General James Delk, now retired, said that gang members' opposition led his group's role to be "more akin to low intensity conflict (or urban warfare) than riot control." [17]

13 Mitchell Landsberg & John Mutchell, "In Gang's Territory, a Weary Hope," *The Los Angeles Times*, 12/5/02, p.A.1.
14 "Rival Gangs Extend Reach to Small Cities," *Houston Chronicle*, 9/20/94, p.20.
15 Reuters New Service, "Gangs Found in Military, Magazine Says," *St. Louis Post –Dispatch*, 7/17/95, p4A.
16 "U.S. Intelligence…Weed and Seed." Alexander Cockburn, "Beat the Devil," *The Nation*, June 1, 1992, pp.738-9. For example, Gang truce leader Dewayne Holmes received a 7 year prison sentence for allegedly stealing $10 at a gang unity dance. Mike Davis, "Who Killed Los Angeles? Part Two: The verdict is given," *New Left Review* 199/1993, p.34-5. WBAI Radio, 4/15/02. FBI work with LAPD in Operation Hammer in Megan Gavery & Rich Winton, "City Declares War on Gangs," *Los Angeles Times*, 12/4/02. Mitchell Landsberg & John Mutchell, "In Gang's Territory, a Weary Hope," *The Los Angeles Times*, 12/5/02, p.A.1. On Bush's Weed and Seed, see Mike Davis, "Who Killed LA? A Political Autopsy," *New Left Review*, 197, 1993, p.7. On Weed and Seed for weeding undercover agents into the gangs: Personal interview, 11/02/03.
17 "Also, by a Presidential…control.'" see Colonel William W. Mendel, US Army (retired), book review of *Fires and Furies*, by James D. Delk, *US Army Foreign Military Studies Office* (FMSO), Fort Leavenworth, Kansas, 1996. See also by Mednel, Combat in Cities: The LA Riot and Operation Rio," *FMSO*, July 1996. Major Christopher M Schnaubelt, "Lessons in Command and Control, from the Los Angeles Riots," *Parameters Magazine*, Summer 1997. William V. Wenger and Frederick W. Young, "The Los Angeles Riots and Tactical Intelligence," *Military Intelligence*, Oct-Dec.

Prison officials collaborated with U.S. Intelligence objectives within the federal prison system. They put Mutulu Shakur in the country's most restrictive confines, apparently due to gang work with young Blacks and his work with Tupac. Out of concern over his "outside contacts and influence over the younger Black element," prison officials transferred Mutulu to the highest maximum-security underground prison in Colorado.[18] U.S. Intelligence would later use the same forces to exert control over Tupac during his incarceration.

1992. *The Federation of American Scientists Military Analysis Network*, "Garden Plot," November 1998. All cited in Frank Morales, "U.S. Has Been Preparing to Turn America into a Military Dictatorship," *What Really Happened*, .whatreallyhappened.com/suppression.html Similar Morales article appeared in print, such as Frank Morales, "The Militarization of the Police," *CovertAction Quarterly*, Spring–Summer 1999, #67, pp.45-50.

18 "Prison...Colorado." A warden's memo said that Mutulu's transfer to the nation's most maximum-security prison was due to his influence over young Black men through his "outside contacts." Bruck, *The New Yorker*, p.54.

16

TUPAC'S FBI
FILE, REPUBLICAN
ATTACKS,
HARASSMENT
ARRESTS, &
SPECIOUS
LAWSUITS

"I never had a record until I made a record."
    —Tupac Shakur, 1994 quote.

U.S. Intelligence and their Republican political supporters increased their focus on Tupac Shakur. The Los Angeles FBI office continued accumulating documents that would eventually come to over 4,000 pages for their file on Tupac, according to a Freedom Of Information Act (FOIA) Justice Department worker. They guarded this file closely as a FOIA request only released 99 partially deleted pages.[1]

But any documentation of operations against Tupac Shakur remained unavailable because of legal changes President Ronald Reagan made in the '80s. Reagan and Bush began keeping documentation of U.S. Intelligence operations under wraps and outside of FOIA requests' reach through President Reagan's Executive Order 123333. The order "'privatized' NSC [National Security Council] intelligence operations and permitted agencies other than the CIA to carry out 'special operations' without reporting its activities...[allowing] any private enterprise the NSC set up to carry out covert operations."[2]

U.S. Intelligence began using new strategies against Tupac and enlisted the White House for help. While Tupac had only one CD at this time, George Bush Sr.'s Vice-President Dan Quayle focused on him and Ice-T, amongst the many so-called "gangsta" rappers. As previously mentioned, on September 22, exactly one month after the Marin Fest attack (see timing tactic discussion in Ch. 13, 14, 27), Quayle made a widely publicized speech condemning Tupac's first CD. *Billboard* also noted how in that speech Quayle used the same words of it "having no place in our society" that he used in a speech against rapper Ice-T three months earlier.[3]

Ice-T had joined Tupac in railing against the government in *Rolling Stone*'s post-riot issue, except Ice-T more directly called for taking the riot to the White House. Like Tupac, Ice-T also proposed

1 Personal interview with Tawanda Monroe of the Department of Justice, Federal Bureau of Investigation, May 9, 2000. Letter from Department of Justice acknowledged this communication and this author's willingness to pay for the copying fee of $405 (see Monroe). Ms. Monroe also disclosed that they charged 10 cents per page, copying 10 at a time, fitting her "over 4,000 page disclosure. Ms. Moroe originally said "I'm not allowed to tell you how many pages are in that file," but then stated the number a few minutes later. The Los Angeles FBI File Number for the Tupac Shakur file is 266A-LA-201807.
2 "Reagan...operations." Michale Montalvo, "Prisoner of the Drug War: An Inside Report from a former Inside Player," *Prevailing Winds* #8, 2000, pp.76-82.
3 On September...earlier." Chris Morris, "Quayles' 2Pac/Interscope Attack Puts New Heat On Time Warner," *Billboard*, October 3, 1992, pp.5, 86.

a violent response to the Rodney King police brutality incident, in his song "Cop Killer." [4]

The case of Ice-T appeared to show Time Warner's true intent in supporting U.S. Intelligence's repressive agenda. Ice-T had sung the song "Cop Killer" with his group, Body Count, at every stop of the sold-out '91 Lollapalooza Tour. No police complaints ensued. He then released the song on his band's CD, which hovered between #32 and #45 on the Billboard charts for weeks. The LA riots ended in early May of '92, and two Texas police groups held a press conference in June protesting the CD. After many Congressmen joined the protest over the next 45 days, Ice-T announced his removal of the song from the album. Despite largely increased sales from the publicity, Time Warner dropped Ice-T within six months. [5]

Tupac likely brought on Quayle's denunciation for a variety of reasons, including Tupac's attacks on George Bush in his debut album. Tupac was also about to release his second CD just before the presidential election, which contained even more attacks on Bush and Quayle. These critiques mentioned Republican leaders by name while also saying "they've got money for war but can't feed the poor." Between Tupac's debut CD on Interscope Records and the release of his second CD, Time Warner increased its ownership of Interscope's music label from 25% to 50%. [6] Time Warner then delayed Tupac's second CD's release for a year, to well after the election. [7]

Other Republican politicians also singled out Tupac in their speeches. Republican presidential candidate Bob Dole and former Bush cabinet member William Bennett said Time Warner needed to ban Tupac's recordings. A former Pennsylvania state office holder who headed a private group she called the National Congress of Black

4 "Ice-T had...Killer'" Allan Light, "L.A. Rappers Speak Out," *Rolling Stone*, June 25, 1992, p.15. Ice-T, "Cop Killer," on Body Count, *Body Count* (Self-titled debut on Sire/Warner, 1992).

5 "The case of...months." All from Barry Shank, "Fears of the White Unconcious: Music, Race, and Identification in the Censorship of 'Cop Killer.'" *Radical History Review* #66, Fall 1996. http://chnm.gmu.edu/rhr/article1.htm . This article cites several articles regarding police groups' and Republicans' protest. These include Bruce Brown, "Quayle Boosts 'Cop Killer' Boycott Campaign," *Washington Post*, 6/20/92, ppB1,5; Avis Thomas-Lester & Marylou Tousignant, "Reaction to Ice-T Song Heats Up: 60 Congressmen Join Complaint," *Washington Post*, 6/25/92, pp.C1,3. On Time Warner dropping Ice-T, Irv Lichtman, "The Billboard Bulletin: Sire/Warner Drops Ice-T," *Billboard*, 2/6/93, p.82.

6 "Tupac was also...50%." Robert Sam Anson, "To Die Like a Gangsta," *Vanity Fair*, March 1997, p.251. Connie Bruck, "The Takedown of Tupac," *The New Yorker*, 7/7/97, p.57. Tupac lyric from "Keep Ya Head Up,"*Strictly 4 My N.I.G.G.A.Z* (Interscope, 1993).

7 "Tupac likely...election." Tupac Shakur, *2Pacalypse Now* (Interscope, 1992). *Strictly 4 My N.I.G.G.A.Z* (Interscope, 1993). This CD was ready for release but held up for a year by Time Warner. Personal interview, Watani Tyehimba, 5/5/00.

Women, C. Delores Tucker, joined Bennett in a suspicious campaign to censor Tupac and other political rappers (explored later in the chapter).[8]

Politicians were brought into the tactical strategy more officially in 1993. Sundance Award-winner Nick Broomfield, who produced the documentary *Biggie and Tupac*, said that a bipartisan Senate subcommittee formed out of a concern over rap's subversive elements in '93. He also said that the FBI began spying on rappers that year, though it has been shown that they started their operations in 1988 or earlier. [9]

The U.S. Intelligence document outlining the tactics for use against political musicians included orders to "send articles to the newspapers" smearing them, using "narcotics and free sex to entrap" them, arrest them "on marijuana charges," and "provoke target groups into rivalries."[10] New police intelligence units were formed to target rappers. New York had a rap intelligence unit trained in the FBI's Counter Intelligence Program tactics that started at least as early as 1995. That unit subsequently trained police in Los Angeles and Atlanta.[11]

After Tupac was publicly denounced by Quayle, police appeared to use these FBI harassment strategies against the up and coming star.[12] In line with Tupac's popular quote, "I never had a record until I made a record," the power that increasing fame brought the radical rapper also brought on more police attacks. In Los Angeles, where the FBI accumulated their file on Tupac, police arrested the rap and film star about a half dozen times on crimes such as public drunkenness, gun possession (note that it is common among celebrities to arm themselves against potential stalkers), and marijuana possession. Except for a fight with the Hughes brothers directorial team in '94, most of the charges were dismissed.[13]

8 Other Republican…Tupac." Nick Broomfield, *Biggie and Tupac*, documentary film, 2002. Cathy Scott, "The Death of Tupac Shakur One Year Later," *Las Vegas Sun*, September 6, 1997.

9 "Politicians…year." Nick Broomfield, *Biggie and Tupac* (documentary, 2002). Broomfield had previously won a best documentary award at the Sundance Film Festival.

10 "The U.S.…into rivalries.'" "Intelligence Activities and Rights of Americans," Book II, April 26, 1976, *Senate Committee with Respect to Intelligence Report*. Excerpted in Alex Constantine, The Covert War Against Rock (Los Angeles: Feral House, 2001), p.9.

11 "It eventually…below)." Dasun Allah & Joshua Fahiym Ratcliffe, "Law and Disorder," *The Source*, June 2004, p.44. Nicole White and Evelyn McDonnell, "Police Secretly Watching Hip-Hop Artists," *Miami Herald*, 3/9/04, p.1A.

12 See August 30, 1967 FBI Memorandum from Philadelphia's Special Agent in Charge to the FBI Director, reprinted in Churchill and Vander Wall, *Agents of Repression*, pp.44-7.

13 "In line…dismissed." Associated Press, "Rapper Shakur Hit with a Gun Arrest Encore," *The Daily News*, May 1, 1994. Personal interview with Ken Ellis, Esq. 5/20/00. Karen Zekan, "4 Sought in Shakur Shooting," *Las Vegas Sun*, September 9, 1996 from lasvegassun.com/news/1996/sep/09/4-sought-in-shakur-shooting/. On celebrities and guns, see, for example, "Names and Faces: Pistol Packing Big Shots," compiled by Chris Richards, *Washington Post*, 8/5/03, p.C3. On Tupac's many arrests for mostly minor charges in areas particularly focusing on Tupac and other rap stars, see "Rapper's Rap Sheet: 10 Arrests," *The New York Post*, 12/22/93.

These harassment arrests and public denouncements further appeared to have the purpose of leading people to believe that Tupac invited strangers' armed attacks as a result of his purported "criminal" behavior. Like the armed attacks after his MTV debut and his movie premiere, a conflict occurred in 1993 while Tupac was in LA. In March, Tupac was filming his first "live" network television musical performance on the set of *In Living Color*. In between takes he took a break with a friend and went to their limousine parked just outside. Tupac reported that the limousine driver started screaming at his friend as if to instigate a fight. He said the driver then attempted to use a gun on them. Police confirmed finding a gun at the scene that didn't belong to Tupac or his friend, supporting Tupac's account and making it the fourth attack by an assailant with a gun.[14] Police detained Tupac and interrupted his television performance.

In Atlanta, police similarly took Tupac away from a national rap convention just before his featured speeches, two years in a row. Police arrested Tupac for marijuana possession, then public drunkenness, and next for allegedly slapping a fan who wanted his autograph. Two of these arrests occurred one year apart during Atlanta's "Jack the Rapper" national rap convention, which scheduled Tupac to speak in '92 and '93. Tupac lost much time and money before judges dismissed all of the charges.[15]

The FBI appeared to have another strategy. They apparently used the Republican denunciations and harassment arrests for a second reason—to get Tupac's shows canceled. In interviews, Tupac said many venues canceled his concerts due to police citing their risk of turning riotous. The FBI had previously used this tactic on others, like the top-selling rap group N.W.A. in 1988. After the FBI sent N.W.A. a warning letter about their "Fuck the Police" song, the FBI then sent faxes to the police department in every city that N.W.A. toured. They told police to find an excuse to cancel each show (though few were at that time). After the success of this tactic against Tupac, they tried to use it again with Rage Against the Machine when they toured with rap group Wu Tang Clan. Rage lead singer Zach De La Rocha said that police called concert venues and said they wouldn't provide security because the show posed too much risk of a riot occurring.[16]

14 "These harassment…gun." Deborah Russell, "Rapper 2Pac Faces Assault Charge in LA," *Billboard*, v105 March 27, 1993, p.94. Also see *New York Post*, and Vibe Editors, *Tupac Shakur*, pp.29, 138.
15 "Similar circumstances…charges." Personal interview with Tupac's Atlanta trial lawyer, Ken Ellis, Esq. 5/20/00.
16 "The FBI apparently…occurring." Tupac said shows cancelled in Vibe eds *Tupac Shakur* (New York: Crown, 1997) p.46. Rage Against the Machine lead singer Zach De La Rocha detailed how police used this tactic against his group

By the mid-to-late '70s, researchers found that U.S. Intelligence started a new version of the harassment arrest strategy in the form of a harassment lawsuit strategy. As early as the '70s, Cointelpro researchers found that the "U.S. Justice Department brought many activists to trial, often on unprosecutable conspiracy charges in order to deplete the funds and energy of the left." [17] A vast number of civil suits began against Tupac and continued against other wealthy, leftist-linked Black entertainers. Over a dozen people risked sanction and penalization for "frivolous" lawsuits when they filed seemingly specious civil suits against Tupac starting in 1992.

The bizarre nature of several of these lawsuits, along with links to U.S. Intelligence and top conservative figures, suggests such a new intelligence tactic. For example, C. Delores Tucker, who had joined in television advertisements against rappers with President Bush's drug czar, William Bennett, filed a civil lawsuit claiming Tupac's lyrics hurt her sex life.[18]

Most of the other lawsuits appeared just as specious and had similarly high level conservative links. Vice-President Dan Quayle's public denunciation of Tupac came in support of a multi-million dollar lawsuit a Texas police officer's widow filed against Tupac. Quayle claimed that "*2Pacalypse Now* bore some responsibility for the fatal shooting of [this] Texas state trooper." [19] Also, the Atlanta autograph-seeker, as previously mentioned, filed suit alleging that Tupac slapped her. Witnesses said that the woman hounded Tupac as he was rushing to an appointment, an associate of Tupac's intervened, and the

when they went on tour with rap group Wu Tang Clan, personal interview, 5/5/99. On the FBI's fax campaign to get police canceling NWA shows, see Bruce C. Brown, "Quayle Boosts 'Cop Killer' Campaign," *Washington Post*, 6/20/92, pp.B1,5. Cited in Barry Shank, "Fears of the White Unconcious: Music, Race, and Identification in the Censorship of 'Cop Killer.'" *Radical History Review* #66, Fall 1996.

17 *Me and My Shadow: Investigation of the political left by the United States Government*, producers Tarabu Betserai and Adi Gevins from "The Pacifica Radio Archives." Track 5.

18 "Over a dozen...life." On "frivolous" lawsuit, personal interview with attorney Dan 5/9/05.C. Delores Tucker, who formed an anti-rap campaign with President Bush's Drug Czar, William Bennett, filed a lawsuit claiming that "her sex life with her husband was adversely affected because of some of Shakur's lyrics." Tupac's lyrics were, "Delores Tucker, yous a motherfucka. Instead of trying to help a nigga, you destroy a brotha." Cathy Scott, "The Death of Tupac Shakur One Year Later," *Las Vegas Sun*, 9/6/97. Randall Sullivan, *LAbyrinth* (New York: Atlantic Monthly Press, 2002), pp.87-88.

Also see, Johnnie Roberts, "Grabbing at a Dead Star," *Newsweek*, September 15, 1997, p.56. "C. DeLores Tucker Files $10 Million Lawsuit Against Tupac Shakur's Estate," *Jet*, September 1, 1997, p.62. On over a dozen lawsuits, see "Another in a long line...nothing about the lawsuit." Associated Press, "$16.6 M of Shakur Estate Sued," *Las Vegas Sun*, November 20, 1996. lasvegassun.com/news/1997/sep/06/the-death-of-tupac-shakur-one-year-later/ .

19 "Most of these...trooper.'" Veronica Chambers, "Ain't Nothing Changed but the Weather," *Premiere*, i1 v6 August, 1993, p.84-88. On Quayle-backed lawsuit claiming lyrics caused teen to kill cop, see Chuck Phillips, "2Pac's Gospel Truth," *Rolling Stone*, 10/28/93, p. 22. Chris Morris, "Quayles' 2Pac/Interscope Attack Puts New Heat On Time Warner," *Billboard*, 10/3/92, pp.5, 86. Barbara Ross, "Cops Widow Sez It's Time to Dump Star," *The Daily News*, 11/24/93.

autograph-seeker started a fight with her. They said that Tupac merely got in between the two to stop the fight. A judge dismissed the case.[20]

Furthermore, a woman claimed she was shot and paralyzed at a Tupac concert because Tupac created a "riotous atmosphere" at the show.[21] And finally, the limo driver who Tupac said tried to use a gun on him during his first live network television performance joined the others in suing the rapper.[22] The driver did this despite the police report that backed Tupac's claim, and this bizarre scenario of an apparent attempt on Tupac's life leading to a lawsuit against him would repeat itself in Atlanta later that year.

U.S. Intelligence attacks continued in direct proportion with Tupac's ever-increasing wealth and influence and this barrage kept him forever on edge. *The Source* magazine reported one particular incident that may have been especially concerning to the intelligence community. It occurred when Tupac exploded in anger and alluded to a latter-day Black Liberation Army.

This incident came about when Tupac awaited trial for the sole charge he agreed he was guilty of—a fistfight on a film set with young Black directors Albert and Allen Hughes. *Source* magazine reporter Dream Hampton followed Tupac at the time. On the day of the trial in a Los Angeles courthouse, Tupac stood outside the courtroom with Hampton and others. He saw the Hughes brothers surrounded by the Nation of Islam's security-for-hire Fruit of Islam (FOI). Tupac walked up to one of the bow-tied FOI and asked why they were protecting the Hughes Brothers from him. Accusations between the brothers and Tupac ensued, when an FOI guard pushed Tupac and he charged the group. Tupac backed the brothers and their four guards against the wall.

"You gon' need mothafuckin' Farrakhan to calm me down! You got that? Farrakhan! You beanpie-slinging, bowtie-wearing bitches! You wear bowties! Remember that! I'll have niggas from Crenshaw wit AK's and rags up here! Nigga you don't even know who you fucking with—these roots run deep!" Tupac's threats apparently alluded to the modest 'rags' attire of his former New Afrikan Panther group in the Crenshaw neighborhood of Los Angeles who lived as revolutionaries and likely backed it up with AK-47 military rifles if ever needed for self-defense. Later in the courtroom, two of the FOI guards assured Tupac

20 "The Atlanta...case." On Atlanta suit, see Personal interview with Ken Ellis, Esq. 5/15/00, and Karen Zekan, "4 Sought in Shakur Shooting," *Las Vegas Sun*, 9/9/96 from lasveagasu\sun.com/sunbin/stories/text/1996/sep/09/505068709.html
21 Ibid, Scott, *Las Vegas Sun*, September 6, 1997.
22 Michael Eric Dyson, *Holler If You Hear Me* (New York: Basic Civitas Books, 2001), p.170.

they were fans of his despite them working for the Hughes brothers. The judge in the case sentenced Tupac to 15 days in jail.[23]

---

23 "Tupac said…in jail." Dream Hampton, "Hellraiser," *Source*, September 1994, pp. 82, 84, 88.

ATLANTA POLICE SHOOT ATTUPAC

"How long will it last 'til the poor get more cash
Until then, raise up!
Tell my young black males, blaze up!...
Pump ya fists like this
Holla if ya hear me—PUMP PUMP if you're pissed!
To the sell-outs living it up
One way or another you'll be giving it up, huh
I guess 'cause I'm black born
I'm supposed to say peace, sing songs, and get capped
on
But it's time for a new plan, BAM!
I'll be swingin' like a one man, clan."

>   —Tupac Shakur, "Holler If Ya Hear Me," *Strictly 4 My
>   N.I.G.G.A.Z*, 1993.

O ne of the most blatant police attempts to murder Tupac
Shakur occurred in 1993. Tupac had recently moved to
Atlanta, buying a house for his mother and sister. He
partly did this to be near his business manager, Watani
Tyehimba, who also helped lead the New Afrikan People's Organization
(NAPO) from there.[1] Witnesses support that "off-duty" cops shot at
Tupac after the unarmed rapper finished a Halloween night concert at
an Atlanta college.

The incident started as Tupac drove back from his performance.
Tupac's car, followed by an entourage of 3-6 cars, stopped at a traffic
light near a hotel driveway. A Black driver with no connection to Tupac
said he pulled into that driveway to turn around when two white cops
on foot in civilian clothes, with two women, screamed racial slurs at the
Black driver. One of the cops also punched him.[2]

White and Black bystanders at the scene, among others, said
that Tupac rolled down his window and asked what was going on.
When one of the white men took out a gun, Tupac rolled his window
back up. A white couple also stopped at the traffic light in their car,
said they saw a group of whites run over to Tupac's car, looking like

---

1 "Tupac had...there." Affidavit by Tupac Shakur, p.1, *New York vs. Tupac Shakur, Supreme Court of State of New York*, Appellate Division, First Department, Indict. No. 11578/93. Sonia Murray, "Rapper's Career Taking Off in Film, Recording Industries," *The Atlanta Journal/the Atlanta Constitution*, November 2, 1993, p.C5.
2 "Tupac's car...him." Personal interview with Tupac's Atlanta trial lawyer, Ken Ellis, Esq, 5/12/00. Ellis reported that his investigator luckily got a hold of the Black motorist and interviewed him.

"a white gang attacking a Black man." One of the men broke Tupac's passenger window with the butt of his gun and shot at him.[3]

Tupac rolled out of his car in time to avoid getting shot. The off-duty cop firing his gun brought Tupac's security guards out of their cars. Tupac grabbed one of their guns and fired three shots back. The people exiting the entourage of several cars sent the white group running with the gunman reportedly running partially backwards still aiming behind him at Tupac. Tupac's shots hit the two men in the leg, butt, and back. Police arrested Tupac for attempted homicide.[4]

The white officers said one of the women was one of the officer's wives and the Black motorist nearly hit her, but the woman would never speak to this. The officers involved in the shooting also gave conflicting reports. They first wrote a police report that described Tupac's group responding to the incident as "niggers came by and did a drive-by shooting." They then changed that to Tupac's group getting out of their cars, surrounding and threatening them, then shooting at them.[5]

However, many aspects of the incident and post-shooting events contradict the police account and even support that the police may have planned this attempt on Tupac's life. During the entire conflict, the officers never identified themselves as police.[6] However, shooting a cop can lead to a death sentence and lawyers say that cops would announce "police" to protect themselves on- or off-duty. The officers also discredited themselves by lying in saying they didn't have a gun on them that night. Furthermore, immediately after the incident,

3 "White and Black...at him." Partly from eyewitness Watani Tyehimba, parked next to Black motorist first focused on by the plainclothes cops. Personal interview, 11/5/03. Also from witness interviews--personal interview, Ken Ellis, 5/12/00. The daily *Atlanta Journal Constitution* gave exact quotes of the police report in which Edward Fields is quoted as saying that "one of the White males...pull[ed] out and point[ed] a Black handgun...started yelling 'Get Down! Get Down! And then fired one shot towards the Mercedes." Kathy Scruggs and Scott Marshall, "Witness says off-duty cops fired first shot: Claims rapper's return fire caused brothers' wounds." *Atlanta Journal Constitution*, 11/03/93, p. D12.

4 "Tupac's reaction...homicide." Personal interview, Billy Lesane, April, 10,1999. Also reported by Edward Fields in describing a person looking like Tupac shooting back. Scruggs and Marshall, "Witness says off-duty cops fired first shot," *Atlanta Journal Constitution*, 11/03/93, p. D12. Ellis said that the prosecutor spent a long cross-examination to get Fields to say that the officer's shots could have been a warning shot and the newspaper then reported it that way, personal interview, Ken Ellis, 5/12/00.

5 "The white officers...at them." On "Niggers came by and..." Ronin Ro, *Have Gun Will Travel* (New York: Doubleday, 1998), p.146. On white officers' accounts, see their lawyer in "Witness says off-duty cops fired first shot." *Atlanta Journal Constitution*, 11/03/93, p. D12.

6 Personal interviews with Ken Ellis, Esq. 5/20/00 and Chokwe Lumumba, 5/5/00. On not announcing "police," common knowledge that killing a cop can bring a death penalty and cops would say "Police" in order to help protect themselves. Ellis supported that Atlanta cops would normally say "police," off duty or not, and Chokwe Lumumba supported this notion that the cops would have protected themselves this way unless they wanted to hide the fact. Personal interview with Chokwe Lumumba, 5/5/00. Also, eyewitness accounts of Tupac's biological cousin, Billy Lesane, personal interview, 4/10/99, and Watani Tyehimba, 5/10/00.

Atlanta police went directly to Tupac's hotel room to arrest him, despite the fact that Tupac had registered himself in six rooms under different aliases. Such an action supports the claim that he was under close police surveillance.[7] Most importantly, prosecution dropped their charges against Tupac when the biggest revelations came to light in court. The state prosecutor's own witness said that the gun one of the cops used on Tupac had been taken from the other cop's police evidence locker.[8] In another trial, a police supervisor explained that officers use such "throwaway guns" for the ease of hiding them after killing someone.[9]

Tupac's lawyer Chokwe Lumumba would also later support the claim that Atlanta police intelligence may have used psychological profiling on Tupac to attempt his murder. Lumumba said police started using psychological profiling on political activists, such as Huey Newton, at the same time they started using it on common criminals in the early '70s. Lumumba believed that police may have attacked the Black motorist in an attempt to lure Tupac into a shooting and thus justify their involvement. [10]

---

7 "The officers...surveillance." Caught lying, saying no guns on them, Scruggs & Marshall, "Witness says off-duty cops fired first shot." *Atlanta Journal Constitution*, 11/03/93, p. D12. On going right to hotel room despite aliases, personal interview with, Ken Ellis, Esq. 5/20/00. Personal interview with Chokwe Lumumba, 5/5/00.
8 "Most importantly, locker." Cathy Scott, *The Killing of Tupac Shakur* (Las Vegas, Nevada: Huntington Press, 1998), p.77. Ken Ellis, Esq. Tupac's Atlanta trial lawyer, and *Spin*, p.46.
9 New York City Police Officer Craig McKernan, *People of the state of New York vs. Charles Fuller and Tupac Shakur*, Indictment no. 11578-93, Trial Excerpt of People's Witness—P.O. McKernan cross-examination, pp.8-9. Cross-examination by Michael Warren, Esqu.
10 "Regarding...shooting." Personal interview, Chokwe Lumumba, 5/10/00.

18

COVER-UPS
AND LINKS TO
TUPAC'S NYC
SHOOTING

"Listen while I take you back and lace this rap
A real live tale about a snitch named Haitian Jack
Knew he was working for the feds, same crime,
different trials…
Set me up, wet me up, niggas stuck me up
Heard the guns bust but you tricks never shut me up."

—Tupac Shakur, "Against All Odds," *Don Killuminati, the 7 day theory*, 1996.

T
wo weeks after the 1993 Atlanta attack, a new "friend" of Tupac's, Jacques Agnant (a.k.a. Nigel, name Ricardo Brown used in court, "Haitian Jack"), helped set up Tupac's most serious charge in New York. Agnant, a purported music promoter who originally came from Haiti, often traveled with his associate, "Trevor" (real name Rick Alinzey). They escorted Tupac to a Greenwich Village dance club in mid-November. That weeknight in the club started out spectacular for Tupac as several professional athletes approached him to say they were fans. Then Agnant and Trevor introduced Tupac to a 19 year-old Black Naval Yard employee named Ayanna Jackson. Jackson said that she was with a man she'd been dating for 2-3 months. Within minutes, she danced with Tupac, put her mouth on his penis on the dance floor, then left her date to have sex with Tupac at his hotel.[1]

In the several days following the dance club and late night tryst, Ayanna Jackson left several messages on Tupac's hotel answering service about wanting to meet up again. When she came over, Agnant, Trevor, and Tupac's road manager, Charles "Man-Man" Fuller, entered her and Tupac's room. She would make several forced sodomy charges against Tupac, Agnant, and Fuller, though she later said Fuller only watched. Police also charged Tupac with illegal gun possession. Trevor eluded arrest.[2] One of the first of many questions about Jackson's honesty regarding the incident came when a doctor examined Jackson

1 "Two weeks…hotel." See Ayanna Jackson in New York v. Charles Fuller and Tupac Shakur, Indictment No. 11578-93. Also Det. Slimak, People's Witness, p.352. New York v. Tupac Shakur, Notice of Motion Pursuant to CPL 530.45 Ind. No. 11578/93 by Michael Warren, p.8, cites trial testimony at 33-38, 40, Jackson's confirming consensual oral and vaginal sex at hotel room. On Jackson's date at the club, see New York vs. Tupac Shakur, Sentencing hearing, p.36.
2 "In the several…arrest." Ayanna Jackson in New York v. Charles Fuller and Tupac Shakur, Indictment No. 11578-93. See Jackson's admission in Fuller's defense attorney cross examination of Jackson at p.232. Also Det. Slimak, People's Witness, p.352. New York v. Tupac Shakur, Notice of Motion Pursuant to CPL 530.45 Ind. No. 11578/93 by Michael Warren, p.8, cites trial testimony at 33-38, 40, Jackson's confirming consensual oral and vaginal sex at hotel room and then leaving telephone message "I like the way you fuck."

at a hospital after the charges and said that there was no evidence of forced sexual activity.[3]

Tupac had become accustomed to police arrests and media groups' seemingly biased criminal portrayal of him by this time. He came to use some of this media as sound bites in his songs and video. One of his music videos even had the actual footage of police arresting him outside the hotel. The cops weren't in uniform, one of the first clues that they were part of New York's infamous plainclothes Street Crime Unit. They walked Tupac into a police van as television news cameras filmed the scene and, just before getting into the car, Tupac leaned back out of the van, looked into a TV camera, and facetiously proclaimed, "Guilty." [4]

Tupac's New York trial attorney for this case, Michael Tarif Warren, had personal experience as the target of New York police intelligence while also gaining notoriety for his activism and success. Warren, a former SNCC organizer, knew much about police intelligence work, as the New York Police Department's Black Desk unit had illegally spied on his Black Liberation Movement work in the '80s.[5] He also represented activist Mumia Abu-Jamal as his European spokesman in the '90s. Warren later represented a majority of the Central Park jogger rape defendants' and had their convictions overturned in 2002, by obtaining evidence that supported the real attacker's confession.[6]

Michael Tarif Warren claimed that Haitian music promoter Jacques Agnant worked for police intelligence to orchestrate Tupac's arrest. Warren's suspicions of Agnant's police intelligence links started when the attorney went to put up Tupac's bail. Warren saw a Policemen's Benevolent Association (PBA—a national police group) representative bail out Agnant.[7] Agnant then had a longtime PBA lawyer represent him.[8] Warren later got Agnant's rap sheet that showed Agnant's long list of arrests up and down the East Coast on major charges, all of

---

3 Dr. M. Diana of St. Luke's Roosevelt Hospital, cited as testifying in *New York v. Tupac Shakur*, Notice of Motion., p.9.
4 "Tupac had become...Guilty.'" Tupac Shakur "Changes," *MTV*, video, 1999. Note that the Street Crimes Unit were special undercover agents who weren't in uniform. They started the same year that police unit, B.O.S.S, targeted Tupac's mother.
5 Barbara Handschu et al, plaintiffs, Rev. Calvin Butts, Sonny Carson, C. Vernon Mason, Michael Warren, Intervenors v. Special Services Division a/k/a Bureau of Special Services et al, Memorandum Opinion and Order, Judge Charles Haight, U.S. District Court, Southern District of New York. 71 Civ.2203-CSH, p.34.
6 Karen Freifeld, "Judge dumps convictions in New York jogger case," *The Baltimore Sun*, 12/20/02, p.3A.
7 "Michael Warren...Agnant." Personal interviews, Michael Warren, 12/25/94, 10/15/96, 11/8/98.
8 Connie Bruck, "The Takedown of Tupac," *The New Yorker*, 7/7/97, p.55.

which had been dismissed. "This was a sure sign Agnant was a police agent," said Warren.[9]

Such evidence supports that U.S. Intelligence may have set up the incident with Tupac and Ayanna Jackson. As we have seen in the aforementioned Intelligence memorandum regarding political musicians, this tactic was specifically addressed. It instructed agents to "Send in women and... [use] free sex to entrap."[10]

Another sign of U.S. Intelligence involvement came when police and the prosecuting district attorney proceeded to use all means possible, legal or not, to keep Tupac Shakur in jail after he made bail. First, police wrote in their interview of Jackson that she spat semen on her dress and the bedspread after the alleged forced oral sex. Instead of trying to verify her claims, police never sent her dress to the evidence lab to test it for semen.[11] Then, police fallaciously claimed to be holding the hotel phone messages supporting Tupac's defense, before a police source leaked to reporters that the officers actually erased them.[12] Police also unsuccessfully tried to intimidate women into making public claims that Tupac had assaulted them.[13] In yet another failed attempt to keep Tupac imprisoned, the Assistant District Attorney (ADA) Melissa Mourges tried to have Tupac's bail revoked, claiming he harassed Jackson before the trial.[14]

Among the many past examples, U.S. Intelligence similarly destroyed evidence that would have exonerated Tupac's godfather, Geronimo Pratt. At the exact time in 1969 when police alleged Pratt murdered a Los Angeles woman, the FBI had him on live audio surveillance tape placing him at a Panther conference hours north in Oakland. When Pratt's defense team finally got the tape records, it was missing the minutes of Pratt's talk at the conference, and only those

9 Personal interviews, Michael Warren, 12/25/94, 10/15/96, 11/8/98.

10 As noted above, one intelligence document a Senate committee found included strategies for use against political musicians such as "Intelligence Activities and Rights of Americans," Book II, April 26, 1976, *Senate Committee with Respect to Intelligence Report*. Excerpted in Alex Constantine, *The Covert War Against Rock* (Los Angeles: Feral House, 2001), p.9. U.S. Senate Select Committee to Study Government Operations, *The FBI's Covert Program to Destroy the Black Panther Party*, U.S. Government Printing Office, Washington. D.C. 1976.

11 "Another sign…semen." Jackson Trial Testimony p. 239, Detective Slimak's Cross-examination by M. Warren , p.344, *New York vs. Tupac Shakur*, Indictment No. 11578-93, p.10.

12 Al Guart, "Tupac-tape Tamper Alleged," *New York Post*, November 24, 1993. Salvatore Arena, "Sex Tapes Erased, Says Shakur Lawyer," *Daily News*, November 24, 1993. Cross-examination of Ayanna Jackson, by Ken Ellis, Esq. *New York vs. Charles Fuller and Tupac Shakur*, Indictment no. 11578-93, Nov. 14, 1994, p.232.

13 Rob Speyer, "Rapper, Minor Had Sex in Video: Cops," *Daily News*, November 26, 1993. Al Guart, "Shakur's Lawyer Raps Cops," *New York Post*, November 30, 1993, p. 15.

14 Al Guart, "Tupac Terrorist Twist," *New York Post*, December 17, 1993, p.3.

minutes. The FBI claimed those parts of the tape were accidentally destroyed.[15]

At Tupac's trial, defense attorneys Michael Tarif Warren and Robert Ellis caught two police officers making a number of false statements under oath. For example, Ellis got the immediate officer on the scene, Officer Craig McKernan, to admit he made a false claim in his pretrial testimony. Initially McKernan claimed that Jackson said Charles Fuller took part in touching her. At the trial, however, he revised his statement and agreed that Jackson said Fuller only watched. Then, Warren was able to Det. Kimberly Slimak to admit that she misled a grand jury in implying that she personally recovered the guns at the hotel scene. She ended up agreeing that in actuality, another police officer had found guns, she didn't even see him pick them up, but they gave her the guns and she then brought them in.[16]

But the state's case became much weaker with Ayanna Jackson's testimony. First, attorneys caught Jackson contradicting many aspects of her written police report, despite a number of pretrial meetings she had with ADA Mourges. Jackson further described different guns at the scene than the ones police said they found there, backing Warren's claim that the guns were planted. And, she said she spat Tupac and Jacques Agnant's sperm on her clothes and the bedspread. However, the bedspread came up negative for sperm and, again, the clothes never made it into evidence.[17]

ADA Mourges became desperate and began making unsupported claims. For example, just after arresting Tupac at the hotel, police took the underwear he had on and, upon testing it, found it contained no traces of semen. Despite the fact that the tested

---

15 "Among many...destroyed." Judge J. Dunn's dissenting remarks, *In Re: Pratt*, 112 Cal. Ap.3d. 795;--Cal. Rptr.—(Crim. Np. 37534. Second Dist., Div. One. 3 December 1980). In Ward Churchill and Jim Vander Wall, *Agents of Repression* (Boston: South End Press, 1989), p. 90.
16 "At Tupac's trial...in." See *New York v. Tupac Shakur and Charles Fuller*, Cross examination of Det. Cragi McKernan, p.23-5. On Det. Slimak, see Cross-examination (Warren), p.331-2, 345 and Redirect/Recross, p.356.
17 But the state's...sperm." See for example, Jackson contradicting many former statements regarding time of arrival and gold jewelry left at the scene and who called her to come there, despite many pretrial meetings with ADA Mourges where details are usually reviewed. New York vs. Tupac Shakur and Charles Fuller, Cross-examination of Jackson by Robert Ellis , pp.215, 230, 240-41, 254 compared to Recross of Det. Slimak by Micheal Warren at p. 359. On evidence examined for semen and found negative, despite Jackson's claim of spitting semen on it, see Cross-examination of Jackson/Ellis, p.239, and Warren's Cross-examination of Det. Slimak pp.342-6, and (Trial Testimony at 239) cited in New York vs. Tupac Shakur Moton of Motion Pursuant to CPL 530.45 for Bail Pending Sentence, p.10, pt.26. On Mourges saying different underwear checked, see same—p.10, pt.26. On guns, see same at p.8, pt.22 (citing Affidavit Testimony p.14 at lines 18-23 and Trial Testimony at p.226).

underwear matched Jackson's description of it, Mourges said that police tested the wrong underwear without any evidence for such a claim.[18]

While the jury deliberated, ADA Mourges offered a mistrial. Mourges offered this mistrial after admitting her office withheld evidence from the defense, allegedly because they had just found misplaced pictures at that time. Even though he would have avoided the possibility of jail, Tupac refused the mistrial offer, believing he had won the case and wanting to clear his name of the charges. ADA Mourges may have offered this mistrial to avoid Tupac's acquittal on all counts, as it would have decreased any negative publicity against Tupac and hurt Jackson's coming civil suit.[19]

The jury found Tupac not guilty of all the major charges including forced sodomy, attempted sodomy, assisting forced sodomy, and gun possession. Since the police claimed that they found guns in Tupac's hotel room, the jury's findings supported attorney Warren's contention that police must have planted these guns. Nonetheless, the jury found Tupac guilty on three counts of sexual abuse, specifically detailed as one count of touching Jackson's butt against her will and two counts of assisting Jacques Agnant's touching her butt against her will.[20]

Because of the judicial irregularities that occurred throughout the trial, Michael Tarif Warren publicially accused the District Attorney of having a personal agenda of putting Tupac in jail. The judicial bias never reached the level of Afeni Shakur's New York Panther 21 trial, but it had a grave effect on Tupac's life. While making an appeal on the sexual abuse conviction, Warren sought bail for Tupac. Warren cited many ways the District Attorney made the denial of Tupac's bail a top priority. The DA claimed that Tupac would try to skip bail and flee, while having no evidence to support the claim. The judge's further improprieties included allowing the jury to consider a second count of Tupac assisting Agnant's touching of Jackson' butt, despite the fact that

18 "ADA…claim." On Mourges saying different underwear checked, see *New York vs. Tupac Shakur* Moton of Motion Pursuant to CPL 530.45 for Bail Pending Sentence, p.10, pt.26. Stockings, p.23 pt.50 A iv. On judicial bias, see same, p.21 , pt.50 A I (Trial Testimony 60-8 and indictment counts Exhibit C).

19 "While the jury…suit." Richard Perez-Pena, "Wounded Rapper Gets Mixed Verdict In Sex-Abuse Case," *New York Times*, 12/2/94, pp. A1, B4. Also, Personal interview, Michael Warren,4/7/99.

20 "The jury found…will." *New York v. Tupac Shakur, Ricardo Brown (a.k.a. Jacques Agnant) & Charles Fuller*, Exhibit A. 2. PL 130.65 Sexual Abuse 1ˢᵗ Degree "forcing contact between the…buttocks of informant and the hands of defendant Shakur, Brown." Also, Richard Perez-Pena, "Wounded Rapper Gets Mixed Verdict in Sex Abuse Case," *New York Times*, 12/2/94, p.B4.

Jackson said Agnant only touched her once and ADA Mourges gave no evidence of Agnant touching her another time.[21]

As seen in Panther frame-ups and trials, the prosecutor showed preferable treatment for suspected police agent Jacques Agnant. First, Warren said that prosecution showed their bias in favor of Agnant in allowing him to sever his case from Tupac's. They then allowed Agnant to plea-bargain down to two misdemeanors. ADA Melissa Mourges' cover-up statements regarding her office's incredible leniency towards Agnant supports their roles in this targeting. *New Yorker* editor Connie Bruck noted how Mourges said her office let Agnant off easy because Jackson didn't want to go through the trauma of another trial. Bruck noted, however, that Jackson had already planned another trial with a civil suit against Tupac. [22]

Furthermore, some of Jackson's actions may raise some doubt as to her motivations. Following the alleged incident at the hotel, 19-year-old Jackson immediately called and employed high profile lawyer, Michael Kaplan. Attorneys say that police and prosecution normally speak on behalf of victims alleging crimes. A victim only retains a lawyer if they decide to file a civil lawsuit, almost exclusively after the criminal case goes to trial, to bar the appearance of a financial motivation for the claim. Also, defense attorneys need to take time reviewing a case before accepting it and addressing the media about it. After the late-night incident and arrest, Kaplan spoke to the media on Jackson's behalf early the following day and proceeded to file a civil suit. When questioned about her retention of Kaplan by defense attorneys at the trial, Jackson lied, saying she doesn't know anyone named Michael Kaplan. It should also be noted that Jackson didn't file a civil suit against Agnant, but exclusively against Tupac.[23]

---

21 "Michael Warren…time." On District Attorney's large, successful effort to keep Tupac from gaining bail, see Letter to Judge Ernst Rosenberger, from ADA Francine James, 2/3/95. And, for example, Robert Morgenthau, District Attorney, Petitioner, for a Judgement of Prohibition Pursuant to Article 78 of the Civil Practice Law and Rules, against Honorable Ernst Rosenberger, Justice of Supreme Court, Appellate Division, First Department, and Tupac Shakur, Respondents, New York, 5/9/95. On judicial bias, see New York vs. Tupac Shakur Moton of Motion Pursuant to CPL 530.45 for Bail Pending Sentence, same, p.21 , pt.50 A I (Trial Testimony 60-8 and indictment counts Exhibit C).

22 "First, Warren…easy." On everything regarding ADA Mourges, see Connie Bruck, "The Takedown of Tupac," *The New Yorker*, 7/7/97, p.54-5. On Warren's comment, personal interview, 11/8/98.

23 Also…Tupac wealth." On only filing a civil suit against Tupac, Bruck, New Yorker, p.55. "Free sex to entrap," in "Intelligence Activities and Rights of Americans," Book II, April 26, 1976, Senate Committee with Respect to Intelligence Report. Excerpted in Alex Constantine, The Covert War Against Rock, p.9. U.S. Senate Select Committee to Study Government Operations, The FBI's Covert Program to Destroy the Black Panther Party, U.S. Government Printing Office, Washington. D.C. 1976.

During the deliberation of the Jackson sexual assault trial, there was a sixth armed attack on Tupac. As with all previous attacks, certain details of the events suggest U.S. Intelligence involvement or police cover-up. Jacques Agnant's link to this event, the gunmen's actions, and police inaction support the theory that U.S. Intelligence attempted to murder Tupac yet again in New York City on November 30, 1994.

By the end of November, Tupac had dumped Agnant as a friend, but Agnant was seen trailing Tupac.[24] Several nights later, Agnant's associate Booker called Tupac. Booker offered him $7,000 to come to a Times Square recording studio and provide vocals for another rapper.[25] Upon arriving, alleged muggers shot Tupac four to five times in the lobby. Contrary to media accounts, a doctor's report gave details that depicted how these gunmen conducted a military-style execution. After the shooters put one bullet through Tupac's scrotum, sending him to the ground, they put two bullets in his head as he lay face down on the floor.[26]

Many curious aspects of this attack include a gunman waiting in the studio for Tupac, the items left behind, and the police presence. First, someone had let one of the gunmen into the locked Quad Studios. With dozens of artists, from Madonna to the Rolling Stones, recording hit records at Quad Studios, it had tight security with a video camera surveillance of the locked doors allowing only the artists recording in the studio to buzz someone into the studio front doors. Someone had to knowingly admit the gunman into the lobby, whether they were aware of his intentions or not.[27]

Secondly, police maintained that the incident was "simply another Times Square mugging."[28] These alleged "muggers" took other jewelry but left a diamond-encrusted Rolex watch on Tupac. With guns in hand they then ran out the door into the extremely well

24 Tupac's biological cousin, Billy Lesane, said that his sister told him she saw Agnant following her and Tupac after Tupac stopped hanging with Agnant, just before the Times Square shooting. Personal interview, Billy Lesane, 4/10/99

25 "Several…rapper." Tupac interview with Kevin Powell in Vibe eds. *Tupac Shakur*, p.46.

26 "Upon…floor." On bullets through the head while on ground, see Deposition of Barbara Justice, MD, New York v. Tupac Shakur, December 21, 1994. On military execution, see Stephen Kinzer, "Commandos Left a Calling Card: Their Absence," *New York Times*, 9/26/01, p. B6.

27 "Many…lobby." On, police statement, Gladwell, *The Washington Post*, 12/2/94, p. F2. On Quad's hit records, Cathy Scott, *The Murder of Biggie Smalls* (New York: St. Martin's Press, 2000), p.65.

28 On, police statement, Gladwell, *The Washington Post*, 12/2/94, p. F2.

lit Times Square area, where a police car, reportedly hovering nearby, failed to go after them.[29]

Even the usually censorial mainstream media cited how a particular amount of police foul play accumulated up to this point. Before the virtually complete media censorship on Tupac's trials and tribulations, a few mainstream journalists reported yet another odd aspect of police involvement in this incident. For example, The *Washington Post* commented how "in another strange twist" to Tupac's trial, the same officers immediately arriving on the scene had first arrived at his alleged sexual assault scene.[30] An NYPD officer implicated these officers as part of the Street Crime Unit, the unit believed to have taken over some Counter Intelligence Program duties.[31] A former police detective later said that he worked for New York's official "Rap Unit" found to have targeted rappers and that plainclothes Street Crime Unit members took part in that unit.

Furthermore, a security officer reported that the lobby's surveillance camera videotape caught the whole shooting incident, but the police investigator told him he didn't want to see the tape. [32] Afeni Shakur and attorney Michael Tarif Warren thought police set up the shooting, and the two removed Tupac from the hospital against doctors' orders because of the large police presence at the hospital.[33] They moved him to another hospital where Tupac received a phone call making a death threat. Afeni and Warren accepted an offer by Tupac's friend, *A Different World* actress Jasmine Guy, and moved him into her apartment. Despite the entrance and exit holes in Tupac's head, the bullets miraculously failed to hit his brain and he survived.[34]

Tupac had first rejected the notion that Jacques Agnant (a.k.a. Nigel) was a police agent. But he eventually said it in lyrics implying that Agnant set the shooting up with his associate Booker on behalf of the

29 "These…them." On police outside lobby doors Warren said cops present when they looked out glass doors, personal interview, Michael Warren, 12/25/94. Also in *Vibe*, eyewitness Randy "Stretch" Walker said cops were slowly rolling up just after gunmen fled, Vibe editors, *Tupac Shakur* (New York: Crown,1996), p.61. Police presence is backed by news accounts of police having Tupac under surveillance at that time. In, "Thoughts and Notes on Tupac," *Amsterdam News*, 12/17/94, p. 24. On Rolex watch left, see Vibe eds. *Tupac Shakur*, p.41
30 Malcolm Gladwell, "Shakur Guilty of Sex Abuse," *The Washington Post*, 12/2/94, p. F1, F2.
31 Officer Heinz, Midtown North precinct, personal interview, May 4, 1999. For the integration of the Street Crime Unit and Counter Intelligence Program duties, see Frank Morales, "The Militarization of the Police," *CovertAction Quarterly*, no. 67, Spring/Summer, 1999,p. 48.
32 Cathy Scott, *The Murder of Biggie Smalls* (New York: St. Martin's Press, 2000), p.65.
33 Charisse Jones, "For a Rapper, Life and Art Converge in Violence," *New York Times*, 12/1/94, pp. A1, B3. Personal interview, Michael Warren, 12/20/01.
34 "They moved…survived." See Deposition of Barbara Justice, MD, New York v. Tupac Shakur, December 21, 1994, Vibe ed.s *Tupac Shakur*, p.48, and Scott, *The Murder of Biggie Smalls*, p.66.

FBI. In the last CD he finished producing, due out within two months of his death, Tupac rapped with slang about " a snitch named Haitian Jacques." [35]

35 "Tupac first...up." On Tupac first rejecting the notion, personal interview with Michael Warren, 2/4/00. Song quote from "Against All Odds" on Tupac Shakur (a.k.a. Ma.k.a.velli), *Don Killuminati: The Seven Day Theory*, 1996.

CIA & TIME WARNER'S GRIP ON THE MUSIC INDUSTRY

Amongst all of the arts, U.S. Intelligence and top conservative corporations appeared particularly concerned about popular youth music. Various writers believe that U.S. Intelligence thought that rock music and then rap would supersede U.S. Intel's attempt to influence the opinions of the people. The FBI now openly admits having started files on musicians such as Elvis Presley in the mid-'50s and other musicians thereafter. Despite such admissions, researchers such as London's *Daily Mail* and *Sunday Express* legal correspondent, Fenton Bresler, said he fought for years with numerous Freedom Of Information Act requests to get copies of even a small percentage of John Lennon's FBI and CIA files. Young conservative Ralph Reed, who headed the Christian Coalition and was a leader in the Republican Party, alluded to popular music when he said in 1996 "the future is an endless and vicious culture war."[1]

In the early '50s, white Jewish Cleveland disc jockey Allan Freed was credited with introducing rock music to large white audiences. White crooners such as Perry Como dominated pop radio at the start of the decade. Freed was the first large city DJ to introduce danceable rhythm and blues musicians to white audiences in 1951. This was at a time when most stations only allowed these songs to air when covered by white musicians. Freed was credited with coining the term "rock and roll" in '51, which he borrowed from Black slang for sex. Freed, under the moniker Moondog, drummed pencils and howled to songs. He inspired other small stations nationwide to develop his R&B format, soon forcing large stations to follow suit.[2]

In '52 Freed's soaring influence was apparent. That year, 25,000 people, two-thirds white, came to a 10,000-seat arena for Freed's first concert.[3] Freed's career continued skyrocketing before it ended abruptly due to bribery charges in 1960.

---

1 "Various writers…war.'" See, for example, Alex Constantine, *The Covert War Against Rock*, p.12 on U.S. Intelligence focus on music. On rap, see Nick Broomfield stating that a Congressional committee convened to discuss rap's subversive element in '93 and how the FBI began spying on rappers at least that early, *Biggie and Tupac* (Documentary, 2002). Constantine also stated that samples of FBI files on Elvis, Jimi Hendrix and Jim Morrison can be found in their reading room. Also see, Fenton Bressler, *Who Killed John Lennon* (New York: St. Marks, 1989), p.9. Quote by Reed in James Ridgeway, "The End of the Road? Convention '96," *The Village Voice*, August 20, 1996, p.25.
2 "In the early '50s…suit." Frederic Dannen, *Hit Men* (New York: Vintage Books, 1991), pp.42-3, 46. On Freed widely credited with coining the term rock and roll from the Black community's slang for sex, see "Allan Freed" at .history-of-rock.com/freed.htm . It cites The Dominoes "Sixty Minute Man," for the slang. This source also told of small stations imitating Freed, and actually used the words "eventually forcing large stations to follow suit."
3 On 25,000 people showing up, http://groups.msn.com/Teddyboyrock/biographyofallanfreed.msnw . This source cites a book on Freed by John A. Jackson, *Big Beat Heat: Allan Freed and the Early Years of Rock and Roll*. Jackson has written many books on music and this book was made into an NBC movie.

Some researchers believe U.S. Intelligence used Allan Freed, without Freed realizing it, and then set up an early end to his career. One example of U.S. Intelligence's stake in the music world may be indicative. Former OSS agent John Elroy McCaw attended meetings of the U.S. Intelligence umbrella group, the National Security Council as he served on their Advisory Council. He also owned WINS, one of New York City's top music stations. The National Security Council is the umbrella group for all of U.S. Intelligence.[4]

Events suggest that John McCaw and U.S. Intelligence obtained help in the music world from a common collaborator—organized crime. As seen above in the MLK assassination and with drug trafficking, U.S. Intelligence collaborations with the Mafia had a long history. And, at least with drug trafficking, the Genovese Mafia family was central to that history.[5]

Fredric Dannen's widely acclaimed bestseller, *Hit Men*, documents the vast number of organized crime figures in the music world, such as Morris Levy. Dannen said Levy was a Genovese Mafia associate who owned top New York jazz clubs and song publishing rights. Levy signed a deal with Allan Freed and influenced him to accept a DJ position at the radio station WINS. McCaw offered Freed a huge salary to join WINS in 1954 and Freed's program became #1 within months. With the help of Freed's popularity, Levy started the jazz and rock record label, Roulette Records, in 1956. An Assistant U.S. Attorney would later claim that Roulette Records was also a way station for heroin trafficking. A well-substantiated drug-trafficking charge was also made against the key rap label that would later undermine Tupac, Death Row Records.[6]

After Freed helped make WINS the country's most popular music station, McCaw implemented changes at the station in 1957 that shaped the rock music world. WINS led the nationwide promotion of

4 "Some researchers...stations." Alex Constantine, *Covert War Against Rock* (Los Angeles, Feral House, 2000) pp.19-22.
5 "Events...history." Constantine, *Covert War Against Rock*, pp.19-22. On Mafia, particularly Genovese, and U.S. Intelligence collaboration in WWII and then drug trafficking, see Alfred McCoy, *The Politics of Heroin: CIA Complicity in the Global Drug Trade* (New York: Lawrence Hill Books, 1991), pp.30, 35-7, 73-4. Also see, Clarence Lusane, *Pipe Dream Blues: Racism and the War on Drugs* (Boston: South End Press, 1991), pp.38-42. McCoy is a professor of Southeast Asian History at University of Wisconsin-Madison and Lusane is a professor at University of the District of Columbia.
6 "Fredric Dannen's...Records)." On Levy and Freed, see, Fredric Dannen, *Hit Men* (New York: Vintage Books, 1991), pp.37-8, 42-6. see, for example, Dannen, pp.164n, 272-99. On charge of Roulette for heroin trafficking, p.53. On McCaw, Constantine, *Covert War Against Rock*, pp.19-22.

the Top 40 music format. This format helped large money interests gain the most dominant influence and control over top music sales through promotion money and radio play menus.[7] It would further aid censorship of political songs by barring them from the radio play menus.

That Paramount Pictures paid Allan Freed $29,000 a day to make a teen movie in 1957 exemplified Freed's immense success in the music world.[8] However, powerful forces started a continuous assault on Freed the following year. In 1958, when violence occurred outside a Boston arena at a Freed show, authorities indicted Freed for inciting a riot. Police Intelligence would later use this same charge against H. Rap Brown, Jimi Hendrix, Tupac, and others.[9]

While charges were eventually dropped for the Boston incident, other attacks were more serious. McCaw fired Freed in '58 for unknown reasons. The day he was fired, a gunman, allegedly an upset concert promoter, looked for Freed in the WINS studio before Freed escaped.[10] Freed went to work for WABC but in 1959, researchers believe Freed was set up and scapegoated when Orrin Hatch's Congressional committee focused exclusively on him in the "payola" scandals. The Payola scandal was in regards to the now illegal practice of bribing radio stations to play certain songs. Morris Levy, the source of much of the payola bribe money, was never called to testify. *Hit Men* author Fredric Dannen said that these deals weren't illegal then and were only considered misdemeanors thereafter. Nonetheless, the scandal effectively ended Freed's career.[11]

The Mafia continued influencing music ownership and work in music clubs, labels, and promotion. It also controlled record distribution and music tours through its power in the Teamsters Union.[12] At least

7 "After Freed...menus." Rick Sklar, *How the All-Hit Radio Stations Took Over* (New York: St. Martin's Press, 1994), pp.11, 17 19.Cited in Constantine, *Covert War Against Rock*, pp.19-22.

8 http://groups.msn.com/Teddyboyrock/biographyofallanfreed.msnw, from John A. Jackson, *Big Beat Heat*.

9 "in 1958...lives)." Jackson, *Big Beat Heat*, cited above.

10 "While charges...day." On Boston inciting riot charge, "Allan Freed" at .history-of-rock.com/freed.htm. John A. Jackson, *Big Beat Heat*. On gunman looking to kill Freed in the music studio, Rick Sklar, *Rocking America: How All Hit Radio Stations Took Over* (New York: St. Martin's, 1984), p.46, cited in *Covert War Against Rock*, pp.19-22. Rick Sklar's wife was at the scene when a gunman came to the station looking for Freed that day. McCaw firing Freed for unknown reasons, Constantine and Dannen, *Hit Men*, p.

11 "Freed...career." Constantine, *Covert War Against Rock*, pp.19-22. Fredric Dannen, *Hit Men*, pp.37-8, 42-6. and on. Payola wasn't illegal at that time, Congress only made it a misdemeanor thereafter, and no one else besides Freed was penalized.

12 "The Mafia continued...Union." On label ownership and promotion, see Dannen, *Hit Men*, pp.34, 59, 164n, 272-99. On Mafia control of Teamsters, Harry Shapiro and Caesar Glebbeek, *Jimi Hendrix: Electric Gypsy* (New York: St.Martin's Griffin, 1990), p.295.

one publisher, Lou Wolfe of Covert Action Quarterly, claimed that the Mafia owned East/West, the sole magazine distributor to kiosks and newsstands. Wolfe further believed that East/West collaborated with the CIA in barring his and most other leftist magazines.[13]

When Time Inc. and Warner merged in the 1980s, it became the world's largest media conglomerate, which gave it vast power to censor Tupac and cover up events in his life.[14] Both Time and Warner have a history of supporting conservative Republicans, such as backing Richard Nixon's presidency. Warner also showed its loyalty to U.S. Intelligence regarding a book, *Counter-Revolutionary Violence*, by professors Noam Chomsky and Ed Herman, printed by Warner subsidiary, Warner Modular Books. After its printing, the parent company destroyed 10,000 copies because it criticized U.S. Intelligence policies.[15]

Of 17 media companies he listed as working closely with the CIA in his seminal article, "The CIA and the Media," Carl Bernstein said that CIA officials singled out Time, Inc. as doing the most collaborative work with the CIA. Bernstein said that *Time* (and ex-*Life*) magazine founder, Henry Luce, was close friends with CIA Director Allan Dulles. The vice-president of Luce's Time-Life media company, Charles Douglas (C.D.) Jackson also worked as a leader of U.S. Intelligence. He co-authored "a CIA-sponsored study recommending the reorganization of the American Intelligence services."[16]

British editor Frances Stonor Saunders also confirmed that the Time-Life vice-president, C.D. Jackson had a historical role in shaping U.S. Intelligence, particularly regarding culture manipulation. By poring through a huge library archive of Jackson's papers, Saunders found that during his decades-long career at Time-Life, Jackson took several breaks for U.S. Intelligence leadership work. He was deputy chief of the Psychological Warfare Division. He then had a job as an " 'outside'

13 Personal interview with Louis Wolfe, 5/10/04. Wolfe has copublished Covert Action Quarterly for over 20 years. This leftist political magazine was co-founded by Phil Agee, a longtime CIA employee who published a memoir tell-all about the CIA, *Inside the Company: CIA Diary* (New York: Bantam, 1975). Covert Action has won numerous annual Project Censored awards and published this writer's Tupac article.

14 Besides music and magazines, Time Warner further had vast holdings in dozens of Cable TV stations, video production, Warner Brothers motion pictures, Warner Brothers (WB) Television, and a half dozen book publishers. Time Warner's merge with Turner Broadcasting around this time brought them another half dozen film production companies, a dozen cable networks such as CNN, and many other entertainment holdings. They had the most media holdings of the four companies that dominated what *The Nation* magazine called, "The National Entertainment State." Mark Crispin Miller, pullout "The National Entertainment State," *The Nation*. 1996.

15 "Bothe Time and Warner…policies." Ben Bagdikian, *The Media Monopoly*, 4th edition, pp.31-33.

16 "Of the 17…services.'" Carl Bernstein, "The CIA and the Media," *Rolling Stone*, p.63.

director of CIA covert operations." He further worked as Special Adviser to the President [Eisenhower] for Psychological Warfare. Jackson proposed and authored the consolidation of the Psychological Warfare and the propaganda units to become a major function of the newly created CIA. He further headed CIA front groups, such as The Congress of Cultural Freedom, which obtained vast amounts of money to influence all facets of the arts.[17]

One of C.D. Jackson's other propaganda projects financed Black musicians, writers and actors who were not vocal about racism in the United States, eroding the livelihood of activist Black writers and performing artists.[18] Time and Warner's actions showed that its top executives, who took over after its long-time Vice-President, C.D. Jackson, had similar goals as they attempted to contain rap activist Tupac Shakur. As mentioned, after Tupac's debut Interscope Records CD, Time Warner bought another 25% of Interscope for a controlling share.[19] Time Warner then excluded songs and censored lyrics on Tupac's second and third CDs. They further withheld the release of these CDs for a year each, which may be due to an attempt to censor Tupac's anti-Bush lyrics from coming out just before the '92 presidential election.[20]

Tupac confidants Watani Tyehimba and Michael Tarif Warren support that Time Warner and large corporate advertisers who helped fund higher distribution for rap magazines, like *Vibe* and *The Source*, also censored much of the more political aspects of Tupac's life.[21] Like

17 "British editor Frances..arts." Frances Stonor Saunders, The Cultural Cold War: The CIA and the World of Arts and Letters (New York:The New Press, 1999), pp.116-17, 146-9, 152-3. See citations that include, C.D. Jackson, 'Notes of meeting,' 3/28/52 (CDJ/DDE) and Dwight D. Eisenhower, quoted in Blanche Wiesen Cook, *The Declassified Eisenhower: A Divided Legacy of Peace and Political Warfare* (New York: Doubleday,1981). C.D. Jackson to Henry Luce, 3/28/58 (CDJ/DDE), C.D. Jackson to Abbott Washburn, 2/2/53 (CDJ/DDE) and Lawrence de Neufville, telephone interview, Geneva, March 1997. Note that CDJ/DDE stands for C.D. Jackson Papers and Records, Dwight D. Eisenhower Library, Abilene, Kansas.
18 "C.D. Jackson...artists." Stonor Saunders, The Cultural Cold War, pp.180-183, 291. Saunders' citations on Rosenbergs include Douglas Dillon to State Department, 5/15/53, (CJD/DDE). Charles Taquey to C.E. Johnson, Psychological Strategy Board, 3/29/53 (CJD/DDE), and C.D. Jackson to Herbert Brownell, 2/23/53 (CJD/DDE). On Blacks and the arts, see C.D. Jackson to Nelson Rockefeller, 4/14/55 (CDJ/DDE). In this letter Jackson warned his CIA colleagues not to get the 'smarty pants' idea of using these artist as intelligence sources—'I don't think that these people are emotionally capable of playing a double role'—but he did agree that 'After they return they can of course be skillfully debriefed.'
19 Robert Sam Anson, "'To Die Like a Gangsta," *Vanity Fair*, March 1997, p.251. Connie Bruck, "The Takedown of Tupac," *The New Yorker*, 7/7/97, p.57.
20 One of the songs they censored was "Holler If Ya Hear Me," *Strictly 4 My N.I.G.G.A.Z*, Interscope Records, 1993. Tyehimba stated that Time Warner/Interscope heavily censored the lyrics to this single along with its accompanying video. The CD *Strictly...* was not allowed to be released for more than a year after it was finished. Personal interview, Watani Tyehimba, May 20, 2000. Tupac's public relations assistant said that his third release, the group project he titled Thug Life, was also held up for a year. Barbara Ross, "Cops Widow Sez It's Time to Dump Star," *Daily News*, November, 24, 1993, p.27. New Yorker editor Connie Bruck also reported on Interscope/Time Warner forcing songs off that CD, Bruck, "The Takedown of Tupac," *The New Yorker*, 7/7/97, p.52
21 Among previously cited personal interviews with Tyehimba and Warren.

many mainstream magazines, *The Source* censored most radical political information (in 2006 these white owners were pushed out by a new board). Time Warner had similar content control over close to 25 other magazines it owned, including *Time, Life,* and *People*.

Rap started dominating music sales by the early '90s and Time Warner dominated rap by that time.[22] After several '80s rap albums broke into the top of Billboard sales charts, including radical political rap, media giant Time Warner began heavily buying into the industry. In 1992, the *Los Angeles Times* said Time Warner's vast record label ownership included "the great bulk of the rap stars." Within eight more years, Time Warner had ownership of twenty formerly independent rap labels, as well as most of the rock music labels.[23] But Time Warner provided huge initial funds to promote its rap label, Death Row Records, which has links to both U.S. Intelligence and the Mafia.[24]

22 Ted Demme, the nephew of noted film producer Jonathan Demme, influenced MTV to let him start a rap show in 1988, which he titled, *Yo! MTV Raps*. That same year, NWA's *Straight Outta Compton* sold 2 million copies and Public Enemy was becoming one of the top rap bands among both Whites and Blacks. Filmmaker Spike Lee featured Public Enemy's radical political songs including, "Fight the Power," in his late Eighties movie, *Do the Right Thing*. One of the first rappers, Grandmaster Flash, started things off in the late Seventies, while Run DMC was the biggest rap group in the mid-Eighties.

23 "Rap started...labels" On the scope of Time Warner's control, Mark Crispin Miller, "The National Entertainment State," *The Nation*. 1996. On Time Warner's rap censorship, see Chuck Phillips, "Putting the Cuffs on 'Gangsta' Rap Songs," *Los Angeles Times*, 12/10/92, p. F1. On music consolidation, also see Tuma Musango, "And Then There Were Four: The Fight For Independents," *The Source*, April 2000, p.50.

24 One source reported that Time Warner's initial funding of Death Row Records was $10 million. Robert Sam Anson, "To Die Like a Gangsta," *Vanity Fair*, March 1997, p.252. A later book by Ronin Ro reported a lesser, but still substantial, $1.5 million initial financing. Ro, *Have Gun Will Travel*, p.315. Time Warner said it sold all links to Death Row in late '95 but it still keeps publishing rights, Sullivan, *LAbyrinth*, p.173.

PENAL COERCION AND FBI COINTELPRO TACTICS SET UP EAST/WEST RAP FEUD

Following the 1994 shooting in New York City, Tupac Shakur suffered through a long and painful recovery from his four or five bullet wounds. Despite requests from doctors for Tupac to continue bed rest near a hospital, a judge forced Tupac to await his sentencing for the sexual assault charges behind bars.

Near the time of Tupac's sentencing, highly suspected undercover agent Jacques Agnant only received two misdemeanors in a plea bargain regarding the heavier charges for which Tupac was acquitted. Meanwhile, with respect to Tupac's conviction on lesser charges of sexual abuse, the judge gave Tupac a 1½ to 4½ year prison sentence at the start of '95. This discrepancy is particularly noteworthy given Tupac only having two misdemeanors on his record versus Agnant's lengthy rap sheet.[1] Tupac's severe sentencing, prison placement, and forthcoming prison manipulation suggest further U.S. Intelligence influence.

For instance, the judge gave Tupac an exorbitant bail to pay—a Counterintelligence tactic previously used against his mother. Legal experts wrote about how, during Afeni Shakur's Panther 21 trial, the judge did Intelligence's bidding by setting costly bail and directly collaborated with the prosecution in an attempt to gain a guilty verdict.[2] Tupac's judge set bail at $3 million. He also refused Tupac's offer of a $1.3 million bail package, despite the fact that only 10% of bail is usually needed for release with a bail bond. Defense attorney Michael Tarif Warren also argued that, as a high profile entertainer, Tupac would jeopardize any future in his professional livelihood if he jumped bail and fled. The judge refused to acknowledge this.[3]

Tupac's third CD, *Me Against the World*, debuted on top of the pop music charts while he was in jail 45 days after his sentencing hearing. Interscope Records ended up selling 2 million copies of the CD

---

1 "Tupac Shakur's severe…sheet." Tupac's criminal record of two misdemeanors were for weapons possession and simple assault when someone came on his stage in Lansing, Michigan and tried to take the microphone away from him. Notice of Motion or Bail Pending Sentence New York v. Ttupac Shakur, Indictment no. 11578/93, Michael Warren, Attorney for Defendant-Petitioner Tupac Shakur. p.19 point 48.

2 See Peter Zimroth, *Perversions of Justice: The Prosecution and Acquittal of the Panther 21*, p.289-292. Zimroth worked for the Justice Department before teaching at New York University Law School while watching the Panther 21 trial and interviewing all involved in the case.

3 "Tupac's judge…this." Several Affidavits regarding bail money raised include those noted from court documents New York v. Tupac Shakur New York County Indict. No. 11578/93 in Supreme Court of N.Y. Appellate Div. 1ˢᵗ Dept. Tupac Shakur told of $350,000 put up by his actress friend Jasmine Guy and by Bert Padell. Watani Tyehimba told of $850,000 put up by Time Warner, which Asst. District Attorney Francine begrudgingly acknowledged in a letter to the judge, 2/3/95, and Ahadi Tyhimba told of $36,000 Tupac gave her as a down payment for Tupac's sister Sekiywa's $115,000 house which Ahadi had to purchase because of Sekiywa's insufficient work record. The house was Tupac's and put up as part of the bail package. On other information, also see Bruck, *The New Yorker*, 7/7/97.

in seven months. Many reporters tried to get interviews with Tupac at the time, giving him a platform for him to express his leftist political views. In one interview, Tupac asked, "What did the USA just do, flying to Bosnia ['95, before full-scale bombing]?" Adding, it has "no business over there." Tupac further said, "America is the biggest gang in the world. Look how they didn't agree with Cuba, so [they] cut them off." [4] Cuba had given a safe haven to his ex-Panther aunt Assata Shakur, as well as other Black radicals. [5]

Early in March of '95, prison officials distanced Tupac from the New York media by transferring Tupac from Rikers Island to Clinton Correctional Facility in upstate Dannemora, New York, a maximum-security prison about 9 hours north of New York City. It's uncertain whether plans for Tupac's prison transfer were already in motion, but *Me Against the World* was released February 27th and Tupac's new prison card issue date was March 8th. This suggests that the CD's chart-topping week may have hastened the transfer of Tupac away from New York City's interviewing journalists. [6]

At Clinton, officials used the same political prisoner tactics on Tupac that they had on Black Panthers and other ethnically diverse activists. More intensive political intelligence work in the prisons started in the '70s, according to a special investigative committee of the California State Legislature. They found that the U.S. Department of Corrections had a "Special Services Division" to carry out operations on prisoners. [7] Researchers working from divergent groups, such as the Bureau of Prisons and Amnesty International, described several particular prison tactics as akin to both "torture" and "brain washing," and referred to them as "penal coercion." [8]

4 "Also, 45 days...off." On sales, see Vibe *Tupac*, p.140. On quote, see Michael Eric Dyson, *Holler If You Hear Me: Searching for Tupac Shakur* (New York: Basic Civitas Books, 2001), p.125.

5 Eugene Robinson, "Exiles," *The Washington Post Magazine*, 7/18/04, pp.23-4, 33-7.

6 "'The increase...visits.'" On Clinton, see Jacob Hoye and Karolyn Ali, ed.s *Tupac: Resurrection* (New York: Atria, 2003), p.153. Cathy Scott, *The Killing of Tupac Shakur* (Las Vegas: Huntington Press, 1997), p.83. Tupac's prison card, *Tupac: Resurrection*, p.152. Album release date, Vibe eds, *Tupac Shakur*, p.140.

7 Reporter Mark Schwartz, covering prison legislative reform, CD, *Me and My Shadow: Investigation of the political left by the United States Government*, producers Tarabu Betserai and Adi Gevins from "The Pacifica Radio Archives." Track 5.

8 "U.S. Intelligence and prison...penal coercion.'" On guards, Tupac told of the better treatment he received from the Black female guards at Rikers Prison in New York City, Vibe eds. *Tupac Shakur*, pp.50-1. U.S. Intelligence influence on judges and prison situations, see Mike Ryan, "The Stammheim Model: Judicial Counterinsurgency," *New Studies on the Left*, Vol. XIV, Nos. 1-2, Spring-Summer 1989, pp.45-69. On political prisoners, see treatment of Weather Underground activists linked to Mutulu, Black Liberation activists and Plowshares activists. On "torture" See *Amnesty International Report on Torture, 1983*. Also see, Thomas Benjamin and Kenneth Lux, "Solitary Confinement as Psychological Torture," California Western Law Review, 13(265), 1978, pp.295-6. And, on "brainwashing," see Dr. Edgar Schein discussing methodology with federal maximum-security prison wardens in 1962, quoted in National Committee to Support the Marion Brothers, *Breaking Men's Minds*, Chicago, 1987. see Churchill and Vander Wall, *The COINTELPRO Papers*, pp.321-4.

University of Wisconsin Professor Alfred McCoy put the "penal coercion" techniques in proper perspective. In his book, *A Question of Torture*, McCoy presented the decades of research the CIA conducted to perfect their techniques at breaking down prisoners with various forms of torture. McCoy found that the CIA came out with their leading manual on effecting these goals that was titled *Kubark Counterintelligence Interrogation* handbook. The *Kubark* book explicitly cited the importance of using the "penal coercion" techniques developed by the Bureau of Social Science Research, headed by Albert Biderman.[9]

A 1983 *Amnesty International Report on Torture* presented the original documents on these CIA-cited techniques, "Biderman's Chart on Penal Coercion" (which writers Churchill and Vander Wall reprinted in *The COINTELPRO Papers*). Biderman listed eight general penal coercion methods prison officials used to psychologically tear down individuals in order to manipulate them. These *methods* are: isolation, monopolization of perception, induced debility, threats, occasional indulgences, demonstrating 'omnipotence,' degradation, and enforcing trivial demands. The *techniques* used to aid these included solitary confinement, restricted movement, exploitation of wounds, death threats, occasional favors, demonstrating complete control over the victim's fate, personal hygiene prevention, taunts, denial of privacy, and enforcing trivial rules.[10]

Reports demonstrated that prison officials used many of these and harsher techniques for accomplishing all eight penal coercion methods on Tupac. One of Tupac Shakur's appeal lawyers, Stuart Levy, visited Tupac at Clinton's Dannemora prison site and stated his disbelief. Levy said that prior to one of his visits, "Tupac had a rectal search when he came in [to the visiting area]...we spent six hours there in full view of the guards. Then the guards started saying 'Tupac! Tupac!' in this falsetto voice, putting up their fingers with these plastic gloves, waving them—'It's time! It's time!' Why a second rectal search,

9 "In a...Biderman." Alfred McCoy, *A Question of Torture:CIA Interrogration, from the Cold War to the War on Terror* (New York: Metropolitan Books, 2006), pp.31-33, 40-43,50-52.
10 See, "Biderman's Chart on Penal Coercion," *Amnesty International Report on Torture, 1983.* Reproduced and discussed in Ward Churchill and Jim Vander Wall, *The Cointelpro Papers: Documents from the FBI's Secret Wars Against Dissent in the United States* (Boston: South End Press, 1990) pp.321-323. Also see tactics used on Tupac's mother, Joan Bird, Afeni Shakur, Lumumba Shakur et. al., *Look for Me In the Whirlwind: The Collective Autobiography of the New York 21* (New York: Vintage Books, 1971), pp. 319-325.

when he'd been sitting there in plain view with his lawyer, why, except to humiliate him?"[11]

These painful rectal searches aided aspects of penal coercion, such as the induced debility. They would painfully force their dry gloved fingers up his rectum after each visitor. They also did this in an area where he had been shot on November 30, through his testicle and femoral artery, a wound that was still healing.[12]

The *Amnesty International Report* described this induced debility's purpose as weakening "mental and physical ability to resist."[13] Prof. McCoy noted how the CIA's *Kubark* research stated that the most long-lasting penal coercion torture techniques came from the victims playing a part in their own pain. Thus, Tupac may have had to endure these painful anal probes in order to see visitors while he was in solitary confinement for eight months. McCoy reprinted Biderman's penal coercion note that "the threat to inflict pain...can trigger fears more damaging than the immediate sensation of pain."[14]

In a court affidavit, the doctor that attended to Tupac after his Times Square shooting described his still healing groin and head wounds. The doctor also noted that Tupac suffered from Post-Traumatic Stress Disorder (PTSD) after the shooting.[15] Tupac's PTSD symptoms continually had him waking up sweating and screaming.[16] Family friend Yaasmyn Fula, who visited Tupac often, said he had both "guards threatening to kill him, [and] inmates threatening to kill him."[17] Tupac confirmed this. Regarding the guards, he said one showed him a Ku Klux Klan T-shirt, saying, "We are the biggest gang in town. Don't ever forget it."[18]

One of Tupac's revolutionary figurative uncles, also imprisoned at Clinton, eventually quelled prisoners' threats. While it's unknown exactly which of his Black Panther elder comrades did this, he had at least several in the New York Prison, including former Bronx Black Panther leader Sekou Odinga. Odinga's wife, Yasmynn Fula,

---

11 Bruck, *The New Yorker*, p.56.
12 On bullets wounding a testicle and femoral artery, see Deposition of Barbara Justice, MD, New York v. Tupac Shakur, December 21, 1994.
13 "Biderman's Chart on Penal Coercion," Churchill and Vander Wall, *The COINTELPRO Papers*, p.323.
14 "Prof. McCoy...pain.'" McCoy, *A Question of Torture*, p.52.
15 Affidavit of Barbara J. Justice, M.D. , *New York v. Tupac Shakur, Indictment No. 11578/93*, pp.2-4.
16 Robert Sam Anson, "To Die Like a Gangsta," *Vanity Fair*, March 1997, p.280.
17 Bruck, *The New Yorker*, p.56.
18 "Tu Klux Klan," *Melody Maker*, November 11, 1995, p.4. Ronin Ro, *Have Gun Will Travel* (New York: Doubleday, 1998), pp.246-247.

helped Tupac with his business matters while their son, Yafeu "Kadafi" Fula, rapped in Tupac's backup group, The Outlawz.[19]

Prison officials also used isolation and monopolization of perception on Tupac by placing Tupac in solitary confinement 23 hours a day for eight months, allegedly for flunking a drug test. They further limited his ability to shower, only granting him the indulgence when news reports said Madonna was coming to visit him.[20] Many reported a vastly negative change in Tupac after prison.[21]

Tupac's confidantes believed that the penal coercion techniques helped U.S. Intelligence manipulate Tupac in other ways. Watani Tyehimba and Michael Tarif Warren say the techniques aided an attempt to have Tupac believe that his friend, rapper Biggie Smalls (a.k.a. Notorious B.I.G., born Christopher Wallace) or Biggie's producer, Sean "Puffy" Combs, orchestrated the Times Square shooting.[22] This eventually became known as the East Coast versus West Coast rap war, since Tupac was most affiliated with California while Biggie and Puffy were based in New York.

As explored earlier, evidence supports that U.S. Intelligence had historically created an East Coast versus West Coast Panther war around 1970. The FBI influenced Oakland, California-based Huey Newton, while he was in and out of jail, to come into conflict with Afeni Shakur's New York Panther 21 fellow prison inmates. As previously detailed, this evolved into the East versus West Panther war that later had Geronimo Pratt and the New York Panther 21 aligned with Eldridge Cleaver.[23]

---

19 Anson, *Vanity Fair*, p.280. Tupac's sister, Sekiyawa Shakur also said his Panther uncle looked out for him in prison. Gustavo Solis and Murray Weiss, "Black Panther Convicted of Trying to Kill 6 Officers Released From Prison," *DNAInfo.com* 11/26/14. dnainfo.com/new-york/20141126/central-harlem/Black-panther-convicted-of-trying-kill-6-officers-released-from-prison/

20 "Of the other...Caryn James, "The Things That People Say," *New York Times*, December 15, 1995, pp. C15, C19. On length of time, see *Tupac: Resurrection*, p.162. Shower for Madonna visit, p.173.

21 Several close to Tupac before and after prison attest to this. Actress Jada Pinket Smith, his best friend from high school, said "he went to jail and turned into a totally different person...part of Pac just died right there." Tupac's first manager and continued friend, Leila Steinberg, said Tupac had a brutalizing prison experience and his shining light and wit and happy persona "was completely changed, dimmed." Michael Eric Dyson, *Holler If You Hear Me: Searching for Tupac Shakur* (New York: Basic Civitas, 2001) pp.215-16. Political prisoner George Edwards noted psychological damage in what he sensed was put in his prison food. He said that prison officials appeared to take the Penal Coercion to new levels with Huey Newton at one particular prison that caused a noticeable change in the Panther cofounder. Personal Interview, 8/10/00.

22 Personal interviews with Tupac business manager Watani Tyehimba, 5/10/00, national lawyer Chokwe Lumumba, 5/5/00 and New York lawyer, Michael Warren, 11/8/00. Nick Broomfield also said this after discussions with Tyehimba, noted in his credits, Nick Broomfield, *Biggie and Tupac* (BBC funded documentary, 2002).

23 Of the many examples cited of FBI's use of fake letters and undercover agents to set up East vs. West Panther war between Afeni Shakur's New York Panthers and Huey Newton's West Coast Panthers, see New York Black Panther leader, Assata: An Autobiography (Chicago: Lawrence Hill Books, 1987), pp.230-232. Also see, copies of FBI correspondence obtained through the Freedom Of Information Act (FOIA) or confiscated in an FBI office raid by activists in 1971. Some of these were reprinted in Ward Churchill and Jim Vander Wall, The COINTELPRO Papers, pp.160-61. Such as, "From: Director, FBI (100-448006) COINTELPRO – BLACK PANTHER

To set up the Panther war, the FBI wrote fake letters from the imprisoned NY Panther 21 and they used undercover agents to pass on false information to both Newton and the NY Panther 21. U.S. Intelligence then used journalists to collaborate in magnifying the conflict into the "East/West Panther war." And finally, the FBI used the created feud to cover up their murders of Panthers.[24]

The FBI similarly instigated a conflict between Tupac and Biggie to create a war in the rap world. Recall that U.S. Intelligence agents were instructed to "Obtain specimens of their handwriting [apparently to generate dissension through fake letters]. Provoke target groups into rivalries," regarding political musicians.[25]

The FBI remains the most likely culprit for writing anonymous letters to Tupac and paying prisoners to influence Tupac into believing that Biggie and Puffy were behind his shooting. Tupac's road manager, Charles "Man Man" Fuller, confirmed that Tupac got anonymous letters in prison saying Biggie set up the Times Square shooting. Strangers in jail also told Tupac that Biggie had him shot.[26] U.S. Intelligence's Special Services Division of the Department of Corrections has a history of placing undercover agents and informants in prison to carry out this kind of work.[27]

Tyehimba tried to convince Tupac that Biggie likely had no part in the shooting. Biggie had visited Tupac in the hospital and also wrote him letters in prison saying he had no connection to the shooting. Tyehimba's words couldn't counteract so many people and letters saying Biggie *was* connected to the shooting. Tupac was largely

PARTY (BPP) – DISSENSION RACE MATTERS 2/10/71," and "Airtel to Albany et al Re: COINTELPRO – Black Panther Party (BPP) – Disssension 100-448006 Newton's …(deletions)…New York 21…San Francisco and New York are already involved in counterintelligence operations…creating dissension between local branch and/or its leaders and BPP national headquarters." Also see FBI undercover agent Louis Tackwood's admissions, Louis Tackwood, Churchill and Vander Wall, *Agents of Repression*, p.80. Tackwood, Lewis E., "My Assignment was to Kill George Jackson," *Black Panther*, April 21, 1980.

24 See former FBI Cointelpro agent M. Wesley Swearingen, FBI Secrets: An Agent's Expose (Boston: South End, 1995, pp.82-3.

25 "But Congress…into rivalries.'" "Intelligence Activities and Rights of Americans," Book II, April 26, 1976, *Senate Committee with Respect to Intelligence Report*. Excerpted in Alex Constantine, The Covert War Against Rock (Los Angeles: Feral House, 2001), p.9.

26 "'The FBI remains…shot." Cathy Scott, *The Killing of Tupac Shakur* (Las Vegas, NV: Huntington Press, 1997, p.153. On anonymous letters, see Tupac's road manager, Charles "Man-Man" Fuller in Connie Bruck, "The Takedown of Tupac," *The New Yorker*, p.58. In personal interviews with Tupac business manager Watani Tyehimba, 5/10/00, national lawyer Chokwe Lumumba, 5/5/00 and New York lawyer, Michael Warren, 11/8/00 the writer of this FBI War on Tupac book proposed these theories to these close associates of Tupac's and they wholeheartedly agreed. Nick Broomfield also said this after discussions with Tyehimba, noted in his credits, Nick Broomfield, *Biggie and Tupac* (BBC funded documentary, 2002).

27 Reporter Mark Schwartz, covering Special Investigative Committee of California Legislature reviewing U.S. Intelligence tactics in prisons, *Me and My Shadow: Investigation of the political left by the United States Government*, Tarabu Betserai and Adi Gevins from "'The Pacifica Radio Archives." Track 5.

convinced by the fall of '95. Still, Tupac's biological cousin, Billy Lesane, said that Tupac eventually came to think that Biggie simply should have either warned him or worked harder to help find out who shot him.[28]

The media escalated the East versus West rap war even before Tupac blamed Biggie for his shooting. By the summer of '95, media outlets began discussing an East versus West rap war that had nothing to do with Tupac or Biggie. Journalists then appeared to take several quotes of Tupac's out of context to magnify the assertions of suspected agent Jacques Agnant's associate Booker, who said Tupac blamed Biggie for his shooting. Agnant and Booker, who offered Tupac the $7,000 to come to the studio that night, were the prime suspects for setting up that shooting. With these suspected intelligence agents' help, several journalists hyped this conflict as the peak of an East/West rap war.[29]

28 Personal interview, Billy Lesane, 3/26/99. Billy Lesane is Tupac's biological cousin.

29 "But this…war." On media role, see, for example, Cheo Hodari Coker, "How the West was Won," Vibe, Vibe eds, Tupac Shakur, p.39, also see suspected intelligence agent Booker. Jacques Agnant's associate who called Tupac to Times Square shooting scene and then "spun" Tupac's first interview to help make it much more contentious and accusatory to aid the rap war's start, in Vibe eds, Tupac Shakur, p. 59. Adario Strange, "Death Wish," The Source, March 1996, pp.87-88. Source in Ro, Have Gun Will Travel, p.163.

21

DEATH ROW SIGNS TUPAC

Tupac's conditions in jail would further aid to influence Tupac into finally signing with Death Row Records. Death Row made several attempts to get Tupac to sign with them, but he refused their offers from the years 1993 to 1995. Death Row paid Tupac $200,000 for one song, and both Death Row owners regularly traveled from Los Angeles to visit Tupac in the upstate New York prison where he was being held. Tupac manager Watani Tyehimba couldn't understand why Time Warner-Interscope also pushed for Tupac to switch from Interscope to their Death Row subsidiary as early as '93.[1]

Tupac finally stopped rejecting Time Warner's requests to sign with its subsidiary, Death Row after he had spent 10 months in jail. Prior to signing, the Appeals Court refused Tupac's $1.2 million bail offer for those 10 months that he waited for his appeal trial. But within days of Tupac's September of 1995 signing with Death Row Records, the Court of Appeals accepted a virtually identical bail offer and released Tupac.[2] Death Row claimed to solely provide the bail money at this time (though writers said Interscope/Time Warner actually did so).[3] Few besides U.S. Intelligence could influence the Court of Appeals.

Other findings further support the notion that Death Row Records dually worked as a front company for various U.S. Intelligence operations. Pulitzer Prize-winning writer Gary Webb was the first to link Death Row Records to the CIA from the record company's inception. Webb quoted the probation officer of national crack trafficker Freeway Ricky Ross. That probation officer cited a silent partner of Death Row, a Michael "Harry-O" Harris, as one of Ross' two understudies.[4] The *New Yorker* magazine and other media outlets described how Vice-President George Bush helped run key components of the CIA/Contra/Crack operations with CIA Director William Casey.[5] Webb detailed the

1 "One of Penal...as '93." Penal Coercion goal, *Amnesty International Report on Torture, 1983* in Churchill and Vander Wall, The COINTELPRO Papers, p.323. $200,000 for one song, Ro, *Have Gun Will Travel*, p.146. Time Warner push for Tupac on Death Row, Connie Bruck, "The Takedown of Tupac," *The New Yorker*, 7/7/97, p.57.

2 After over...1995." On 90% of Tupac's bail already raised, see Tupac's aunt, Jean Cox, and mother, Afeni, put up personal bonds. His actress friend, Jasmine Guy put up $350,000 with a man named Bert Padell. Tyehimba got Atlantic Records to agree that if Tupac promised $850,000 from his next CD, they'd put that much into the bail package to bring it to $1.2 million. See New York v. Tupac Shakur, sentencing hearing transcript, p.70 and Affidavits from Tupac Shakur, 2/2/95, Watani Tyehimband Ahadi Tyehimba. Atlantic is a Time Warner subsidiary. On, Tupac's release just after signing to Death Row, see, eds. Jacob Hoye and Karolyn Ali, *Tupac: Resurrection* (New York: Atria, 2003) pp.193-4, and Bruck, *New Yorker*, p.58.

3 Ronin Ro said Knight actually only provided $250,000 of the bail money with Interscope and Time Warner providing the rest. Ro, *Have Gun Will Travel*, p.250. Also see Bruck, *New Yorker*, p.58.

4 Gary Webb, *Dark Alliance: The CIA, the Contras, and the Crack Cocaine Explosion* (New York: Seven Stories, 1998), p.148. On Harris as silent partner, Ronin Ro, *Have Gun Will Travel: The Spectacular Rise and Violent Fall of Death Row Records* (New York:Doubleday, 1998) pp.76-80. Bruck, *New Yorker*, p.58.

5 Murray Waas and Craig Unger, "In the Loop," *New Yorker*, 11/2/92, p.64ff. Referenced in Craig Unger, House of Bush, House of Saud (New York: Scribner, 2004), pp.74. One writer, Michael Montalvo, described Bush's role and how the Reagan/Bush administration could set a new standard for cover-up of their cocaine trafficking. Montalvo said that Marine Lt. Col. Oliver North's own diary entries disclosed much of his role in supervising the transportation of "over 500 tons of cocaine...to the poor masses of the inner cities and across the USA," purportedly only for saving Central America and the U.S. from Communism. Montalvo said that former CIA Director George Bush,

CIA cocaine trafficking network that went from Nicaraguan Contras, such as Danilo Blandon, to Freeway Ricky Ross. A CIA Inspector General backed these findings about the CIA trafficking cocaine in 1998.[6] Webb claimed that Ross was their national point man, trafficking "multimillion-dollar cocaine shipments across America."[7] This would have made Michael Harris and Death Row Records important assets for the intelligence community.

Evidence suggests that Ricky Ross worked closely with CIA-collaborating cocaine traffickers such as Danilo Blandon and Ron Lister in the '80s. Also, at that time, Lister met regularly with former CIA Covert Operations director Bill Nelson, who had worked under George H. W. Bush at the CIA.[8]

As Vice-President, Bush appeared to renew this relationship when researchers say he also oversaw the National Security Council, which supervises the CIA.[9] This became the Iran-Contra-Crack scandal of the '80s that involved illegal arms sales to Iran, as well as drug trafficking, to illegally provide funds to the Nicaraguan Contras. The Contras tried to overthrow the socialist Sandinistas that had usurped the Nicaraguan government in 1979 from a U.S.-backed brutal dictator, and then won an '84 election. U.S. Congress held hearings investigating Reagan/Bush officials and CIA-linked associates indicted on drug trafficking, murder, and related charges. Some were convicted but Bush pardoned many others as President from '88-'92. Retired U.S. Navy Lt. Commander Al Martin, who worked in the Office of Naval Intelligence, blew the whistle on Iran-Contra. Martin detailed how Bush Sr. oversaw most of these operations before Bush Jr. nominated Iran-Contra co-conspirator Robert Gates to Secretary of Defense.[10]

Of further note, Death Row silent partner Michael Harris' work with Ricky Ross in this CIA-supplied network on the West Coast reflected a similar CIA cocaine network on the East Coast which

the Vice-President at the time, was heading the National Security Council (NSC) for the White House, with North as a National Security Advisor. They were able to keep documentation of these operations under wraps through President Reagan's Executive Order 123333. The order "'privatized' NSC intelligence operations and permitted agencies other than the CIA to carry out 'special operations' without reporting its activities…[allowing] any private enterprise the NSC set up, to carry out covert operations." Michale Montalvo, "Prisoner of the Drug War: An Inside Report from a former Inside Player," *Prevailing Winds* #8, 2000, pp.76-82.

6 Dale Russakoff, "Shifting Within Party to Gain His Footing," *The Washington Post*, A1, A8, 7/26/04.

7 Webb, *Dark Alliance*, p.558.

8 "Ricky…Bush." Nelson's background came from the Department of State's Biographical Register, 1973, and from CIA-BASE, a computer database operated by former CIA officer Ralph McGehee, in Garry Webb, *Dark Alliance*, pp.196-7, 513n.

9 On National Security Council overseeing U.S. Intelligence, see Victor Marchetti and John D. Marks, *The CIA and the Cult of Intelligence* (New York: Dell, 1974), p.117. The authors are CIA and Intelligence veterans, respectively. On Bush directing the National Security Council, see Michale Montalvo, "Prisoner of the Drug War: An Inside Report from a former Inside Player," *Prevailing Winds* #8, 2000, pp.76

10 "'This became…others." On U.S-backed brutal dictator, Webb, *Dark Alliance*, pp.22-3, 46-7. On officials and CIA-linked associates indicted, convicted, and pardoned, Webb, pp.553-561. On Bush directing Iran-Contra and the drug trafficking operations, as well as Robert Gates part, see, Al Martin, *The Conspirators: Secrets of an Iran-Contra Insider* (Pray, Montana: National Liberty Press, 2002).

affected Afeni Shakur's life. The primary owner of Death Row Records was attorney Dave Kenner. He represented drug kingpin Harris. Kenner introduced Harris to Death Row's managing partial owner, Suge Knight. Kenner then created a shell company with oversight ownership to gain ultimate control.[11]

As previously detailed, a member of the crack dealing East Coast network also appeared to do undercover work against the Shakur family. Ken "Legs" Saunders, got close to Afeni Shakur and may have sabotaged her life by repeatedly pushing crack on her in the '80s. This bore a striking similarity to the way Kenner got close to Afeni's son Tupac and subsequently manipulated him.[12] Also, the insertion of a spy as an activist entertainer's manager had at least one historical precedent with CIA spy Jay Richard Kennedy becoming a manager for activist entertainer Harry Belafonte.[13]

A Los Angeles police whistleblower, Detective Russell Poole, provided the best evidence that Death Row Records both produced rap albums and provided cover for U.S. Intelligence operations run by many working inside the record company. Death Row started its operations in early 1992 during George H.W. Bush's presidency. Poole found that "dozens and dozens" of his fellow police department officers were doing more than just moonlighting as security guards at Death Row Records.[14] Poole investigated Death Row with fellow LA Officer Ken Knox. When the two asked their superiors about all the cops working for Death Row, they were "told that some of these cops who worked for Death Row weren't considered security guards, but were more like confidants or troubleshooters or *covert agents*" [emphasis added].[15]

Suge Knight's apparent police intelligence collaboration likely started around 1990, as seen in his 11 guilty pleas from 1990-1995, mostly on violent charges, without the authorities ever revealing he violated his earlier probation. In 1990, a judge had issued him a 2-year suspended sentence and 3 years' probation for felony assault with a deadly weapon. Knight pled guilty to at least five more criminal charges

11 "The real...control." Ronin Ro, *Have Gun Will Travel: The Spectacular Rise and Violent Fall of Death Row Records* (New York:Doubleday, 1998) pp.76-80.

12 "Mutulu Shakur...'Mr. Untouchable.'" According to a 1976 "Top Secret" Justice Department report. Jefferson Morley, "The Kid Who Sold Crack to the President," *The City Paper*, 12/15/89, p.31. On Barnes acquittals and *New York Times* label, see Hank Messick, *Of Grass and Snow* (Englewood, CA: Prentice-Hall, 1979), p.148. Both cited in Clarence Lusane, *Pipe Dream Blues: Racism and the War on Drugs* (Boston, MA: South End Press, 1991), pp.41-42, notes 76 and 79. Mutulu Shakur also alluded to Nicky Barnes as a "rat," suggesting that he, too, thought Barnes worked for the government. See the momentary display of Mutulu's Thug Life Code in *Tupac: Resurrection* DVD at the Mutulu Shakur interview.

13 Elaine Brown, *Taste of Power*, p.86. William Pepper, *Orders to Kill*, p.82.

14 Police Detective Russell Poole said this on film in Nick Broomfield, Biggie and Tupac (documentary, 2002), as well as Randall Sullivan, *LAbyrinth: A Detective Investigates the Murders of Tupac Shakur and Notorious B.I.G., the Implications of Death Row Records' Suge Knight and the Origins of the Los Angeles Police Scandal* (New York: Atlantic Monthly, 2002). Poole lists many of the cops' names working in Death Row throughout this book.

15 Randall Sullivan, *LAbrynth*, p.166.

within the next two years, but he never spent a day in jail during that time.[16]

From 1993-1995, Knight violently assaulted people many times without police charging him with a crime. For example, a security guard said Knight pounded him at musician Prince's Glam Slam Club, causing spleen injuries that required multiple surgeries in 1993. Witnesses said Knight got into a shoot-out at the same club and beat up a music promoter inside the club seven months later.[17] As previously noted, Intelligence used the tactic of recruiting someone facing jail time to acquire agent infiltrators against the Panthers, such as one recruited in 1968 and used against Fred Hampton's Panthers in Chicago.[18]

Some writers suggest that one California assistant state's attorney, Lawrence Longo, protected Knight after the Death Row manager gave his daughter a recording contract. But interactions with any of the Longos only started in the middle of 1995, whereas only one of Knight's eleven guilty pleas came after 1992. In a 1995 trial on a 1992 case, some writers believe Longo got Knight a suspended sentence despite very credible charges. In that case, two Death Row-contracted employees brought police (curiously accompanied by the FBI) back to Death Row studios to show them the bullets lodged in a wall where they said Knight shot at them after first beating them. Knight received one of many suspended sentences at the trial (One of Knight's consulting attorneys who only represented him for that charge, Johnnie Cochran, said Longo was at first only a "low man on the totem pole" for that case. And then Longo was removed from the case).[19]

Desperate to get out of prison, Tupac signed a record deal with Death Row. This led to a tearful parting with his manager Watani Tyehimba. Tyehimba said he knew enough about Death Row Records that involving himself or his New Afrikan People's Organization with the record company could risk their safety. While Tyehimba's

---

16 Ro, *Have Gun Will Travel*, pp.36-7. Sullivan, *LAbyrinth*, "Timeline," p.301

17 "For example, after...his own record label." Ro, *Have Gun Will Travel*, p.118, 130-1, 154.

18 "Later trial...infiltrator work." See, *Appeal*, PL WON #3 showed that FBI Chicago SAC Mitchell personally posted bond on one of O'Neal's charges and neither of his charges were prosecuted. On FBI collaboration with gang intelligence, see *Appeal*, PL #413 and *Transcript* at 26909. Churchill and Vander Wall, *Agents of Repression*, pp.64-6, .endnotes 5, 24.

19 Some writers...case)." Sullivan, *LAbrynth*, p.107. Ro, *Have Gun Will Travel*, p.197. And secondly, lawyers working on the case said Longo had nothing to do with the settlement because he was "the low man on the totem pole" in that case. Ro, *Have Gun Will Travel*, p.197. Furthermore, Death Row hadn't signed a contract with Longo's daughter, Gina, until January of '96, while Knight's continued arrests, convictions, and jail-free suspended sentences included several as early as 1990. Gina Longo's brother reportedly first met with David Kenner in June of 1995 to talk about an Eazy-E film project, when he first mentioned his sister. In 1996, Kenner also rented a home from Longo, before Kenner had Knight stay there. Longo had only submitted plans for the home to be built in December of 1994. Ro, pp. 300-303. It's also interesting to note that Knight received a glowing probation report despite having nine separate charges with many convictions by that time of '95. This is particularly pertinent when compared to a probation report supervisors changed from positive to negative in Tupac's sexual assault case.

son continued to work for Tupac, Watani Tyehimba had to resign as business manager. Tupac's top legal consultant, NAPO Chair Chokwe Lumumba, also stopped working with Tupac for this reason.[20]

Death Row owners Suge Knight and Dave Kenner appeared to continue the prison authorities' penal coercion tactics on Tupac. Two documented penal coercion tactics, as laid out in the previous chapter, involved physical threats and demonstrations of omnipotence by those making the threats.[21] Among other actions, Tupac was made to watch the physical beatings of Death Row employees who showed signs of leaving the record company.[22] Knight also encouraged Tupac to take several trips with him to Hawaii, as if to isolate Tupac further. This took Tupac further away from his mentors and likely surrounded him more with police intelligence who were Knight's close associates.[23]

Knight further appeared to use weed and alcohol in an attempt to manipulate Tupac. As previously explored, evidence suggests that U.S. Intelligence had agents attempt to use drugs and alcohol to manipulate Huey Newton upon his prison release, as well as Afeni Shakur.[24] Death Row supplied a constant amount of weed and alcohol to Tupac who, before entering prison, reportedly had a daily weed habit.[25]

Other people close to him described Tupac as having marijuana and alcohol abuse problems. A close friend, Jada Pinkett Smith, described Tupac as brilliant, well-read, and both a brother and father to her. But she also said that Tupac later became an addict and an alcoholic—"he was high all the time."[26] Closer to the time Tupac was breaking from Death Row, that behavior appeared to change. Possibly due to the insistence of his fiancée, Kidada Jones, among others, Tupac began trying to avoid alcohol and marijuana by the end of the summer of 1996. Rap music mogul Russell Simmons said that, at one party, Tupac danced with a woman for four hours rather than drink and smoke with everyone.[27]

20 "Tupac's signing …lawyer." Personal interview, Tyehimba, 5/10/00. Bruck, New Yorker, p.58.
21 See, "Biderman's Chart on Penal Coercion," Amnesty International Report on Torture, 1983. Reproduced and discussed in Ward Churchill and Jim Vander Wall, The Cointelpro Papers: Documents from the FBI's Secret Wars Against Dissent in the United States, pp.321-323.
22 Ro, Have Gun Will Travel, p.271-272, 319-20. Randall Sullivan, LAbrynth, pp.35-38.
23 Bruck, The New Yorker.
24 "As previously…Belafonte." Elaine Brown, Taste of Power (New York: Doubleday, 1992), p.86. Pepper, Orders to Kill, p.82.
25 See, for example, Bruck, New Yorker, p.58. Robert Sam Anson, "'To Die Like a Gangsta," Vanity Fair, March 1997, p.280. Alcohol and weed at Death Row, also see Ro, Have Gun Will Travel, pp.104, 110. 116. Kevin Powell interview with Tupac, Vibe editors, Tupac Shakur, p.45-6.
26 "Others also…all the time.'" On Tupac as well-read and always teaching Pinkett Smith, see Michael Eric Dyson, Holler If You Hear Me (New York: Basic Civitas, 2001), p.71. Pinkett Smith described him as brilliant and incredible, crying about his death in an interview for the promo outtakes of Tupac: Resurrection, DVD (MTV, 2003). Second part from Dyson, Holler If You Hear Me, p.240.
27 Rob Marriott, "Ready To Die," Vibe, November 1996, p. T3.

DEATH ROW POLICE AND SUGE KNIGHT WORK TO END GANG TRUCE

"When they ask me when will the violence cease?
When your troops stop shootin' niggas down in the streets
Niggas had enough, time to make a difference
Bear witness, own our own business…
Take the evil out the people they'll be actin' right
'Cause both Black and White is smokin' crack tonight
And the only time we deal is when we kill each other
It takes skill to be real, time to heal each other…
And ain't a secret don't conceal the fact
the penitentiary's packed, and it's filled with Blacks…
Cops give a damn about a Negro
Pull a trigga, kill a nigga, he's a hero…
Rather be dead then a poor nigga…
and if I die, I wonder if heaven's got a ghetto…
Just think, if niggas decide to retaliate (soulja in the house)."

—"I Wonder if Heaven's Got a Ghetto," Tupac Shakur, *R U Still Down? [Remember me]*. Released in 1997.

D ave Kenner and Suge Knight appeared to have an agenda to negatively manipulate rap from the time they first founded the record label at the end of 1991. Suge Knight first targeted top '80s rappers such as N.W.A., whom the FBI had targeted with a warning letter and attempts to cancel their concerts in the late '80s. After influencing rappers D.O.C and Andre "Dr. Dre" Young to leave N.W.A., Knight got Dr. Dre involved in negative promotion and behaviors. After Dre rapped against marijuana use on an NWA track, "Express Yourself," Knight convinced Dre to promote weed use, titling his CD *The Chronic*.[1] Knight also started public brawls around Dre, in which only he, not Dre, avoided arrest.[2]

Suge Knight next set his sights on getting East Coast rappers with links to activism to leave their labels and join Death Row. Knight tried to get New York's Def Jam rappers to sign to his label. Def Jam produced top political rappers Public Enemy and former N.W.A. star Ice Cube. Suge Knight and Death Row also attempted to sign New York rappers Wu Tang Clan, who were affiliated with Black Liberation

1 "Suge Knight…*Chronic*." Ro, *Have Gun Will Travel*, pp.97, 109. On FBI letter to, and attempt to cancel concerts of, NWA see Bruce C. Brown, "Quayle Boosts 'Cop Killer' Campaign," *Washington Post*, 6/20/92, pp.B1,5. Cited in Barry Shank, "Fears of the White Unconcious: Music, Race, and Identification in the Censorship of 'Cop Killer.'" *Radical History Review* #66, Fall 1996.
2 Ronin Ro, *Have Gun Will Travel*, pp.83-4.

Movement leader Sonny Carson and Panther-inspired Hip Hop activists, Zulu Nation. Def Jam and Wu Tang Clan rebuffed Knight's advances.[3]

Suge Knight and Death Row further tried to disrupt rap events. Knight instigated violence in rap venues nationwide. These included the national rap convention in Atlanta at which Tupac was to speak, and in Miami where rap group 2 Live Crew had a music label.[4] That Knight provoked violent conflicts at these events, yet police failed to arrest him much of the time, provides further evidence of an amicable relationship with law enforcement agencies.

As detailed in previous chapters, FBI Cointelpro undercover agents aided U.S. Intelligence in pitting activist leaders and groups against each other, such as creating the East/West Panther war, as an apparent excuse for agents' murders of Panthers. Similarly, Death Row's Suge Knight helped instigate the East/West rap war. Knight initiated these actions before Tupac had even signed with Death Row and before Tupac directly accused Biggie and his producer, Sean Puffy Combs, of orchestrating his shooting in Times Square. Knight criticized Combs at an awards ceremony in the summer of '95 and blamed Combs for the murder of a Death Row associate. Knight also threatened and beat rap industry figures associated with Combs' Bad Boy Records. Combs, on the other hand, had no history of violent behavior.[5] Knight and his employees, however, did.

Knight was charged with many attacks and his police guards were highly suspected of murdering rap manager Bruce Richardson, who was popular with both Bloods and Crips. Richardson, a 6'5" black belt, easily defended himself against Knight and his guards in public, after Richardson had confronted Knight about stealing rappers. When Richardson ended up dead in his home, Tupac called the rap manager's father to tell him he had no part in the murder. Tupac wouldn't say the same about Knight.[6]

Knight and others at Death Row appeared to use FBI Cointelpro tactics in trying to create divisions among top rap figures, particularly

3 "Death Row next set….advances." Ro, *Have Gun Will Travel*, pp.122-3, 158, 174-6. On Death Row and Wu Tang, also see Sullivan, *LAbyrinth*, p.85. Zulu Nation Afrika Bambata said his Zulu hip hop activist organization partly modeled itself after the Panthers, Black Panther Film Fest III, CUNY, NYC, 2002. Zulu Nation founder Afrika Bambatta reported first organizing the group around principles of the Black Panthers, Third Black Panther Film Festival, CUNY, 2003. The Black Liberation Movement leader was Sonny Carson, who had a recording studio. He worked with Tupac's New York lawyer Michael Warren in the 80s when New York police illegally targeted them with their Black Desk unit.
4 "Death Row next set….Miami." Ro, *Have Gun Will Travel*, pp.122-3, 158, 174-6. On Death Row and Wu Tang, also see Sullivan, *LAbyrinth*, p.85.
5 "Similarly, Death…behavior." Ro, *Have Gun Will Travel*, pp.156-157, 226-227, 232, 258. And, Cathy Scott, *The Murder of Biggie Smalls* (New York: St. Martin's, 2000) pp.54-5.
6 "Knight and his…answer." Also many witnesses said Death Row employees beat a Crip gang member to death unprovoked. Sullivan *LAbyrinth*, pp.37-9, 190-1.

between Tupac and anyone outside of their sphere of influence. It has been suggested that it was Death Row who encouraged Tupac to switch from writing songs promoting other rappers, to penning lyrics that attacked other rappers. Knight also fueled the notion in Tupac's mind that Biggie and Combs set up his shooting. In doing so, he continued the U.S. Intelligence agenda, involving the paid inmates and fake letters in jail, to promote this unsubstantiated claim about Biggie and Combs. Knight also continually encouraged violence between Death Row and Bad Boy Records.[7] Knight even convinced Tupac to turn against the rap producer he formerly idolized, Dr. Dre, after Dre split with Knight and Death Row early in 1996.[8]

Furthermore, Los Angeles police detective Russell Poole found evidence that police working inside Death Row Records were trafficking cocaine and guns. In documented interviews, one Tupac bodyguard at Death Row, former police and FBI employee Kevin Hackie, told Det. Poole that some of Suge Knight's closest associates were trafficking drugs and guns. Hackie identified three police officers who were close associates of Knight's and worked with Death Row in these activities: Reggie Gaines, David Mack, and Ray Perez. Poole found abundant evidence of these officers' involvement in drug dealing, as well as in laundering money.[9]

Bodyguard Kevin Hackie said that Suge Knight and his Death Row security director, former cop Reggie Wright Jr., also had a history with Knight's drug dealing friends. Hackie said that when Reggie Wright Jr. worked for the Compton, California police, he ripped off drug dealers and helped Knight's dealing friends when they got in trouble. And, finally, a Death Row employee told police detectives that she could provide information that Death Row owner Dave Kenner "was a major drug dealer." While police superiors said they failed to substantiate her claim, they also told Poole to drop his findings. Police further failed to act on other informants' reports of Death Row's drug and gun trafficking, and money laundering.[10]

---

7 "Knight and...records." On Tupac's change from promoting unity amongst rapper to divisiveness, see, for example, the first CD *2Pacalypse Now*'s naming of activist rappers on "America's Nightmare," and then "Representin' '93" on his second CD, *Strictly for My N.I.G.G.A.Z.* Despite the divisive sounding CD title, Tupac promotes White and Hispanic rap groups House of Pain and Cypress Hill along with Black rappers in this song. On his Death Row CDs, especially over half the tracks he produced within days of leaving prison, he has attacks on his former friend and top rapper, Biggie Smalls (Notorious BIG). His next CD then included attacks on many other New York rappers. Also see for example, Tupac's quotes of Knight's advising him to beat down Biggie and Puffy if they don't respect him. Vibe eds. *Tupac*, p.102.
8 Ro, *Have Gun Will Travel*, p.267-268.
9 "Furthermore...laundering money." Randall Sullivan, *LAbrynth* , pp.40, 124, 192, 197.
10 "Furthermore, highly...acted on." Sullivan, *LAbyrinth*, pp.40, 124, 169-70, 191.

While Death Row participated in these criminal operations, they also aided another U.S. Intelligence objective. As detailed earlier, U.S. Intelligence had a massive reaction to the LA 'riots'/rebellions against the oligarchs and U.S. Intelligence repression, and the gang peace truces that extended from it. One of the ways in which U.S. Intelligence worked to oppose this was by using police working with Death Row Records.

Besides running operations through Death Row, writers and activists such as best-selling author Mike Davis said police outside of Death Row worked with the FBI in framing individuals who helped lead the Bloods and Crips gang peace summit and conversion to activism. Despite the fact that Crips gang leader Dewayne Holmes led the drive for gang members to shift their work into legal community businesses, a judge jailed him on a ten-dollar theft charge at a gang unity dance. Congresswoman Maxine Waters and former governor Jerry Brown spoke on behalf of Holmes but couldn't keep him from getting a multi-year jail sentence for petty theft.[11] Also, people convicted of murdering unarmed gang peace leaders got off surprisingly easy. For example, Rodney Compton received just one year of probation for the murder of peace truce activist Tony Bogard.[12] Furthermore, under Operation Hammer, LA police agents specifically targeted the gangs coordinating the peace summits. That operation included 100 FBI agents assigned to assist them after the LA riots.[13]

Regarding these police activities, Det. Russell Poole failed to comment on what appeared to be a larger goal of Death Row Records on behalf of U.S. Intelligence—ending the gang peace truce. At least several moonlighting police officers in Death Row Records worked in these groups to disrupt gang peace summit events. One group included the aforementioned Death Row-linked Raphael "Ray" Perez, who worked for the elite undercover CRASH (Community Resources Against Street Hoodlums) anti-gang unit in the Rampart precinct.[14]

---

11 Mike Davis, "Who Killed Los Angeles? Part 2," *New Left Review*, #199, 1993, p.35. Davis authored the *New York Times* best-selling book, City of Quartz, on the history of Los Angeles.
12 Jesse Katz, "Man Freed in Death of Gang Leader Courts: Rodney Compton is to get one year probation in the slaying of Tony Bogard, who helped reach a truce between the Crips and Bloods," *The Los Angeles Times*, 6/1/94, p.3.
13 "The L.A...riots." Mike Davis, "In L.A., Burning All Illusions," *The Nation*, 6/1/92, p.745. For example, Gang truce leader Dewayne Holmes received a 7 year prison sentence for allegedly stealing $10 at a gang unity dance. Mike Davis, "Who Killed Los Angeles? Part Two: The verdict is given," *New Left Review* 199/1993, p.34-5. WBAI Radio, 4/15/02. FBI work with LAPD in Operation Hammer in Megan Garvey & Rich Winton, "City Declares War on Gangs," *Los Angeles Times*, 12/4/02. One activist was taped speaking to a large assembly and broadcast on the Pacifica Radio Network. He told how the LAPD's Operation Hammer—an "anti-gang operation" disrupted the gang peace summit meetings. He said that while he was helping run the peace summit meetings, it was only then that this operation had their police officers break up the meeting with a charge of "unlawful assembly. Heard by this writer on 99.1, WBAI radio station in New York City, April 29, 2001.
14 Sullivan, *LAbyrinth*, pp.197, 201-7.

A government report said that Operation Hammer was run inside of Perez's CRASH undercover anti-gang unit.[15]

"Former" LA cop Reggie Wright Jr. supervised Death Row's moonlighting cops. Wright's father, Reggie Wright Sr. was the Compton Police Gang Chief. He formerly worked with his son in Compton, and likely directed him later.[16] Similarly, in the '60s Richard W. Held had led the LA's FBI Cointelpro unit and directed his agents inside the "Black nationalist cultural group," the United Slaves, to murder Panthers (see chapter 5), before targeting Newton, Bari, and Tupac. Held was also directed by his father, one-time FBI associate director, Richard G. Held.[17]

Wright and Perez supervised the dozens of police officers following Suge Knight's orders. These orders included conducting anti-gang peace truce work inside Death Row. Early on, Suge Knight hired many Bloods and Crips gang members from his teen Compton neighborhood to work at Death Row Records, though he subsequently showed favor to his friends in the Bloods.[18] Compton's gang leaders were some of the first to ratify the 1992 gang peace truce and conversion to activism.[19] Insiders described how Knight provoked huge brawls between Crips and Bloods at his recording studio and further used his armed moonlighting police guards to protect him as he assaulted anyone who tried to stop the fights.[20]

At least one of these conflicts ended up with Death Row-employed Bloods murdering a Crip in the presence of, if not with the active participation of, Death Row cops. At a Soul Train Music Awards after-party that Death Row held, a group of Death Row Bloods killed a Crip named Kelly Jamerson. Some of these Bloods could have been undercover cops, as some Death Row cops were known to dress in Bloods colors. Jamerson had flashed a gang sign to Death Row rapper Snoop Dogg, a former Crip, and the Bloods beat Jamerson to death. Witnesses gave reports about this murder to uniformed police, but the police department never followed up.[21] In a separate incident, when a Death Row Crip said he communicated with a gunman by cell phone in an attempt to retaliate against Knight for hunting him down, a police car immediately intervened as if monitoring his phone.[22]

15 OJJDP Summary, August 2000—Youth Gang Programs and Strategies, "Suppression Programs" .ncjrs.org/html/ojjdp/summary_2000_8/suppression.html
16 On Wright, Sr. as Gang chief, see Nick Broomfield, *Biggie and Tupac*. On Wright, Jr. working with his father on Compton police force, Sullivan, *LAbyrinth*, p.191.
17 Churchill and Vander Wall, *Agents of Repression*, p.465 n.86
18 Ro, *Have Gun Will Travel*, pp.88, 102, 105, 111, 114-115,
19 Mike Davis, "Who Killed Los Angeles? Part Two: The Verdict is Given," *New Left Review* 198/1993, p.35.
20 Ro, *Have Gun Will Travel*, pp. 68, 92, 104-5, 120, 193-4.
21 "At least one…reports." Sullivan, *LAbyrinth*, pp.37-39. Also see, Ro, *Have Gun Will Travel*, pp.208-11.
22 Ro, *Have Gun Will Travel*, p.166.

MURDER IN MOBLAND

By August of 1996, Tupac Shakur appeared to have had more success at divorcing himself from the effects of Death Row's coercive tactics. In interviews, Tupac talked about how he would soon leave Death Row. He settled down, moving in with his fiancée, Kidada Jones, the daughter of *Vibe* magazine-owning, music-producing mogul Quincy Jones. Kidada said that Tupac also had found a new apartment for them to move into so they could get out of their Death Row-leased home. And, she said, he talked about having kids.[1]

While many said Tupac's energy was lower and his mood dimmer due to his concerns about his enchainment to Death Row, he started regaining his more fun-loving side that summer of '96. In one video, Tupac was filmed working in the studio. Grabbing a Death Row employee wearing a tank-top and pointing to the young guy's Chinese letters tattoo, Tupac said the guy had "Chinese letters like he's been somewhere. Shit, you ain't never left the block." Looking right into the video camera, Tupac pointed at the tattoo and added, "You know what this says? 'Two egg rolls with hot sauce, to go.'"[2]

The last month of Tupac's life also marked his return to radical leftist politics. Tupac completed production of his last CD, *don killuminati: the 7 day theory*, and it included one of his most explicitly radical political tracks since his first CD. Besides his track "Against All Odds," which, as mentioned earlier, named "Haitian Jacques" Agnant as working for the FBI to set up his shooting, his "White Manz World" included excerpts of radical activist speeches.

"White Manz World" included excerpts from one of his own speeches, as well as one from a Malcolm X speech. In his own speech he dedicated himself to his Panther political prisoner mentors—Mutulu Shakur, Geronimo Pratt, Sekou Odinga, and Mumia Abu-Jamal. The Malcolm X excerpt quoted, "the masses of the people—white and black, red, yellow and brown and vulnerable—are suffering in this nation.... Native Americans, Blacks, and other non-white people were to be the burden bearers for the real citizens of the nation."[3] Tupac further

---

1 "U.S. Intelligence...Quincy Jones." Robert Sam Anson, *Vanity Fair*, p.281. Scott, *The Killing of Tupac Shakur*, p.81.
2 Frank Alexander with Heidi Siegmund Cuda, *Got Your Back: Protecting Tupac in the world of gangsta rap* (New York: St. Martin's Griffin, 1998, 2000) p.144.
3 "In Tupac Shakur's...nation.'" Tupac under pseudonym, Ma.k.a.veli, *don killuminati: the 7 day theory* (Death Row, 1996).

signaled a return to leftist activism in his interviews. He discussed some of his political plans, including finishing a movie script he was writing about his mother's Black Panther experience. He was also planning to organize around independent electoral politics and to open community centers.[4]

By this time, Tupac defied continued Intelligence attempts to keep rappers in conflict, saying he wanted to reunify East and West coast rappers. Tupac said that his "W" hand signs didn't stand for "West" anymore, but for "War" on behalf of a unified Black America.[5] He also talked about politicizing various ethnic groups, reading Mao Tse Tong, and returning to his family's political work, which, once having left Death Row, he could do again with his revolutionary mentors in the New Afrikan People's Organization.[6]

By his 25th birthday in June of '96, Tupac Shakur had reached megastardom. Tupac's first Death Row release, *All Eyez On Me*, debuted in January of '96 as a chart-topping double CD with $10 million in sales—the second highest first week sales ever at that time (only topped by *The Beatles Anthology* in '95).[7] It had sold 7 million units by August.

Tupac's percentage of profit would soon massively increase by producing his own CDs as he had imminent exit plans from Death Row Records. He then started his own record and film production company, headed by imprisoned ex-Bronx Panther leader Sekou Odinga's wife, Yaasmyn Fula.[8] By that summer, Tupac argued with Knight about the advance money his contract promised, almost to the point of getting into a fistfight.[9] At the end of August, Tupac finished the CD he claimed should have completed his 3 CD contract and fired his contracted lawyer, Death Row co-owner Dave Kenner.[10]

---

4 Robert Sam Anson, "To Die Like a Gangsta," Vanity Fair, March 1997, p.280. On organizing around independent electoral politics, see Vibe eds. *Tupac Shakur*, p.280.

5 Rob Marriott, "Last Testament," Vibe Editors, *Tupac Shakur*, pp.125-126.

6 Vibe Editors, "Inside the Mind of Tupac Shakur," *Tupac Shakur* (New York: Crown Publishing, 1996), p.97. Armond White, *Rebel for the Hell of It* (New York: Thunder's Mouth Press, 1997), p.168. "Bits and Pieces," The Source, October 1996, p.6. Rob Marriott, "Last Testament," Vibe Editors, *Tupac Shakur*, pp.125-126.

7 Ro, Have Gun Will Travel, p.281.

8 Fula ran Tupac's record company, Euphenasia, Bruck, *New Yorker*, p.61. Molly Monjauze, Tupac's 4 hour personal assistant, also helped run this company. On Odinga's fathering Yafeu Fula with Yaasmyn, see a letter by Mutulu Shakur in Alex Constantine, *The Covert War Against Rock* (Los Angeles: Feral House, 2001), p.159. Yaasmyn Fula had also done jail time in connection with Mutulu Shakur's indictment in the 80s. See Kuwasi Balagoon, *A Soldier's Story: Writings by a Revolutionary New Afrikan Anarchist* (Montreal: Solidarity, 2001), p.34.

9 Both of Tupac's personal bodyguards, Fran Alexander and Kevin Hackie, reportedly said this in Det. Russell Poole's interviews. In Sullivan, *LAbyrinth*, pp.188, 192.

10 "Tupac had immediate exit…Death Row co-chair Dave Kenner." Connie Bruck, "The Takedown of Tupac," The New Yorker, 7/7/97, pp.61-63. Also see a copy of Tupac's handwritten contract signed in jail, ed.s Jacob Hoye and Karolyn Ali, *Tupac: Resurrection 1971-1996*, pp.192-93.

Ten days after Tupac fired Dave Kenner, concretely signaling his Death Row departure, he was scheduled to attend a Mike Tyson boxing match with Suge Knight in Vegas. Tupac tried to back out of attending, even though he usually congratulated his fan and friend, Tyson, just after the matches.[11] Tupac was wary of this event's timing and locale. Death Row employees said that Kenner's connection with a New York Mafia family was common knowledge, as was the New York Mafia's gambling-based development of Vegas.[12]

U.S. Intelligence had a history of collaborating with the Mafia in various operations. A researcher got family members of one Albert Carone to provide statements and official documents showing how Carone had straddled the Mafia, the U.S. military (as a colonel), and New York police.[13] Among other instances, Martin Luther King's family trial lawyer, William Pepper, provided two examples of such corroborative work, each backed by press reports from the BBC. Pepper explained how Mafia work against MLK provided the CIA with "an officially deniable local contract and assassination operation ostensibly carried out exclusively by organized crime."[14]

Death Row was suspected of having many links to Mafia figures who, in turn, had links to U.S. governmental agencies. Several researchers mentioned Death Row's links to the Genovese Mafia family,[15] the Mafia family with the longest history of U.S. Intelligence work.[16] Death Row attorney Oscar Goodman acted as the consigliere

11 See both Yaasmyn Fula in Bruck, *New Yorker*, p.62 and Kidada Jones in Anson, *Vanity Fair*, p.281.

12 On Kenner's East Coast Mafia ties, Sullivan, *LAbyrinth*, p.192. Las Vegas gambling had a notorious Mafia history. Organized crime figures made Las Vegas their "Mafia money machine." Cathy Scott, *The Murder of Biggie Smalls* (New York: St. Martin's Press, 2000), p.130.

13 See the booklet of documents created by Michael Rupert on Albert Carone, with assistance from Carone's daughters. Michael Ruppert, *Albert V. Carone: The Missing Link Between CIA and the Mob* (Los Angeles, CA, From the Wilderness Publications, 1998). copvcia.com/free/ciadrugs/casey_letter.html ,fromthewilderness.com .

14 William Pepper, *Orders to Kill: The Truth Behind the Murder of Martin Luther King* (New York: Warner, 1998), p.146-7, 485. Also note that despite Warner Books' republishing of Pepper's book originally published by Carrol and Graf, this author needed to order the book from Warner's warehouse and Warner generally appeared to buy the rights to it in order to keep it hidden. Other Mafia overlap with the FBI in Boston and the NYPD have also received wide press. See for example CBS News/Associated Press, "Ex-FBI Agent Charged in Mob Hit," .cbsnews.com/ stories/2003/11/21/national /main584890.shtml. FBI documents also cited their attempts to provoke a Mafia hit on Panther-supporting comedian, Dick Gregory. See FBI letter From: SAC, Chicago, To: FBI Director,(100-4480006). 4/15/68. Copied in Churchill and Vander Wall, *The COINTELPRO Papers*, p.104.

15 Randall Sullivan, *LAbyrinth* (New York: Atlantic Monthly Press, 2002), p.99. And Ronin Ro *Have Gun Will Travel* book flap. An associate of Ro's told this author that much information was censored out of the American reprinting of his book originally published in Britain. Anson also mentioned this connection. Anson, *Vanity Fair*, p.281. *New Yorker* editor Connie Bruck also mentions Death Row's connections to New York organized crime families, Bruck, *The New Yorker*, p.64.

16 For Genovese Mafia family and U.S. Intelligence work, see Lucky Luciano and his Lieutenant, Vito Genovese. They led New York's five largest Mafia families that controlled heroin traffic in the fifties while helping oppose Communists/Socialists. *Newsday* Editors, *The Heroin Trail* (New York: Signet, 1973), p.199, cited in Clarence Lusane, *Pipe Dream Blues: Racism and the War on Drugs* (Boston, South End Press, 1991), p.39, 117-18. When Luciano, Genovese and Meyer Lansky exited due to death and old age, the next leading member of their network, Santo Trafficante, furthered business with CIA- and U.S. military-supported drug trafficking generals. Alfred McCoy, *The*

for the Mafia, keeping members jail-free for years. Goodman was to be elected mayor of Las Vegas by the end of the '90s. Goodman's partner, Death Row attorney Dave Chesnoff, was a former assistant U.S. attorney.[17]

Despite his worries about Vegas as a setup, Tupac decided to attend the Tyson fight with Knight on September 7, 1996. His decision was partly due to a benefit concert that he was scheduled to take part in later that night in Vegas. The benefit show stemmed from a summer trial in Los Angeles for weed possession that an elderly white judge had presided over. After reading a report on Tupac's life, the judge called him "remarkable" and sentenced him to do a benefit concert, shocking an LA District Attorney who tried to get Tupac's bail revoked.[18]

That weekend, Death Row made several changes to leave Tupac virtually unprotected for the first time. A day before Tyson's boxing match, Death Row fired one of Tupac's two main bodyguards, Kevin Hackie. The reasons given for this vary, but Hackie reportedly had been encouraging Tupac to move to Atlanta, which Suge Knight and Reggie Wright found out about.[19] The following day, Tupac's other bodyguard, Frank Alexander, said that Reggie Wright told him he couldn't carry his gun because Death Row had forgotten to register it. Wright then gave Alexander a cell phone, which happened to have a dead battery.[20]

Hours before the Saturday night Tyson fight, Suge Knight held a rollicking party at his Vegas mansion. Moonlighting cops attended this party with the moonlighting LA cops in Death Row.[21] They then went to the MGM Grand Hotel which housed the boxing arena where they watched Tyson knock out his opponent in the first round.

Politics of Heroin: CIA Complicity in the Global Drug Trade (New York: Lawrence Hill Books, 1991), pp.32-9, 43-4, 73-7, 255-6.

17 "Death Row…attorney." Scott, *The Murder of Biggie Smalls*, p.81, 130. Scott told how Goodman and Chesnoff worked as Death Row's lawyers. Sullivan also told how Goodman billed himself as the "mouthpiece for the Mob." *LAbyrinth*, p.99. Cathy Scott was a veteran police reporter for the *Las Vegas Sun* who has written for the *New York Times* and written for or appeared on a dozen other newspapers and television news programs. She has also won a dozen journalism awards. Randall Sullivan has written articles for *Rolling Stone* and *Esquire*. On Chesnoff, see Sullivan, *LAbyrinth*, p.99

18 "Tupac finally…revoked." Dyson, *Holler If You Hear Me*, pp.247-8.

19 "The biggest…setup." Sullivan, LAbyrinth, pp.192-3.

20 "That weekend…battery." Sullivan, *LAbyrinth*, pp.188, 192-3. In official notes taken by Los Angeles Detectives Russell Poole and Frank Miller, cited within. See, LAPD notes of interview of Frank Alexander, written by Det. Russell Poole, dated 4/28/98, 7 pages. Most comments of Alexander's come from this source, except where otherwise noted. Alexander was also an auxiliary police officer in Los Angeles. Also see, Scott, *Tupac*, p.5. Anson, *Vanity Fair*, p.282.

21 On alcohol and weed at the party, Anson, *Vanity Fair*, p.282. On the Vegas moonlighting cops joining the LA moonlighting cops that night, Scott, *The Killing of Tupac Shakur*, p.6.

After the match, the Death Row group walked through the MGM's huge lobby. Death Row employee Travon Lane and others influenced Tupac to join them in a conflict with a young guy they saw standing in the lobby named Orlando Anderson. The Death Row employees convinced Tupac that Anderson had previously been with several Crips who attacked them. That Tupac may have drank or smoked at the party, as well as the fact that two Crips had once punched him for no reason, may have helped the Death Row group get Tupac to join in this beating. The group briefly attacked Anderson in the hotel lobby and then left, unstopped by the many guards and police who immediately came to the scene.[22]

Soon after the incident, the large Death Row entourage began the drive to Tupac's post-match benefit concert. Many disclosures about the drive support that it was a U.S. Intelligence-planned procession to Tupac's murder.

Knight convinced Tupac to drive with him rather than taking the Hummer Tupac had originally planned to drive. A Death Row bodyguard also said that the security for the drive was unlike any he had previously done for Death Row. He said that two armed bodyguards would normally ride in the car with Knight and Tupac, but no one rode with them on this occasion.

Unarmed guard Frank Alexander followed in the car behind Knight and Tupac. Alexander rode with several of Tupac's backup rappers, in a group Tupac dubbed The Outlawz, giving each of them a name of a world leader who opposed American and European imperialism. The most important of these backup rappers was Tupac's 'cousin' Yafeu Fula. In the 60s, Sekou Odinga had founded The Bronx Black Panthers before coupling with fellow Bronx Panther Yaasmyn Fula, Yafeu's mother.[23]

Just-fired bodyguard Kevin Hackie, who also worked for the FBI but had grown loyal to Tupac, claimed that he had FBI documents to prove that an FBI agent and an ATF agent were in the entourage of cars following Knight, Tupac, and Fula's cars.[24] *Las Vegas Sun* police

22 "After watching a ...scene." Eyewitness Frank Alexander in Sullivan, *LAbyrinth*, p.188. Cited in Dream Hampton, "Hellraiser," *The Source*, September 1994, p.85.
23 "Many disclosures...Tupac." Bruck, *New Yorker*, p.63.
24 Stated in Broomfield, *Biggie and Tupac*. Hackie's "informant," meaning paid work for the FBI, also came out in many news sources when they reported on rapper Biggie Smalls' family's wrongful death trial. See, for example, Charlie Amter, "B.I.G. Revelations in Biggie Trial," *Yahoo! News*, 7/24/05.

reporter Cathy Scott concurred about the FBI presence. She wrote that it had been widely printed that Tupac "was under surveillance by the FBI at the time of his shooting."[25] Many reports also placed Death Row's Los Angeles police officers, such as Richard McCauley, accompanying other Death Row security in Vegas.[26]

Tupac sat in the passenger seat as Knight, followed by the Death Row entourage, stopped at a light by a crowded sidewalk in front of the Maxim Hotel just off The Strip. With a Death Row car in front of them and behind them, Death Row employee Travon Lane pulled up to the left of Knight and Tupac, but a little ahead of them. A car full of women stopped just behind Lane's car. The women grabbed Tupac's attention by calling out to him. Just then, a white Cadillac stopped to Tupac's right partly ahead of him and one or two gunmen from the car fired over thirteen rounds. Four bullets hit Tupac, including two in the chest. Knight's forehead was reportedly cut, though most say that only a ricocheting bullet fragment or glass shard hit him. Reports also claimed that no guards in the following cars fired at the assailants. The Cadillac fled from the scene and was never apprehended.[27]

25 Cathy Scott, *The Murder of Biggie Smalls* (New York: St. Martins, 2000), p.94.

26 Sullivan, *LAbyrinth*, pp.157, 159, 162-5. "security detail," p.165.

27 "Knight and Tupac…apprehended." This scene has been described in many ways by many sources. Cathy Scott did excellent work, particularly in uncovering many police irregularities regarding this scene. The only weak point in her depiction came in regards to Suge Knight. Scott claimed Knight was hit by a bullet "fragment," implying a ricocheting fragment, Scott, *The Killing of Tupac*, Shakur, p.7. Scott later changed the wording to Knight being "hit by a bullet," in Scott, *The Murder of Biggie Smalls*, p.72. This small difference is important in people's attempt to defend Knight. Investigating Police whistleblower, Det. Russell Poole, documentary filmmaker Nick Broomfield, and *LAbyrinth* author Randall Sullivan, all believe that Knight was only injured as described in this writer's paragraph, by flying debris. Sullivan, *LAbyrinth*, p.144. *New Yorker* editor Connie Bruck did an extensive article saying "Knight's forehead was grazed," without saying by what. Connie Bruck, "The Takedown of Tupac," *The New Yorker*, 7/7/97, p.63. Vibe's Rob Marriot said "bullet fragments" grazed Knight, Vibe ed.s, *Tupac Shakur*, p.120. On Travon Lane's car also blocking Tupac in, *documentary Tupac Assassination* (2007) dir. Richard Bond, co-produced with Frank Alexander.

POLICE COVER-UPS AND THE REIGNITION OF THE BLOODS VS CRIPS WAR

"In the event of my demise
When my heart can beat no more
I hope that I die 4 a principle
or a belief that I had lived 4
I will die before my time
because I feel the shadow's depth
so much I wanted 2 accomplish
before I reached my death
I have come to grips with the possibility
and wiped the last tear from my eyes
I loved all who were positive
in the event of my demise."

> —Tupac Shakur, "In the Event of My Demise," from *The Rose That Grew from Concrete*, his collected poems.

The events of Tupac Shakur's shooting both suggest Suge Knight's involvement and that he may have even been a low man on the U.S. Intelligence's operation hierarchy. While 170-pound Tupac was hit four times, 330-pound Knight miraculously avoided getting directly hit by any of the 13+ bullets.[1] The danger of the scenario suggests Knight didn't know how precarious it would be, but the care the gunmen took not to hit Knight supports that they must have done so on purpose.

Tupac reportedly tried to jump into the back seat and Knight said in a police interview that he pulled him down. Knight implied that he tried to cover Tupac's body with his own, thereby risking taking the bullets himself, despite their recent fights and Tupac leaving his label.[2]

Knight's actions immediately following the shooting implicate him more forcefully. After the shooting stopped, Knight did a U-turn and raced in the opposite direction from the closest hospital, which was located on the block of the club holding the benefit show. Knight worked several years to purchase that club and went to college in Vegas,

---

1 Knight argued that he got a bullet lodged in his head that required an overnight hospital stay, though most researchers say he was merely grazed by ricocheting glass or shrapnel. Of the many researchers' insistence of Knight not getting directly hit by a bullet, see Sullivan, *LAbyrinth*, Broomfield *Biggie and Tupac*. Scott, *The Killing of Tupac Shakur*, p.8. Knight's walking around fine a day or two later attests to no direct shots hitting him. For their approximate weights, see his prison identity card in Tupac: Resurrection 1971-1996, p.152, where it also lists him as 5'11". For Knight, he's listed as 6'4" and" and 330 lbs. Scott, *The Murder of Biggie Smalls* (New York: St. Martin's, 2000) p.52.
2 "'Tupac reportedly...label." Bruck, *New Yorker*, p. 63.

which would suggest that he knew the area. Knight also failed to call for an ambulance with the cell phone on his dashboard.[3]

Knight drove wildly through lights and over concrete medians back towards the MGM Hotel. Many in the Death Row entourage followed him, as did two cops on bicycles at the scene. Knight flattened all of his tires on the medians and stopped when he got stuck on one. Police surrounded his car, ordered all at the scene to lie on the street, and then paramedics helped take blood-drenched Tupac to a hospital.[4]

Veteran *Las Vegas Sun* police reporter Cathy Scott described Vegas police actions as aiding the escape of Tupac's murderers. Scott presented a "long list of questionable decisions" by police.[5] First, the bike cops were within yards of the shooting and failed to secure the scene. They also either failed to call in the location or the police chiefs ignored their calls.[6] Then, police also lost the opportunity to gather evidence and interview witnesses due to the fact that they spent 20 minutes searching for evidence at the location where Knight ended up getting his car stuck on an embankment and not at the scene of the shooting, several miles away.

Scott said that police officials further decided to go against other standard procedures. They didn't put out an All Points Bulletin (APB), they didn't use a police helicopter to search for the killers, and they didn't take any aerial photos.[7] These actions occurred despite Las Vegas cops saying that Tupac's shooting was the biggest murder case in Vegas history.[8]

Bunglings like this appeared to continue for months. Eyewitnesses to the shooting said that Vegas police ignored them and some officers contradicted official police statements that said they had no forthcoming witnesses.[9] Tupac's back-up rappers and bodyguard in the car following his all said they saw the assailants. Rappers Yafeu Fula and Malcolm Greenridge both said they thought they could identify the shooter, while bodyguard Frank Alexander said he saw the assailants before the gunfire. Police appeared to ignore the three's assertions until the *Los Angeles Times* reprinted their statements.[10]

3 "Knight then raced...dashboard." Scott, *The Killing of Tupac Shakur*, pp.9, 41, 95.

4 "Knight drove...hospital." Scott, *The Killing of Tupac Shakur*, pp.7-10.

5 Scott, *The Killing of Tupac Shakur*, p.59.

6 "First...calls." Scott, *The Killing of Tupac Shakur*, pp.8-9, 39, 42-43.

7 "Then, police lost...photos." Scott, *The Killing of Tupac Shakur*, pp.9, 40, 43. Also see, "Investigative Reports: Interview with Cathy Scott," *XXL Magazine*, October, 2000, p.131.

8 Scott, *The Killing of Tupac Shakur*, p. 40.

9 Scott, *The Killing of Tupac Shakur*, pp.18-19, 35-39, 112. Scott, *The Murder of Biggie Smalls* (New York: St. Martin's Press, 2000), p.89.

10 "Tupac's backup...assertions." Chuck Phillips, "2 Say They Saw Attackers of Slain Rapper; Members of Tupac Shakur's entourage say they haven't been asked to view photos of suspects." *The Los Angeles Times*, 2/28/97, A3.

Police then failed to cooperate with media groups trying to assist with the investigation, including TV's *Unsolved Mysteries'* coverage of the murder and promotion of the police call-in tip line. Police reporter Cathy Scott said that police shows like *Unsolved Mysteries* usually help police, and this particular program inspired many phone calls that would later lead to arrests. However, following the episode on Tupac's murder, police later reported that they got "too many calls" and stopped answering phones on the tip line.[11]

Furthermore, Los Angeles police officer Ken Knox found fellow LA police officer Richard McCauley working at the front desk in the Death Row Records recording studio in early 1996. Knox reported this to his superiors whom he successfully influenced to officially reprimand McCaulley. A police chief ostensibly ordered him to quit this side work but many witnesses and hotel records showed that McCaulley was still working for Death Row in Las Vegas when Tupac was shot there.[12] Despite this open defiance of an order, McCaulley was promoted to sergeant shortly after Tupac's murder.[13]

The details about a possible police operation against Tupac came out much later. Las Vegas police investigators of Tupac's murder told Los Angeles police detective Russell Poole that they had loads of evidence on Tupac's murder and that they didn't plan to follow up on any of it. The Vegas detectives revealed to Poole that police superiors told them that they were not supposed to actually investigate Tupac's murder.[14]

U.S. Intelligence appeared to have several motives for helping Knight and Death Row cops orchestrate Tupac's murder. U.S. Intelligence first feared Tupac's political use of his new mega-stardom financed by his large wealth and power. While he was alive, each of Tupac's solo CDs sold more than twice the preceding one. Producing his own CDs would exponentially increase Tupac's already multimillion-dollar profits. He also had movie role offers pouring in, and his planned marriage to Kidada Jones would have had him marrying into her *Vibe*-owning father Quincy's wealth and influence.[15]

---

11 "Police then failed...line." Scott, *The Killing of Tupac...*, pp.47-8, 59.
12 "Furthermore...there." Sullivan, *LAbyrinth*, pp.157, 159, 162-5. "security detail," p.165.
13 See official police documents that confirm witness statements about McCauley's promotion just after Tupac's murder, as well as his work permit revocation before the murder. For example, LAPD "Intradepartmental Correspondence" from Commander Keith D. Bushey of Human Resources Bureau, Personnel Group, "Subject: Work Permit "Revocation, Police Officer III Ricahrd McCauley," dated 1/8/95 2 pages. And LAPD "Supplemental Investigation to Personnel Complaint Investigation IA No 96-1408," resulting in "one additional allegation of misconduct against Sergeant I Richard McCauley," dated 6/25/97 5 pages. p.157, 163, 316-17. Police superiors only punished McCauley after other police joined Knox and Poole in complaints about McCauley.
14 "Las Vegas...murder." Sullivan, *LAbyrinth*, p.143.
15 "U.S. Intelligence...influence." Robert Sam Anson, *Vanity Fair*, p.281. Scott, *The Killing of Tupac Shakur*, p.81.

Tupac's expanding influence and appeal, which went well beyond Black America, may have also concerned U.S. Intelligence. Tupac's fans included fashion designers who feted Tupac and Kidada, a model, with free clothes, and mainstream magazines that ran features on him. Tupac also starred in two new films, *Gridlock'd* and *Gang Related*, both of which hit theaters within months of his death. His close friends ranged from Black entertainers and pro athletes to Madonna, Mickey Rourke, and Interscope Entertainment mogul Ted Fields. Furthermore, about 70% of people who bought his albums were white. Many entertainment stars cited Tupac's incredible charm that even won over the elderly white judge who sentenced him to do the benefit concert scheduled after the Vegas Tyson fight. That judge was so moved by Tupac that he wouldn't cancel a post-death review hearing on the case just so he could be around people who knew the rapper.[16]

As mentioned before, by the last months of his life, Tupac had many activist projects. Tupac promised to set up a new community center after each CD, the first of which had already opened in LA. Tupac also stated his intent of returning to his family's revolutionary politics. In one of his last interviews he said that now he would "mix the street life with respected, known, and proven military philosophy." And finally, he stated his plans to collaborate with LA Crip gang leader-turned author, Sanyika Shakur (a.k.a. Monster Kody Scott), a converted revolutionary socialist. This would have particularly set off U.S. Intelligence alarms.[17]

Regarding Tupac's plans with Sanyika Shakur, U.S. Intelligence had yet another motive for murdering the rap star. They apparently saw an opportunity to both end Tupac's goal of radicalizing gangs while also using his shooting to reignite the Bloods versus Crips gang war. Eyewitness Frank Alexander believed Suge Knight had paid alleged Crip Orlando Anderson to wait for the Death Row group in the hotel lobby after the Tyson fight and take a beating from them as a false motive for Tupac's murder.[18] Det. Russell Poole said that Alexander and Tupac's other bodyguard, Kevin Hackie, both said that they believed Knight, Reggie Wright Jr., and Anderson all helped set up Tupac's murder.

16 "Tupac's expanding...rapper." See fashion modeling picture and film list, Vibe ed.s Tupac Shakur, pp.114, 141. Also see picture of Tupac with Donatella Versace in Frank Alexander, *Got Your Back*. On judge, see Dyson, *Holler If You Hear Me*, p.248. Tupac's last film include *Gridlock'd* with actor Tim Roth, and, ironically, *Gang Related*, with Jim Belushi. The latter movie used the same theme most media used to cover up corrupt police murders of Blacks, in saying it was "gang-related."
17 "Tupac promised...alarms." On community centers after each CD, military philosophy and Monster Kody, Vibe ed.s, *Tupac*, '97, p.51, 97-8. LA community center was for "at-risk youth," Robert Sam Anson, "To Die Like a Gangsta," *Vanity Fair*, March 1997, p.280.
18 Sullivan, *LAbyrinth*, pp.188-189.

Documentary director Nick Broomfield even got Hackie to say on film that Death Row was behind Tupac's murder.[19]

Years after Tupac's death, Hackie disclosed publicly that he had worked undercover for the FBI the whole time he worked for Death Row, from 1992 to 1996.[20] He had apparently become close to Tupac and defied his employer in telling Tupac to move to Atlanta and avoid Las Vegas. Afeni Shakur concurred with Hackie about Tupac's animosity towards Knight, saying Tupac's work for Knight was living "in bondage." Tupac's Aunt Yaasmyn [Fula] agreed with Hackie on Tupac trying to go to Atlanta instead of Vegas on that fateful weekend. Hackie encouraged Tupac to move near his family and mentors in Atlanta, likely for protection. NAPO Security Director Watani Tyehimba lived there near Afeni, while Tyehimba's son worked for Tupac in LA.

After Poole tried to use his reports from Hackie against Death Row cops, Hackie said authorities framed him and he spent months in jail. Expert researchers have said agents in such positions are usually given only partial knowledge of the entire operation. Hackie said the FBI set him up with gun possession charges, for having guns in his trunk, despite his status working for both the Los Angeles police department and the FBI.[21]

Hackie's disclosed working undercover for the FBI when he sat as part of a panel discussion for a presentation of the film *Tupac: Assassination,* and got into a debate with a police officer in the audience.[22] This DVD presented Death Row bodyguard Michael Moore, who was a back-up guard for Tupac. Moore also backed Frank Alexander's assertion that Reggie Wright told all of the Death Row bodyguards they were not to carry guns that night due to a lack of state permits. Moore said this shocked him and he alone said that he has a personal gun and permit. Moore said he then debated Wright all day about guarding Tupac, as the regular substitute for the recently fired Hackie. Moore finally gave in and left Tupac's side to go directly to Club 661 with Wright. Moore

19 Nick Broomfield, *Biggie and Tupac*, 2002. Sullivan, *LAbyrinth*, p.189.
20 AllHipHopStaff, "Tupac's Former Bodyguard Claims To Be FBI Agent," *Maven*, 08/18/07. http://allhiphop. com/news/ Jullianne Shepherd, "Death Row Bodyguard=Undercover FBI Agent," Vibe.com vibe.com/news headlines/2007/10/death_row_undercover/
21 "Kevin Hackie's…jail." See former Panther attorney, Paul Chevigny, Cops and Rebels: A Study of Provocation (New York: Curtis/Pantheon Books, 1972), p.113. On Afeni's description of Tupac's business relationship with Knight, as well as Fula and Jones about Atlanta, see Bruck, *The New Yorker*, pp.61, 63. Hackie said authorities set him up for that arrest in Broomfield, *Biggie and Tupac*.
22AllHipHopStaff, "Tupac's Former Bodyguard Claims To Be FBI Agent," *Maven*, 08/18/07. http://allhiphop. com/news/ Jullianne Shepherd, "Death Row Bodyguard=Undercover FBI Agent," Vibe.com vibe.com/news headlines/2007/10/death_row_undercover/

said that at about the time Tupac was shot, he heard a voice come over Wright's radio saying, "Got him!"[23]

Within several days of Tupac's shooting, Knight visited the Las Vegas police department at least twice and talked to the FBI at least once. Sources described only one of these three communications as related to the shooting. One reason given for talking to the FBI, including reporting as an ex-felon in a new state, remains dubious since Knight owned a house in Vegas and often traveled there.[24]

But most curiously, within those first 72 hours after Tupac was shot and he lay dying in the hospital, Knight was talking to the FBI and the police in Los Angeles.[25] In the LA neighborhood of Compton, a police informant's affidavit stated that Suge Knight and his anti-gang CRASH unit confidants helped spark the war by having their Bloods spread the rumor that lobby scuffle victim Anderson killed Tupac. Anderson lived with his uncle, known Compton Crip Dwayne Keith "Keffy-D" Davis. Death Row employees such as Travon Lane who encouraged Tupac's scuffle with Anderson, along with Bloods working at Death Row, quickly spread the word that the Compton Crips killed Tupac.[26]

Poole said that another police informant claimed that Knight delivered an entire load of AK-47 assault rifles to Bloods gang members at the Nickerson Gardens housing project in LA the night after Tupac was shot. The following night, the Bloods versus Crips violence started. It began with shootings of Compton Crip leaders within a 5-10 minute drive of the Nickerson Gardens Bloods.[27] This is particularly tragic because the Bloods and Crips gang sets living in the Nickerson Gardens project in the Watts area of LA had been the first to agree to the peace truce several years before. Other Watts gangs and Compton's Bloods and Crips gang sets were the next to join the truce.[28]

23 Richard Bond, dir. *Tupac Assassination* (2007), Bond-Age Films/Ste N' UP Enterprises, produced with Frank Alexander.

24 "Within several…often traveled there." Scott, *The Killing of Tupac*, p.105. Knight's Vegas lawyer, David Chesnoff, claimed Knight went to police headquarters a second time to register as an ex-convict. Chesnoff said the FBI "reminded" Knight of this because of a Nevada law saying you had 72 hours to do so. This reason for the FBI talking to Knight seems dubious. Knight had driven the 300 miles from LA to his Las Vegas mansion many weekends. Since Knight had a home in Las Vegas and spent much time there, why wouldn't they have asked him to register in the past? This makes the reported "registration as an ex-con" reason for Knight's contacts with the FBI and police sound like a cover story for a debriefing and consultation on how to handle the murder aftermath. Scott, *The Killing of Tupac*, p.104.

25 "But most curious…shooting." Sullivan, *LAbyrinth*, pp.141-143.

26 "In LA…Tupac." Sullivan, *LAbyrinth*, pp.141-143. On Travon Lane reporting Anderson and Crips killing Tupac, *Tupac Assassination* (2007) documentary, Rich Bond and Frank Alexander producers.

27 "Police said…Bloods." Sullivan, *LAbyrinth*, p.145.

28 Davis, "Who Killed Los Angeles? Part Two: The Verdict is Given," *New Left Review* 199/1993, p.35.

In the days following his shooting, Tupac fought for his life in the hospital while Knight helped restart the Bloods versus Crips gang war. The Bloods and Crips fatally shot each other on September 9 in L.A., two days after Tupac's shooting, and the shootings continued later that week.[29] The murders revived the Bloods/Crips gang war after their several-year truce and political activist conversion.[30] In Las Vegas, hospital spokesmen held press conferences for the mass of national and international reporters asking about Tupac's health status as he lay dying for 7 days. Political activists, entertainers, and athletes joined Tupac's family and extended family at the hospital. Fiancée Kidada Jones described sitting by Tupac's bedside, asking Tupac if he knew she loved him. She said he gave a slight head nod and movement of his foot.

Kidada then played Don McLean's "Vincent," a song Tupac loved because it was about Vincent Van Gough, whose art Afeni Shakur had given him as a child. McLean sang, "now I understand, what you tried to say to me, how you suffered for your sanity, how you tried to set them free. They would not listen, they did not know how, perhaps they'll listen now." People close to the reignited Bloods/Crips gang violence might have felt this way about Tupac as they soon spread a message to stop the violence. Tupac slipped into a coma, his heart failed several times, and Afeni decided to pull the life support on September 13, 1996.[31]

Twenty Crips and Bloods died in the revived gang war in the seven days after Tupac's shooting. But on September 13, while many mourned Tupac's death, activists spread the word that the Crips may not have been behind Tupac's murder, and the shootings ended.[32]

---

29 "But most curious…shooting." Sullivan, *LAbyrinth*, pp.141-143.

30 Mike Davis, "Who Killed Los Angeles? Part Two: The Verdict is Given," *New Left Review* 199/1993.

31 "In Las Vegas…1996" Anson, *Vanity Fair*, p.282. Some of the people that came to Tupac's bedside included Jesse Jackson, Al Sharpton, Jasmine Guy, Diana Ross, MC Hammer and Mike Tyson. Tyson left his post-boxing match press conference without talking to reporters so that he could rush to the hospital and come to Tupac's bedside. On Afeni deciding to not revive him, Scott, *Biggie*, p.102.

32 "Twenty…shootings." Sullivan, *LAbyrinth*, pp.141-143. Crips Darnell Brims was shot three times on 9/9/96. A Blood working for Death Row's Wrightway security was shot several times by a Crip. 30 yr-old Bobby Finch was fatally shot on Compton's Southside. Police found arms and ammunition inside the homes of Jerry Bonds and Orlando Anderson. On many in mourning, the movie *Tupac: Resurrection* showed people mourning worldwide. In the U.S., Princeton Professor Cornel West said his son attended a Tupac memorial of hundreds at Howard University that had people crying. West also asked for a moment of silence for Tupac on the anniversary of his death, at the start of West's keynote address at the AFL-CIO Labor Conference at Columbia University this writer attended. Personal interview, 9/13/97. Many white activists appeared not to understand why West cared.

THREAT-TIMING
TACTICS AND A
SUSPECT KILLED

"In time I learned a few lessons, never fall for riches
Apologize to my true sisters, far from bitches
Help me raise my black nation
Reparations are due, it's true...
Especially black, bear with me, can't you see
We're under attack
I never meant to cause drama
To my sister and Mama
Will we make it to better times
in this white man's world...
This is dedicated to my motherfuckin' teachers:
Mutulu Shakur, Geronimo Pratt, Mumia Abu-Jamal,
Sekou Odinga."

> —Tupac Shakur, "White Man'z World," *Makavelli: Don Killuminati, The 7 Day Theory*, released 8 weeks after his death, 11/5/96.

The cover-up of Tupac's murder appeared as large of an operation as the accumulated attempts to murder him, and it continued for years. *Las Vegas Sun* reporter Cathy Scott heavily investigated Tupac's murder and found out that Yafeu Fula was a forthcoming witness. After Scott pressed police spokesmen on the issue of Fula, they admitted to her that he said he thought he could identify Tupac's murderer in a photo line-up. But in press conferences police maintained that there were no forthcoming witnesses. Scott detailed how police then proceeded to ignore Fula for two months.[1]

In November of '96, the night of Mike Tyson's next boxing match, a gunman shot Yafeu Fula in the head in his girlfriend's stairwell while he reportedly wore a bullet-proof vest.[2] Media repeated police saying Fula's murder was drug related, despite no evidence to support the claim and Fula not having a criminal record.

This suggests that U.S. Intelligence used their threat-timing tactic. This tactic gives a conscious or subconscious warning threatening

---

1 "The cover-up of...months." On police ignoring Fula, Scott, *The Killing of Tupac Shakur*, pp.18-19, 35-37, 112-113. On police saying murder was drug-related, Scott, *The Murder of Biggie Smalls*, p.88. Media repeated this lie. *Time Magazine*, "The Year in Review," 12/30/96, p.130. This police/media concoction is a worse case cover-up than that around Newton's death.

2 On details of killing, Scott, *The Killing of Tupac Shakur*, p.112.

people to not go forward, in this case, with identifying the gunmen or giving other evidence as to who killed Tupac. Experiencing the murder of someone close to you can cause a form of Post Traumatic Stress Disorder in others linked to that person such as friends, family, and fellow musicians. Psychology Today states: "Anniversaries of the event and similarities in person, place, or circumstances can trigger symptoms." Psychology Today further says that symptoms include "Avoiding people, places, or activities associated with that event."[3]

U.S. Intelligence had several reasons to use a timing tactic on Tupac's backup rapper Fula. Fula was the top witness in Tupac's murder. Fula also represented another radical political potential entertainment star, as he had Hollywood good looks and his father was the imprisoned former Bronx Black Panther leader, Sekou Odinga. Also, Yafeu's mother, Afeni's longtime friend Yaasmyn, managed Tupac's new record company.[4]

Past incidents suggest they had already used this tactic in their dealings with Tupac. As mentioned, gunmen attacked Tupac on the anniversary of Huey Newton's death and other gunmen murdered the top forthcoming witness to Tupac's previous New York shooting, Randy "Stretch" Walker, exactly one year after gunmen shot Tupac in Times Square.[5] As previously detailed about Newton and MLK's deaths, the use of this threat timing would provide a conscious or subconscious warning to others.

Tupac's former business manager and political mentor, Watani Tyehimba, said that his eldest son, Yakhisizwe, had followed Tupac to keep working with him after he signed to Death Row Records. Yakhizwe also turned up dead around the time of Tupac's murder.[6] This left three former Black Panthers with the loss of a child. Other murders linked to Tupac's support a continuing cover-up around Tupac's death. Increasing evidence supported that hotel lobby beating victim, Orlando Anderson, played a part *in helping set up a false motive* for Tupac's murder. As mentioned, Death Row bodyguard and eyewitness

3 "Post Traumatic Stress Disorder," *Psychology Today*. psychologytoday.com/us/conditions/post-traumatic-stress-disorder Also see, "What are PTSD Triggers?" WebMD. webmd.com/mental-health/what-are-ptsd-triggers#1-2
4 "There are several...company." Scott, *The Killing of Tupac Shakur*, pp.11-115, *The Murder of Biggie Smalls*, pp. 70-1, 89.
5 "There are several...Odinga." Walker was killed by three gunmen after a high speed car chase in Queens. Scott, *The Murder of Biggie Smalls*, pp. 70-1, 89.
6 Personal Interview with Tupac's business manager, former Panther Watani Tyehimba, 3/10/2003.

Frank Alexander believed that Death Row paid Anderson to take that beating to set the stage for Tupac's murder.[7]

Not only did Anderson contradict himself as to why he was at the MGM, he was also caught lying about how he got a ticket to the Tyson fight. Previous analysis of Atlanta police shooting at Tupac supports that they used psychological profiling in an attempt to cover-up how they planned to murder Tupac that night. U.S. Intelligence appeared to have the world's most popular Black entertainer under intense scrutiny, likely knowing some Crip gang members had ripped a chain off his neck.

Tupac was walking with his Death Row label associates through the extensive MGM Grand Hotel hallways leading from the boxing arena to the main lobby when they came upon Orlando Anderson standing in the main lobby. Coming upon Anderson, a Death Row associate named Tray, in a record label with dozens of undercover cops working there, told a drunk and stoned Tupac that the man in front of him, Orlando Anderson, ripped a chain off of Tray's neck. This led Tupac to join in the twenty second physical attack on Tray by Suge Knight and others there with Death Row.

Many said that Anderson acted very strangely after the assault that night. MGM security said Anderson didn't want to file a complaint or say who attacked him and they said he "wasn't angry at all—he just wanted out of there." A friend said he saw Anderson a few minutes after the incident and he "didn't appear to be too upset about what happened, saying 'everything was cool.'"[8]

Reports on the next two days after the shooting further incriminated Anderson. An affidavit filed in court by Compton police said that the Tupac-murdering gunmen's vehicle was taken to an auto shop in Anderson's Compton neighborhood two days after the shooting (Vegas detectives reportedly had a vast amount of such evidence they inexplicably ignored).[9] Also, within 48 hours of Tupac's shooting, a woman saw Anderson transporting guns into his Crip uncle Keffy-D

---

7 LAPD notes of interview of Frank Alexander, written by Det. Russell Poole, dated 4/28/98, 7 pages. LAPD notes of interview of Frank Alexander, written by Det. III Fred Miller, dated 4/28/98, 2 pages. Referenced in Randall Sullivan, LAbyrinth (New York: Atlantic Monthly Press, 2002), pp.188-189.

8 "For one…cool.'" On ticket purchase day of match and saying he got free MGM room as a big gambler without a known source of income, see Scott, Murder of Biggie, p.81. On Orlando's actions and quote after scuffle, see Sullivan LAbyrinth, p.147.

9 "Reports on…shooting." Scott, Murder of Biggie, pp.80-83, 157-158.

Davis's house with other known Crips. The gang peace truce would end that very night in Compton.[10]

Several key people believed Anderson played a role in Tupac's murder set up. Det. Russell Poole believed Suge Knight staged the lobby scuffle with Anderson to have "it on [hotel security] videotape to set up a motive for the killing of Tupac Shakur that would point the blame at the Compton Crips."[11] Filmmaker Nick Broomfield even referred to Anderson as the Lee Harvey Oswald of Tupac's murder.

During off-film interviews with Orlando Anderson's friends, family, and lawyer, Broomfield learned that Anderson received payments from an unknown source, and that he'd acquired a very expensive car shortly after Tupac's murder.[12] Also, Afeni Shakur filed a wrongful death lawsuit in 1997, claiming that Anderson shot her son and that Crip Jerry Bonds drove the gunman's car.[13] Afeni apparently did this to try and find out more details of Anderson's possible government links. She also backed U.S. Congresswoman Cynthia McKinney's bill to have the government release all of their documents on Tupac.

Further investigation into Orlando Anderson's life supported the police intelligence funding to which Broomfield alluded. Writers said Anderson lacked the regular gang trappings. Friends said that he didn't drink, smoke, use drugs, or sport tattoos, and he didn't have any criminal convictions. However, he did appear to attain illicit funds from somewhere. Anderson, known also as "Baby Lane," lived a lower middle-class lifestyle in the Compton area of Los Angeles. He fathered four children by the age of 23 and had never been gainfully employed. He had never filed a federal tax return and had no obvious means of support. Anderson was also starting up his own record company without any known source of financing.[14]

A gunman murdered Anderson in May of '98 at a Compton car wash. Police reported that it happened in a shootout over money. The shooting ended in two other deaths and one arrest.[15] Russell Poole said he found a mixed amount of reliability among police department

10 "Also, within…fled." Sullivan, *LAbyrinth*, pp.142-147.
11 "Det. Russell Poole…Crips." Sullivan, *LAbyrinth*, pp.147,189,193.
12 "Filmmaker…murder." Darrin Keene, "Nick Broomfield Blows the Lid Off of Biggie and Tupac," *ChartAttack. com*, October 15, 2002. wysiwyg://25/http://chartattack.com/damn/2002/10/1502.cfm
13 Cathy Scott, *The Murder of Biggie Smalls* (New York: St. Martin's Press, 2000), pp.80, 157.
14 "Further investigation…financing." Scott, *Murder of Biggie*, p.158. Sullivan, *LAbyrinth*, p.146.
15 Scott, *Murder of Biggie*, pp.155-157.

reports and found more consistent credibility in informants such as Death Row guard Kevin Hackie, who believed the Death Row Security Director and "former" police officer Reggie Wright participated in Anderson's murder. Hackie said Wright owned a champagne-colored Chevy Blazer that matched the description of the suspect's car in the shooting of Anderson. For these reasons, Hackie believed Death Row killed Orlando Anderson as further cover-up of the events surrounding Tupac's death. U.S. Intelligence surely didn't want Anderson testifying in court regarding Afeni Shakur's lawsuit.[16]

---

16 "Russell Poole…shooting." Sullivan, *LAbyrinth*, p.193.

FBI & ATF WATCH AGAIN AS DEATH ROW COPS ARE NAILED IN BIGGIE'S MURDER

Six months after Tupac Shakur's murder, a gunman murdered chart-topping rapper Biggie Smalls (a.k.a. Notorious B.I.G., born Christopher Wallace). The gunman fatally shot Biggie from his car after midnight on March 9, 1997 in Los Angeles, a few months after the murder of Yafeu Fula and a year before that of Orlando Anderson.

Los Angeles police detective Russell Poole first took an interest in Biggie's murder investigation after he investigated the murder of Death Row cop Kevin Gaines. Working on that case led to him stumbling upon the corrupt activities of Death Row's Los Angeles police officers. In doing so, he gained an assignment as an investigator in Biggie's case—the next Tupac-linked murder.[1]

Det. Poole proved a highly credible source on the activities of the Los Angeles police. Poole's father worked for decades in the LAPD, and Poole himself had 10 years of homicide investigation experience. During those years, he received regular commendations and promotions to reach the high level Bureau of Special Operations. Poole's investigation led filmmaker Nick Broomfield to feature him in a major theatrical release, *Biggie and Tupac*. *Rolling Stone* and *Esquire* magazine writer Randall Sullivan also featured Poole in his book, *LAbyrinth* (2002). Both the film and the book were released after Poole's resignation due to the LAPD stonewalling his investigation.[2]

Poole's investigation, with the help of fellow officer Ken Knox, accumulated solid evidence that LAPD cops working with Death Row orchestrated Biggie's murder, trafficked drugs, and orchestrated Tupac's murder). According to Poole, these cops murdered Biggie to further divert people's attention from their orchestration of Tupac's murder. They wanted to make it look as if Tupac's murder stemmed from the East/West rap rivalry. When Poole communicated these findings to his LAPD superiors, they ignored his reports, transferred him to another division, and threatened him.[3]

Biggie was murdered when a gunman pulled up next to his car and fatally shot him outside an Automotive Museum party in early

1 "While investigating...Smalls." Nick Broomfield, *Biggie and Tupac* (2002, documentary film) and Sullivan, *LAbyrinth*.
2 "LAPD...investigation." Sullivan, *LAbyrinth*, pp.6, 44,116, 200, 248, 322-4. Broomfield, Biggie and Tupac. On Stallone's project, Joseph Patel, "Actor Will Play LAPD Detective Russell Poole in 'Rampart Scandal.' MTV.com 6/6/03. Conservative forces apparently stopped that project.
3 "Poole's investigation...investigation." Sullivan, *LAbyrinth*, pp.208-209. Broomfield, *Biggie and Tupac*.

March of 1997. Quincy Jones' Quest Records and *Vibe* magazine held the party in conjunction with the Eleventh Annual *Soul Train* Music Awards. Many Los Angeles police officers were present at the high publicity event, including some who were moonlighting as bodyguards for the record label that produced Biggie, Sean "Puffy" Combs' Bad Boy Records. But few attempted to pursue the gunman, and the guards reportedly couldn't even get a partial license plate number or a good enough description for police to trace the gunman's car.[4]

Biggie's friends, rapper James "Lil' Cease" Lloyd and Damien "D-Rock" Butler, were riding in the back seat of Biggie's car when he was murdered. They described the shooter for a police artist to make a composite sketch of the gunman the next day. When *Las Vegas Sun* reporter Cathy Scott asked the Los Angeles police for a copy of the sketch, they said it wasn't kept on file. That sketch took 36 months to get to the media and then only when it was leaked.[5] Butler and Lil' Cease Lloyd's police sketch of the killer reportedly matched Harry Billups (a.k.a. Amir Muhammad)—a close friend of Death Row-employed moonlighting cop David Mack.[6]

Another witness more clearly identified Billups. Filmmaker Broomfield showed a photo line-up to Eugene Deal, a New York State Parole Officer working as a bodyguard for Sean Puffy Combs. From that line-up Deal picked Harry Billups as Biggie's killer. Deal's description of the killer also matched Lloyd's description of Biggie's murderer.[7]

Det. Poole presented witness Damien Butler another photo line-up and Butler identified police officer David Mack as standing just outside the Automotive Museum party in streetclothes, shortly before Biggie's murder.[8] More evidence implicating Mack was that Biggie's murderer used a German made brand of bullets rarely found in LA, yet the same kind of bullets were found in Mack's home. And, Mack owned a dark-colored Chevrolet Impala, the type that Biggie's assailant used for the drive-by murder, but LAPD superiors wouldn't allow Det. Poole to do forensic tests on Mack's car.[9]

4 "Biggie's murder...car." Cathy Scott, *The Murder of Biggie Smalls*, pp.1-5, 8, 14-15. Sullivan, *LAbyrinth*, p.120, 136.
5 "Biggie's friends...leaked." Scott, *Murder of Biggie Smalls*, pp.9-10, 120-1.
6 Scott, *Murder of Biggie Smalls*, p.120.
7 "Another witness...murderer." Broomfield, *Biggie and Tupac*. Sullivan, *LAbyrinth*, pp.180-4, 282-3.
8 "Furthermore, Damien...home." Sullivan, *LAbyrinth*, pp.180-4.
9 Scott, *Murder of Biggie Smalls*, p.120 and Sullivan, *LAbyrinth*, p.184.

People also saw Orlando Anderson at Biggie's murder scene. As previously detailed, evidence supports Anderson's work with Suge Knight in the Vegas lobby scuffle to help set up a false "gang retaliation" motive for Tupac's murder. That people saw Anderson with his Crip uncle, Keith Davis, and the Death Row cops furthers the evidence of connections between the Death Row cops and the murders of Biggie and Tupac.[10]

Other prominent witnesses to Death Row's murder of Biggie included Death Row accountant Mark Hylland. Hylland described how Suge Knight, accompanied by Death Row's police associates Raphael "Ray" Perez and Dave Mack, gave him money to obtain the gun that they said they would use to kill Biggie. Hylland gave details of these incidents on film for Nick Broomfield as well as for Det. Poole when he was officially investigating the murder. Poole found that Hylland's story matched his airline flights and hotel stays from LA to Phoenix, where Hylland said a Phoenix cop gave him the murder weapon, with which he apparently drove back to LA.[11]

Most importantly, similar to reports of an FBI agent amongst the Death Row entourage tailing Tupac's car at his murder scene, an FBI agent was present at Biggie's murder. Det. Russell Poole and Nick Broomfield confirmed the *Los Angeles Times'* report that New York police agents were present when the gunman shot Biggie.[12] Poole and Broomfield further confirmed that one agent was a New York detective who also worked for the FBI and took pictures of Biggie minutes before his shooting.[13] Award-winning reporter Cathy Scott further said it became widely reported that the FBI watched both Biggie and Tupac's murders. She also stated that FBI agents told her they are supposed to stop their surveillance and intervene if a crime takes place during their surveillance.[14]

In his book *LAbyrinth*, Randall Sullivan reported on Poole's investigation. Poole gave Sullivan copies of all his police documents

10 Broomfield, *Biggie and Tupac*. Sullivan, *LAbyrinth*, pp.282-3. Also see Cathy Scott, *The Murder of Biggie Smalls*, pp.5-6. On Davis, see Sullivan, *LAbyrinth*, p.126.Also, "Investigative Reports: Interview with Cathy Scott," *XXL Magazine*, October, 2000, p.131.
11 "Other...LA." Nick Broomfield, *Biggie and Tupac*. Also, Sullivan, *LAbyrinth*, pp.279-80.
12 Chuck Phillips, "Officers May Have Seen rap Killing; Crime: Off-duty Inglewood police member was behind vehicle when rap star Notorious B.I.G. was slain and undercover New York agents were trailing the singer that night, sources say." *The Los Angeles Times*, 4/23/97, B,1:2.
13 Nick Broomfield, *Biggie and Tupac*
14 Scott, *The Murder of Biggie Smalls*, pp.94, 128-9. "Investigative Reports: Interview with Cathy Scott," *XXL Magazine*, October, 2000, p.131.

and they backed Sullivan's note that the FBI/New York detective taking pictures of Biggie within minutes of his murder was Detective William Oldham. Accompanying Oldham was another member of the New York police working with a federal agency, Special Agent Timothy Reilly of the Bureau of Alcohol, Tobacco, and Firearms (ATF).[15] Former FBI informant Kevin Hackie, who claimed to have documents proving that an FBI agent followed in the line of cars behind Tupac's when he was murdered, also claimed that agent was accompanied by an ATF agent.[16]

Larry Shears, a former ATF agent, said that the ATF had a history of placing murder contracts on left-wing activists. In the '70s, Shears testified in court that the ATF contracted out the (unsuccessful) murders of Black Panther Eldridge Cleaver and labor organizer Caesar Chavez. The ATF also collaborated with the FBI to target Huey Newton at that time.[17] And finally, the FBI and ATF worked in the riot unit Joint Task Force-LA that waged a war on gangs just *after* the riots and Bloods/Crips peace truce.[18]

In their questioning of Biggie's friends, police incidentally revealed agents' surveillance of Biggie within minutes of his murder. Lil' Cease Lloyd, one of the passengers sitting behind Biggie, said that police showed him these FBI photos of the Soul Train Music Awards after-party at the Automotive Museum. "Do you know who this is?" they asked him, not realizing that they were pointing at Lloyd himself. The photos were taken "as late as ten minutes before the killing," according to a *Los Angeles Times* story.[19]

15 "Evidence placed…scene." See Sullivan, *LAbyrinth*, p.136, and "LAPD photocopies of business cards of Det. Oldham, New York Police Department, and Timothy Reilly, Special Agent, U.S. Department of Treasury, Criminal Investigation Division, with handwritten notes, dated 3/9/97 1 page." This was under section, "Documents: Biggie Smalls Murder," *LAbyrinth*, pp.313-4. ATF as Division of the Treasury Department, Christopher Lee, "ATF Eyes Bargaining Exemptions," *Washington Post*, 6/24/03, p.A19. Also, Nick Broomfield, *Biggie and Tupac*.
16 "That the FBI…murdered." Nick Broomfield, *Biggie and Tupac*
17 "A former Bureau…time." ATF agent Larry Shears in court, on Channel 23, Los Angeles, CA, news broadcast, 12/17/71. Drew McKillips, "Amazing Story by Hell's Angels Chief," *San Francisco Chronicle*, 12/12/72, p.1. "ATF Agent Says He Was Part of Coast Plot to Kill Cesar Chavez," *New York Times*, 1/ 2/72, p.31. All referenced in Alex Constantine, *The Covert War Against Rock* (Los Angeles, CA: Feral House, 2001), pp.55-59. George Bush Sr. oversaw U.S. Intelligence when the Hells Angels twice attempted to kill the Rolling Stones and Barger got paroled early due to a Republican senator. Karen Brandel, "Angels in Arizona," *Tucson Weekly*, 8/15/96, p.1. A.E. Hotchner, *Blown Away: A No-Holds-Barred Portrait of the Rolling Stones and the Sixties Told by the Voices of the Generation* (New York: Fireside, 1990), p.320.
On Newton see, Edward J. Epstein, *Agency of Fear: Opiates and Political Power in America* (New York: G.P. Putnam's Sons, 1977), pp201-201, 207, 213-215. Cited in Huey Newton, *War Against The Panthers* (New York: Harlem River Readers and Writers, 1991), pp 50-52.
18 See, for example, *The Federation of American Scientists Military Analysis Network*, "Garden Plot," November 1998. Cited in Frank Morales, "U.S. Has Been Preparing to Turn America into a Military Dictatorship," *What Really Happened*, .whatreallyhappened.com/suppression.html .
19 "Police incidentally…story." Sullivan, *LAbyrinth*, p.136.

For his documentary, *Biggie and Tupac*, Nick Broomfield filmed his discussions with Biggie's mother, Voletta Wallace, who asked Biggie's old friend Lloyd to come over and talk with Broomfield. Lloyd told Broomfield about the police showing him the pictures who then tracked down the FBI/NYPD Detective Oldham, who took the pictures. In his attempt to question Oldham, Broomfield filmed at least one scene that was both grave and humorous. He showed himself driving through traffic as he called Det. Oldham with his cell phone, miking both sides of the conversation. Broomfield asked if this was "Detective…" blanking out the name. Oldham said "yes" and confirmed that he was the one who took the pictures in L.A., but he wouldn't say why he was investigating Biggie Smalls. Oldham said he couldn't talk because he was in court at Sean Puffy Combs' gun possession trial and, despite three years passing, Biggie's murder was an open case.

Then Broomfield dodged Oldham's attempt to get information and further exposed him for a humorous moment in this otherwise bleak film:

"Where did you get my number?" asked Oldham.

Broomfield remained quiet.

"Where did you get my number?" Oldham repeated.

"Sorry?" responded Broomfield, feigning poor reception.

"Where did you get my number?"

"Where did I get your number?"

"Yes."

"Your number was one of the numbers I was given as somebody who was actually following Biggie at the time that he was shot and who might be able to give me some information."

"Who gave you my number?"

"You know I just… Sorry?"

"Who gave you my number?"

"I really don't know off hand who that was."

"Okay, well when you figure it out, beep me. I'll call you back and we'll talk."[20]

---

20 "But Lil' Cease also said… he couldn't remember." Nick Broomfield, Biggie and Tupac, 2002.

MEDIA FUELS THE GANG WAR AND BIGGIE'S FAMILY FIGHTS FOR JUSTICE

Many insiders at Death Row blamed the heads of the label for Tupac's murder. Tupac's bodyguards Frank Alexander and Kevin Hackie said Security Director Reggie Wright and Executive Director Suge Knight threatened their lives if they said anything about Tupac's murder. The two bodyguards also said they believed that Knight and Wright orchestrated Tupac's murder. Nick Broomfield described the long depression and paranoia Alexander exhibited after going against Death Row and talking to Det. Russel Poole. This likely led to his changing reports, in a book as well as a movie, about what happened. Still, his statement to Poole stands as his first report. Hackie said he also believed that Death Row orchestrated Biggie's murder as a mock retaliation for Tupac's death. Others, such as Death Row's former rapper Snoop Dogg, stated their belief that Suge Knight had Tupac killed.[1]

These accounts received little attention from most media organizations. Except for the investigation by *Las Vegas Sun* reporter Cathy Scott, virtually all media groups ignored the possibility that Tupac's murder was committed by Las Vegas police, Death Row cops, and top Los Angeles Police Department officials. Media sources such as the *LA Weekly* repeated false claims exemplified by Sgt. Richard McCaulley's statement that he was the sole officer working for Death Row. LAPD officers Russell Poole, Ken Knox, and even Death Row security chief Reggie Wright cited many other LAPD officers working with Death Row Records.[2]

The largest apparent cover-up story on Tupac's murder was a widely reprinted *Los Angeles Times* article by Chuck Philips. Philips wrote that Biggie Smalls brought a gun to Las Vegas and then paid the Crips a million dollars to kill Tupac with that gun. Philips said it was all set up between the lobby scuffle with Orlando Anderson and the shooting. But Philips had apparently revealed his biased support of Suge Knight in advance. When Philips' article came out, Randall Sullivan's book

1 "Both Hackie and…killed." Sulivan, *LAbyrinth*, pp.192-4. Broomfield, *Biggie and Tupac* (2002). On Alexander's book and film, Frank Alexander with Heidi Siegmund Cuda, *Got Your Back: Protecting Tupac in the World of Gangsta Rap*. The book appears to be mostly to cover up the damage done by his initial disclosures. But it is interesting that Alexander said an MGM security guard stood next to Orlando Anderson when Tupac and the Death Row entourage attacked him, yet no one was stopped by the police. *Got Your Back*, p.155.
2 "These accounts…Records." Sullivan, *LAbyrinth*, pp.166-7, 284-5.

was already in stores reporting Philips' previous statement vowing to vindicate Suge Knight in the Biggie murder case.[3]

Veteran mainstream magazine journalist Robert Sam Anson wrote a long dismissal of Chuck Philips' piece for *Vibe*. Anson's article pointed out how Philips claimed to have many sources but named few of them. Anson's article also quoted Randall Sullivan questioning Phillips' lack of witnesses to the 395-pound, easily recognizable Biggie's presence in Vegas the weekend of Tupac's murder.[4]

Vibe further interviewed people in Vegas and found that the timing of Philips's explanation also did not line up. And finally, lawyers for Biggie Small's mother, Voletta Wallace, sent proof of Biggie's presence in the New York area the night of Tupac's murder, but the press barely mentioned it.[5] Other writers who similarly dismissed Philips' piece included noted former *Vibe* writer Kevin Powell and Hip Hop writer Davey D.[6]

Meanwhile, it seems telling that author Randall Sullivan had three conservative groups trying to stop him or smear him in the time between his publishing an article on Death Row cops' corruption and the release of his book on the subject, *LAbyrinth*. Sullivan first published his findings in an extensive *Rolling Stone* article that announced *LAbyrinth*'s coming release. Sullivan expressed his particular surprise that the *LA Times* joined Death Row Records and the LAPD in trying to persuade him to leave out certain information from *LAbyrinth*. Sullivan said that when he refused to edit out parts of his book, these groups then tried to discredit him.[7]

Furthermore, Death Row's whistleblowing accountant Mark Hylland revealed further corruption of the LAPD officers working with Death Row. Hylland said he worked to launder drug money for two

3 "The largest apparent…Smalls." Chuck Philips, "Who Killed Tupac Shakur; How a Fight Between Rival Compton Gangs Turns into a Plot of Retaliation and Murder," *The Los Angeles Times*, September 6, 2002, p.A1. On Phillip's vow to vindicate Knight, Sullivan, *LAbyrinth*, p. 285.
4 "*Vibe* further…mentioned it." Sam Anson, "Reasonable Doubt," *Vibe*, December, 2002, p.148-156. On Biggie's mom, Voletta Wallace, Salim Muwakkil, "The Sad Saga of Biggie and Tupac," *Chicago Tribune*, 9/16/02, p.1.15.
5 "Vanity Fair…mentioned it." On Biggie's mom see Salim Muwakkil, "The Sad Saga of Biggie and Tupac; the latest rap on two unsolved murder mysteries fingers a gang element and corrupt cops," *Chicago Tribune*, September 16, 2002, p.1.15. Sam Anson, "Reasonable Doubt," *Vibe*, December, 2002, p.148-156. Anson has written articles on Tupac Shakur for *Vanity Fair* and *Esquire* magazines. Quotes *Rolling Stone* and *Vanity Fair* writer Randall Sullivan. On timeline that contradicts Phillips' account, Geoffrey Gray, "Time Bomb," *Vibe*, December 2002, pp.152-156. The many reprints include: Michele Orecklin, "Who Killed Tupac," *Time* magazine, 9/16/02, p.91. Chuck Philips, "The Rap on B.I.G.: Rival reportedly paid $1M and supplied guns to kill Tupac Shakur," *Newsday*, p.A3.
6 *Davey D's Hip Hop Corner*, FNV Newsletter, "Former Vibe Writer Kevin Powell Speaks Out…" .daveyd.com/ fnvsept62002.html
7 "Meanwhile, it seems…him." David Walker and Zach Dundas, "Living and Dying in L.A: Interview with Randall Sullivan." wweek.com/portland/article-935-to-live-and-die-in-l-a.html .mumblage.com/story.php?id=27

Death Row cops, including David Mack, who he and others implicated in Biggie's murder. A police investigator found a long paper trail backing up Hylland's claim of laundering money for Mack and three other Death Row-linked cops, including Mack's longtime partner, Ray Perez, and two others (Kevin Hackie also claimed that Perez was Suge Knight's close confidant). Hylland said the four cops made a fortune dealing drugs and even had a real estate scam involving Hispanic gang members they had arrested in the Rampart Division.[8]

When Det. Russell Poole came forward with his findings, the Los Angeles District Attorney's office appeared to force the LAPD superiors to stop stonewalling Poole and investigate their own officers' illegal activities. An LA Assistant District Attorney, for one, cited Poole's work as opening the lid on Los Angeles Police Department's "worst scandal in decades"—the Rampart Scandal. This scandal refers to the widespread police corruption in the Community Resources Against Street Hoodlums (CRASH) anti-gang unit of the Los Angeles Police Department's Ramparts Division.

Los Angeles police superiors first formed a Robbery / Homicide Task Force, allegedly to follow up on Poole's investigative findings. The Task Force's name was changed to the Rampart Task Force when it found that many of the cops involved, such as Death Row-linked Perez, came from the special anti-gang CRASH unit.[9]

Poole said that the Rampart Task Force became intent on covering up his findings. These findings, which focused on the illegal activities by Death Row-linked cops, included the murders of Tupac Shakur and Biggie Smalls. Poole said the Task Force completely diverted its attention away from the murders of Tupac and Biggie. The Task Force also worked to hide the scandal of Death Row cops' drug and gun trafficking, and the reignition of the gang war. The Rampart Task Force initially made CRASH cop Ray Perez its star witness. This allowed Perez to protect most of his fellow Death Row-linked cops that were involved in the illegal activities while getting dozens of other cops suspended for similar activities.[10]

8 "Furthermore, Death Row's…Division." Sullivan, *LAbyrinth*, pp.180-184, 279-80.
9 "When Det. Russell…precinct." Sullivan, *LAbyrinth*, pp.205-8. On Rampart Scandal in mainstream news, see Don Terry, "Rackets Law Can Be Used Against Police in Los Angeles," *The New York Times*, August 30, 2000, p.A14. Scott Glover and Matt Lait, "30 L.A. Officers Called to Testify Before Grand Jury," *Los Angeles Times*, 4/14/2000.
10 "Poole said the…cops did." Sullivan, *LAbyrinth*, pp.201-212, 228. Also see PBS's *Frontline* report crediting Poole and his investigation opening the lid on the Rampart Scandal and how Frontline also suggested that the Rampart

Poole resigned from the LAPD, got censored in media coverage, and ended up filing a lawsuit against the LAPD. He said that he saw this as his last resort to get at least some of this information to the public. Poole also stated that everyone around him told him not to share his information with the FBI, but he did anyway, in a case of false hope. Poole later decided to help out Biggie Smalls' bereaved mother, Voletta Wallace, in a wrongful death lawsuit against the LAPD.[11]

Wallace's lawsuit, filed with Biggie's wife Faith Evans, reached trial in June of 2005. By the first week of July, the judge declared a mistrial because the LAPD withheld documents from the Wallace family. These documents revealed that an LAPD informant told police that officers Raphael Perez and former officer David Mack acknowledged working for Death Row and murdering Biggie. This also supported Wallace's claim that they hired Mack's college roommate Amir Muhammad (a.k.a. Harry Billups) to pull the trigger.[12]

Wallace and Evans probably received one of their biggest judicial decisions in January of 2006. Their trial judge ordered the city of Los Angeles to pay the family $1.1 million in legal costs. The judge made the order due to her finding that the LAPD intentionally withheld tapes and over 200 pages of documents that supported the Wallaces' charges, after they were "found hidden" in two drawers of an LAPD detective.[13]

A month prior to this, Randall Sullivan published his most far-reaching article on the case in *Rolling Stone* magazine. The article detailed the documents related to assorted hearings and investigations regarding prison inmate Kenneth Boagni. Boagni said that Raphael Perez confessed to his involvement in crimes that included the murder of Biggie when they were cellmates. A panel member overseeing one

Task Force diverted the focus of the corruption away from what Poole originally found. PBS, *Frontline*, "LAPD Blues, Interviews: Detective Russell Poole." .pbs.org/wgbh/pages/frontline/shows/lapd/interviews/poole.html .
11 "The LAPD...still awaits trial." Sullivan, *LAbyrinth*, p.292. While the *LAbyrinth* ends with Poole saying the FBI told him they're investigating Suge Knight in his part in setting up the murder of Tupac and Biggie in 2001, nothing has come of it as of February 2005 as Voletta Wallace's lawsuit against the LAPD awaits trial in April 2005.
12 "Wallace's...trigger." Nolan Strong, "Victory for B.I.G., Family Closes in on Rogue Cop Theory," 7/8/05, allhiphop.com/news/ .
13"Biggie's family...detective." Jessica Robertson, "B.I.G. Family Paid $1.1 Million," *The Rolling Stone*, January 23, 2006. rollingstone.com/music/music-news/b-i-g-family-paid-1-1-million-105034/. "Biggie's family...detective." Associated Press, "Judge Orders LA to pay 1.1M to family of Notorious B.I.G." *Boston Herald.com*, 1/21/06. http://news.bostonherald.com/national/view.bg?articleid=122328

of those hearings said he found Boagni "totally credible" but said that an LAPD representative quickly cut Boagni off.[14]

Sullivan packed a lot into his 23-page article, including testimony from the Wallace/Evans trial against Los Angeles. Several other witnesses' testimony stood out. For example, another witness at the Biggie family trial said his brother worked with Amir Muhammad/Harry Billups as part of a group of contract killers. A cellmate of Suge Knight's named Mario Ha'mmonds also testified that Suge Knight said he had Biggie killed with the help of "Reg" [Reggie Wright Jr], as well as Mack and Muhammad, both of whom Ha'mmonds said he previously met through Knight before their jail stints. Ha'mmonds further stated that Bay Area rappers Too Short and E-40 offered him money to kill Knight in retaliation for Tupac's murder. The judge rescheduled the Wallace/Evans retrial for late 2006 (and then apparently rescheduled it again). The plaintiffs' attorney said political figures called the Wallace family attorney. They worried that he would win the case and the jury would award the rappers' estimated lost earnings to his family. They said that those lost earnings were estimated at over $360 million and could bankrupt the city of Los Angeles.[15]

14 "A month…off." Randall Sullivan, "'The Notorious B.I.G.: The Murder and Cover-up," *Rolling Stone*, 12/15/05, pp.142-4.
15 "A month…2006." Sullivan, "'The Notorious B.I.G.: The Murder and Cover-up," *Rolling Stone*, 12/15/05, pp.138,140,147.

DEATH ROW & FEDS TARGET AFENI, SNOOP DOGG, AND DRE

The murder of Tupac, attacks on rap figures, and provocation of Bloods/Crips gang members appeared to be the key objectives of Death Row director Suge Knight. Only after Knight accomplished these tasks did a judge finally sentence him to jail, possibly suggesting U.S. Intelligence no longer backed him. Judges had previously allowed Knight to stay out of jail for seven years, despite at least nine guilty pleas or convictions, ranging from shooting at the Stanley brothers to beating a club security guard seriously enough to send him to the hospital in critical condition. Within 45 days of Tupac's death, Knight received a 9-year prison sentence for kicking Orlando Anderson in the MGM hotel lobby the night of Tupac's murder.[1]

Poole and his collaborating LA police officer, Ken Knox, revealed enough in their investigations to help send several Death Row figures to jail but intelligence operations continued. When Knight and several of his corroborating cops went to prison, Reggie Wright Jr. took the helm.[2] Det. Russell Poole and the partner of Ray Perez said that Perez worked with Wright in Death Row Records' criminal operations. Poole and Perez's partner also claimed that Perez regularly stole cocaine from dealers and the police evidence locker, and then resold it. They further alleged that Perez had shot at unarmed gang members. Perez ended up doing three years jail time on a five-year sentence for one count of cocaine theft. He then got a two-year sentence for shooting an unarmed gang member.[3]

After his October of '96 incarceration, Knight was released from prison in August of 2001. In 2003 he violated his parole for punching a nightclub valet and did ten more months in jail.[4] Knight's imprisonment suggests he remained lower on the totem pole regarding U.S. Intelligence operations at Death Row Records. Dave Kenner and Reggie Wright Jr. likely had the upper hand in directing the U.S.

1 "Judges had...murder." Sullivan, LAbyrinth, Timeline, pp.301-9. Cathy Scott, The Murder of Biggie Smalls, pp.82-4, 97. Ro, Have Gun Will Travel, pp.323-4. Broomfield, Biggie and Tupac.
2 Former FBI agent, LA cop, and Tupac's whistleblowing bodyguard Kevin Hackie told Poole that no matter what else he heard, Reggie Wright ran Death Row while Knight was in jail. Sullivan, LAbyrinth, p.193.
3 "Det. Russell...member." Sullivan, LAbyrinth, pp.278-9. PBS Frontline, "LAPD Blues: The Rampart Scandal Timeline," pbs.org/wgbh/pages/frontline/shows/lapd/scandal/cron.html.pbs.org/wgb/pages/frontline/shows/lapd/scandal/cron.html . Also see John S. Gordon, U.S. Attorney, Central District California press release, "Former LAPD Officer Raphael Perez Sentenced to Two Years for Federal Civil Rights Violations," 5/6/02. Matt Lait and Scott Glover, "Secret LAPD Testimony Implicated Nine Officers," Los Angeles Times, 2/26/03.
4 Knight gained...jail." Associated Press, "Rap Mogul Out of Jail," 8/7/01. CBS News.com. Reuters, "'Suge' Knight Arrested After Police Find Marijuana in Truck," HighTimes.com.

Intelligence work. As previously detailed, Kenner was the attorney for national cocaine trafficking Freeway Ricky Ross' associate, Michael Harris, and had an indirect link to Intelligence. He had also set himself up as the primary owner of Death Row Records and had represented various Mafia figures in the past. Reggie Wright Jr., through his Compton police gang unit chief father, also remained free of any legal charges.

Death Row Records' actions involving Tupac's estate further support that they had a U.S. Intelligence agenda. Death Row tried to devalue the estate that former Black Panther Afeni Shakur had inherited from her son. While working for her son in his last years of his life, Afeni, with her imprisoned former partner Mutulu Shakur, aided the successful campaign to gain Geronimo (Pratt) ji Jaga's prison release in 1997, after his 1970 frame-up. U.S. Intelligence had used vast resources in their 20-year campaign to keep ex-Panther leader Geronimo ji Jaga incarcerated. Tupac recorded three songs a day in the 11 months between his prison release and death. Afeni Shakur won a lawsuit to obtain the master tapes of these songs, which had an estimated worth of over $100 million. But Death Row defied the judge's orders, delivering only a third or fewer of Tupac's hundreds of unreleased songs.

Death Row also allowed over a hundred songs on closely guarded master tapes to reach the underground bootlegging market. One bootlegged CD became Europe's top seller. With little-to-no profit to be made by the original release of these bootlegs, Afeni's estate was greatly devalued and worked to confound her own future activism.[5]

Besides the apparent targeting of Biggie, Orlando Anderson, and Afeni's estate, Death Row also created problems for Tupac's backup group, The Outlawz. Evidence supports that U.S. Intelligence murdered the rap group's Yafeu Fula by the end of '96. The Outlawz then claimed that Death Row stymied their new work and filed a lawsuit against the record label in 2000.[6]

U.S. Intelligence appeared to also focus on Tupac's Death Row friend, chart-topping rapper Snoop Dogg (Calvin Broadus). Snoop had

5 "Death Row actions...activism." Veronica Lodge, "Jackin' beats," *Rap Pages*, September 1998, pp.65-71. Also, Cathy Scott, *Biggie*, p.106. Ben Charney, "Family of Tupac Sues Rapper's Bootleg Recordings," December 2, 1999. http://search.newschoice.com/AngTr_storydisplay.asp?story=d:\inetpub\wwwroot\newsarchives\angtr\ fpg\19991202\52686_t2as202.txt. Personal interview, Watani Tyehimba, 5/10/00.
6 Michael Datcher, "The Good Die Young: Snapshotz from the Outlawz Photo Album," *The Source*, October 2000, p.195.

accompanied Tupac at activist rallies where they spoke in support of various progressive causes.[7] Snoop also defied Suge Knight's attempts to heighten the East vs. West rap war. Snoop agreed to a unity pact and joint tour with New York's Sean Puffy Combs shortly after Tupac's death.[8] Reports claimed that Suge Knight regularly bullied Snoop and badly beat Snoop's cousin, RBX, at gunpoint when RBX tried to stop Knight from beating up Crip gang members working at Death Row.[9]

More serious attacks on Snoop started when he left Death Row Records for another music label in 1998. At a concert on his first tour with the new label, a crowd of Death Row guards attacked Snoop backstage. Snoop ran to the police for help. Rather than taking the attackers into custody, police arrested Snoop for weed possession.[10] Then, Suge Knight used the FBI's "bad jacketing" Cointelpro tactic, the practice of spreading misinformation to discredit, by implying that Snoop Dogg was a police informant. Death Row also physically threatened the rapper on their website. Police later charged Snoop's bodyguards with illegal gun possession charges, forcing them to go unarmed. Months later, in 2003, gunmen shot at Snoop's car.[11]

Evidence suggests that U.S. Intelligence may have used a harassment lawsuit tactic against Snoop Dogg as he faced a number of specious lawsuits from 2000-2006. For example, in 2005 the lawyer for a makeup artist dismissed her $25 million lawsuit with prejudice that contended Snoop Dogg drugged and raped her. Under these "with prejudice" conditions she could never refile her suit nor threaten Snoop again. Snoop was never charged with a crime and he said the woman had been trying to extort $5 million from him since 2003.[12]

With virtually all the notable rappers having abandoned Death Row by the late '90s, one of the only rappers who stayed, Kurupt, deserves scrutiny. Kurupt's real name, itself, may or may not be a bizarre coincidence. Kurupt was apparently born Ricardo Brown Jr. Jacques Agnant had used the name Ricardo Brown when he appeared in

7 See picture of Snoop with Tupac at rally in ed.s J Hoye and K. Ali, *Tupac: Resurrection*, p.232.
8 Cathy Scott, *The Murder of Biggie Smalls* (New York: St. Martin's, 2000), p.56.
9 Ro, *Have Gun Will Travel*, p.119-20. Sullivan, *LAbyrinth*, p.194.
10 Randall Sullivan, *LAbyrinth* (New York: Atlantic Monthly Press, 2002), p.194.
11 "Then Suge…2003." Suge Knight and Death Row website, Nick Broomfield, *Biggie and Tupac*, 2002. Police unarming Snoop's guards, Rodd, McLeod, "Above the Law," July, 2000, *XXL Magazine*, p.86. Gunmen shooting at Snoop's car. Wire Reports, "Snoop Dogg in Convoy of Cars Shot at in LA," *The Baltimore Sun*, April 12, 2003, p.2D.
12 "In 2005…2003." Lawrence Van Gelder, "Arts, Briefly: Accuser Drops Rape Case Against Snoop Dogg," *The New York Times*, 8/12/05, p. E5.

court in connection with the sexual assault charge made against Tupac. Attorney Michael Tarif Warren and Tupac were convinced after an investigation that Jacques Agnant was an FBI agent. Only after Warren's investigation was Brown's real name of Jacques Agnant revealed. Warren had also found that police had arrested Agnant numerous times up and down the East Coast for major crimes, though all the charges had been dismissed. Kurupt got his break in LA but originally grew up in Philadelphia, within the vicinity of Agnant.[13]

Kurupt collaborated with Suge Knight in promoting conflict within the rap community. As an older teen, Kurupt moved to LA, where he befriended Snoop Dogg and joined in his back up group, Tha Dogg Pound. After Snoop's breakout albums, Tha Dogg Pound produced their own album and a 25-year-old Kurupt subsequently co-founded his own music label in Philadelphia in 1998. That same year, Kurupt "called out" married rapper, DMX, for allegedly flirting with Kurupt's ex-fiancee, Foxy Brown, who was on Def Jam Records.

In 2001, Kurupt joined with Suge Knight's attack on Snoop Dogg, calling his former friend a "snitch" in a song. Kurupt also defended Knight's release of Tupac's songs attacking Biggie and Bad Boy Records that year. In 2002, Knight and Dave Kenner appointed Kurupt senior vice-president of Death Row Records, which had changed its name to Tha Row.[14]

In 2005, police intelligence work appeared to continue at Tha Row / Death Row. Legendary rap producer Dr. Dre had left Death Row in 1996, abandoning any stake in the record company he made hugely profitable to avoid any retaliatory acts by the label. Dre then founded Aftermath Records, which also became wildly successful. Dre would go on to produce 50 Cent and Eminem. While only Eminem became the more radically political of the two, one-time collaborators 50 Cent

13 "With virtually...Coast." On Kurupt history, see Dan Deluca, "Taking his Rap from Death Row to Phila. Former Dogg Pound Member Kurupt Has Big Plans: His Own Label, a Double CD, and Forthcoming Collaborations," *The Philadelphia Inquirer*, 10/7/98, p.E1. On real name as Ricardo Brown Jr. see Sullivan, *LAbyrinth*, p. 291. On Jacques Agnant as Ricardo Brown Sr., see New York vs. 1. Tupac Shakur (M 22) 2. Ricardo Brown (M 30) 3. Charles Fuller (M 23), Defendants, Deposition of Police Officer Craig McKernan by ADA Mourges, 11/19/93. Kurupt was raised by his mother in Philadelphia. While the elder Brown listed his age as 30 in 1993, Warren suggested he was older, believing Tupac first saw Agnant as a substitute father figure. Tupac had a hard time initially accepting that Agnant was likely an agent until after his trial started a year after the sexual assault charge. Kurupt was 20 at that time in 1993. Michael Warren's investigations found out Brown Sr.'s real name was Agnant, as well as his dismissed charges up and down the East Coast.
14 "Kurupt had moved...time." Deluca, "Taking his Rap from Death Row to Phila..." *Philadelphia Inquirer*, 10/7/98, p.E1. Elon Johnson, "Kurupt is 'Calling Out' DMX," *MTV.com*, 10/8/99. Shaheem Reid, "Kurupt Hits Big Screen, Talks Lisa Lopes Album, Tha Row: Rapper puts music aside for roles on big screen and as senior VP of Tha Row," *MTV.com*, 11/11/02.

and Eminem both supported the Hip-Hop Summit Action Network and both produced free Tupac songs on behalf of Afeni Shakur.[15] The Vibe Music Awards granted Dre a Lifetime Achievement Award at their ceremony in 2005. According to police accounts, as Dre went to accept the award, a man seated near the front row named Jimmy Johnson went up to the microphone and punched him. Johnson stated that Suge Knight paid him $5,000 to assault Dre, who had a restraining order on Knight due to past threats.[16]

---

15 "In 2005, police...Afeni Shakur." On Dre, Ronin Ro, *Have Gun Will Travel*, pp.269-279. On Eminem and 50 Cent, see Tupac's posthumous CDs, *Tupac: Resurrection* and Tupac following CD, *Loyal to the Game*.
16 "'The Vibe...threats" Nolan Strong, "Man Who Assaulted Dr. Dre Claims Suge Knight Paid for Punch," 1/16/05 allhiphop.com/news/ .AllHipHopNews.com . Johnson's brother also reportedly owed Knight money.

FBI AND
NEW YORK'S
NATIONAL
POLICE
COINTELPRO
TARGETING OF
RAPPERS

L eaks eventually led to findings that by the mid-90s, U.S. Intelligence had combined their '60s Counter Intelligence Program (Cointelpro) against leftist Blacks and their targeting of musicians into an official New York police rap intelligence unit.[1] In the spring of 2001, *New York* magazine and other media revealed that the New York Police Department had directed a rap intelligence unit to compile a database containing more than 40 rappers, including Jay-Z, DMX, Sean Puffy Combs, and Wu Tang Clan rapper ODB's cousin Frederick Cuffie. A police source said the unit distributed information on rappers—including their photos, vehicles, and record labels—to precincts nationwide. NYPD spokesman Sergeant Brian Burke first denied the charges. He then admitted that the Police Commissioner launched it, citing rappers' "reckless behavior." Journalists helped police minimize these disclosures by referring to the activity as merely "rapper profiling."[2]

A 2004 leak by a Miami police officer led to a series of articles that revealed much more. These articles began with a Miami police whistleblower saying that New York's rap unit trained other police departments to help them develop rap intelligence units nationwide.[3] The training included distributed binders on rap industry figures that had detailed personal information dating back to 1995, suggesting that the New York unit's collection of data started at least that early.[4] One journalist reported that in some California communities the police chief determines what rap acts are allowed to perform.[5]

After this leak in Miami, former NYPD detective Derrick Parker disclosed information about his work in the New York rap unit. Parker said that his New York unit started well before Biggie Smalls's spring of '97 murder.[6] Reporter Dasun Allah interviewed Derrick Parker while investigating that rap unit for articles in the *Village Voice* and *The Source*.

1 As noted above, one intelligence document a Senate committee found included strategies for use against political musicians, "Intelligence Activities and Rights of Americans," Book II, April 26, 1976, *Senate Committee with Respect to Intelligence Report*. Excerpted in Alex Constantine, *The Covert War Against Rock* (Los Angeles: Feral House, 2001), p.9. U.S. Senate Select Committee to Study Government Operations, *The FBI's Covert Program to Destroy the Black Panther Party*, U.S. Government Printing Office, Washington. D.C. 1976.
2 "Starting in the…behavior.' " Andrew Lee and Carl Swanson, "NYPD Raps," *New York*, 4/30/01, p.13.
3 Nicole White and Evelyn McDonnell, "Police Secretly Watching Hip-Hop Artists," *The Miami Herald*, 3/9/04, p.1A. Nicole White and Evelyn McDonnell, "Monitoring of Rap Stars Disputed," *Miami Herald*, 3/17/04, p1B.
4 Evelyn McDonnell and Nicole White, "Arresting Data in Rap Binder," *Miami Herald*, 5/14/04, p.1B.
5 "Rock and Rap Confidential…are allowed to perform." Dave Marsh, "And the Beat(ing) Goes On… Counterpunch," 11/9/2002, counterpunch.org/2002/11/09/and-the-beat-ing-goes-on/counterpunch.org/marsh1109.html Also daveyd.com
6 Dasun Allah, "NYPD Admits to Rap Intelligence Unit," *The Village Voice*, 3/23/04.

Allah stated that Derrick Parker was trained in the FBI's Cointelpro tactics.[7] (*The Source* appeared to print one of its few revelatory articles to make up for the criticisms it received from the Hip Hop Summit Action Network. Also note that Dasun Allah rose, briefly, to Editor-in-chief, but was fired by his top editor/publisher within a year or two. That publisher was then ousted himself. Months later, Allah was sentenced to 6 months jail time for a suspiciously motiveless assault).[8]

Parker's disclosures further support evidence that New York police targeted Tupac Shakur with a frame-up and then a murder attempt. Parker said that several undercover units, including the Street Crime Unit, had officers who also worked in the rap intelligence unit. Parker said that a particular [former] Street Crime Unit officer arrested many rappers.[9]

The Street Crime Unit was thought to have replaced the FBI-overlapping, Panther-targeting BOSS unit. The NYPD disbanded BOSS in 1971, when the FBI "officially" ended its Counter Intelligence Program (Cointelpro), after the activist raid on an FBI office that year exposed the program. Nonetheless, former Cointelpro agents said that the FBI continued Cointelpro activities after 1971, but just used different names. Researchers believe that the Street Crime Unit, which started in 1971, continued BOSS activities. A police officer named Heinz inadvertently admitted that one or more officers who had Tupac under surveillance were part of the Street Crime Unit. These cops also had erased voicemail tapes that supported Tupac's defense in the sexual assault charge and they refused the evidence on a security camera videotape of the gunmen shooting Tupac in the Times Square recording studio.[10]

Parker contradicted some NYPD officials' denials of "exporting" their rap cops, saying that the NYPD sent him down to Houston and Miami to aid police in this work.[11] Events support that

7 Dasun Allah & Joshua Fahiym Ratcliffe, "Law and Disorder," *The Source*, June 2004, p.44.
8 Houston Williams, "Former Editor-In-Chief of the The Source Jailed," 5/25/06 allhiphop.com/news/.allhiphop.com/hiphopnews
9 "Dasun Allah, who…on the rappers.'" Dasun Allah, "The Hiphop Cop," *The Village Voice*, 4/6/04.
10 "The Street Crime…studio." As mentioned in a previous note, this writer had a personal interview with an Officer Heinz of Midtown North precinct, 5/4/99, who inadvertently implicated one of several cops who came to Tupac's Times Square shooting and his sexual assault charge hotel scene. Also see report of three cops at that scene all at hotel scene, *Vibe* ed.s Tupac Shakur, p.41. Salvatore Arena, "Sex Tapes Erased, Says Shakur Lawyer," *Daily News*, November 24, 1993. On refusing surveillance videotape, Cathy Scott, *The Murder of Biggie Smalls* (New York: St. Martin's Press, 2000), p.65.
11 Dasun Allah, "The Hiphop Cop," *The Village Voice*, 4/6/04

these New York-trained rap unit officers used the same murderous Cointelpro tactics that had been used against the Panthers. *The Miami Herald* failed to note but incidentally revealed the important timing of rap murders *after* the Miami police had been trained by the New York unit to focus on rappers in the summer of 2001. The *Herald* article noted no problems with rappers in Miami until a September 2001 murder of a popular rap DJ, a January 2002 murder of a hip-hop promoter and a September 2003 murder of a rap record company owner.[12]

Furthermore, *The Miami Herald* stated that the NYPD had trained police officers from "other major cities like Los Angeles and Atlanta."[13] New York, Atlanta and Los Angeles were the three cities where, as previously detailed, police officers were either directly involved in, passively watched, or covered up the murder and attempted murders of Tupac Shakur.

A final key support for the existence of this new Cointelpro against rappers came from filmmaker Nick Broomfield, writer Randall Sullivan, and former Det. Russell Poole. They helped reveal that some cops on this New York police intelligence rap unit also worked for the FBI. For example, as mentioned earlier, the NYPD's Det. Oldham took pictures of New York rapper Biggie minutes before his death in LA and monitored Sean Puffy Combs' gun possession trial in New York, three years later. Det. Oldham's dual role as an FBI agent aided the ease of his work in other jurisdictions such as LA.[14]

---

12 "Events support...owner." Nicole White and Evelyn McDonnell, "Police Secretly Watching Hip-Hop Artists," *Miami Herald*, 3/9/04, p.1A.
13 Nicole White and Evelyn McDonnell, "Police Secretly Watching Hip-Hop Artists," *Miami Herald*, 3/9/04, p.1A.
14 Broomfield, *Biggie and Tupac*, and Sullivan, LAbyrinth, pp. 136, 314.

TARGETS: SPEARHEAD, RAGE AGAINST THE MACHINE, WU TANG, DEAD PREZ, THE COUP

"Organize the hood under I Ching banners,
Red, Black and Green instead of gang bandannas
FBI spying on us through radio antennas
I'll take a slug for the cause like Huey P.
While all you fake niggas try to copy Master P...
Bring the power back to where the people live
I'm sick of working for crumbs and filling up the prisons
Dying over money and relying on religion
For help. We do for self like ants in a colony
Organize the wealth into a socialist economy
A way of life based on the common need
And all my comrades are ready
We just spreading the seed.
—Dead Prez "Police State." *Let's Get Free*, 2000.

A
s previously mentioned, in a memorandum revealed by a Senate Intelligence committee in 1976, U.S. Intelligence detailed particular tactics to use against political musicians. The excerpt of that memo on '60s anti-war musicians bears repeating. It directed agents to "show them as scurrilous and depraved. Call attention to their habits and living conditions, explore every possible embarrassment. Send in women and sex, break up marriages. Have members arrested on marijuana charges. Investigate personal conflicts or animosities between them. Send articles to the newspapers showing their depravity. Use narcotics and free sex to entrap. Use misinformation to confuse and disrupt. Get records of their bank accounts. Obtain specimens of their handwriting. Provoke target groups into rivalries that may result in death" (Ch.13).[15]

Evidence detailed above supports that U.S. Intelligence used these tactics to target Tupac from 1991-1996. Even a small sampling of news in the music world presents evidence supporting that U.S. Intelligence also used these tactics against other Black musicians with links to leftist political activists. Tupac's friend Michael Franti, a politically radical San Francisco musician, headed an auspicious

---

15 "But Congress...into rivalries.'" As noted above, one intelligence document a Senate committee found included strategies for use against political musicians such as "Intelligence Activities and Rights of Americans," Book II, April 26, 1976, *Senate Committee with Respect to Intelligence Report*. Excerpted in Alex Constantine, The Covert War Against Rock (Los Angeles: Feral House, 2001), p.9. U.S. Senate Select Committee to Study Government Operations, *The FBI's Covert Program to Destroy the Black Panther Party*, U.S. Government Printing Office, Washington. D.C. 1976.

political rap debut in 1991, The Disposable Heroes of Hiphoprisy (Sunday morning news shows interviewed Franti due to his excellent political lyrics).

After Franti ended work with his partner in Disposable Heroes and started the band Spearhead, he said that intelligence agents showed a group member's mother years of surveillance pictures they'd taken of his band, Spearhead. These included pictures at Seattle's riotous World Trade Organization protests that Spearhead members supported. They did this apparently to frighten the musician and his family from doing any more activist work. Franti further noted how British press reported that MTV had sent emails to their affiliates banning any bands' videos that had anti-war messages. Their multinational corporate owner Viacom apparently had a pro-war agenda.[16]

While U.S. Intelligence unsuccessfully tried to get N.W.A.'s rap shows canceled in '88, they had a larger program and more success against Tupac in '93 (Ch.15). They also worked to cancel the shows of Oakland-based political rapper Paris, according to at least one news article, likely due to his 1992 lyrical attack on the President, "Bush Killa." (Paris also produced a Public Enemy comeback CD in 2005).[17] Besides the previously mentioned Rage Against the Machine shows canceled with Wu Tang Clan. Rage Against the Machine collaborated with several rappers, *such as Wu Tang Clan*. Besides the police failing to cancel those shows, *as previously mentioned, police also unsuccessfully tried to* cancel Rage Against the Machine's show with Public Enemy's Chuck D for a Mumia Abu-Jamal benefit.[18]

U.S. Intelligence put much focus on Wu Tang Clan for several reasons. Besides touring with Rage, the Grammy nominated Wu Tang Clan worked with a founding member of the Republic of New Afrika, Brooklyn's Sonny Carson (Mwalimu Amiri Abubadiki). Carson had also worked with Tupac's New York lawyer Michael Tarif Warren on

16 "A radical...videos." Michael Franti with Amy Goodman, Democracy Now, broadcast on FISTV, Comcast Cable Ch.5, Baltimore, MD, 5/16/03, 7:30 p.m. On friend of Tupac's, Franti told this writer in discussion as he stopped in New York on an activist tour funded by Zach De La Rocha in 2000.
17 "While U.S. Intelligence...Killa.'" On the FBI's fax campaign to get police canceling NWA shows, see Bruce C. Brown, "Quayle Boosts 'Cop Killer' Campaign," *Washington Post*, 6/20/92, pp.B1,5. Cited in Barry Shank, "Fears of the White Unconcious: Music, Race, and Identification in the Censorship of 'Cop Killer.'" *Radical History Review* #66, Fall 1996. On Tupac, see Vibe eds *Tupac Shakur* (New York: Crown, 1997) p.46. On Paris, see "Sonic Jihad release from Paris," http://polsong.gcal.ac.uk/news_archive.html . Also see attempted use against Jimi Hendrix, Harry Shapiro and Caesar Glebbeek, *Jimi Hendrix: Electric Gyspy* (New York: St. Martin's Griffin, 1995) pp.190, 426.
18 This writer attended that Rage Against the Machine benefit concert, just outside New York City in New Jersey. Radio stations such as KROK discussed police attempts to cancel the show in 2000.

Black liberation causes. Papa Wu, the brother of one of Wu Tang's lead rappers, Ol' Dirty Bastard (ODB, birth name, Russell Jones), founded a music studio with Carson in the Bedford Stuyvesant neighborhood of Brooklyn. Wu Tang also worked with the Panther-inspired, worldwide hip hop activist organization, Zulu Nation.[19]

U.S. Intelligence had many reasons for concern over Sonny Carson's work with rappers topping the pop charts. As detailed more later, Zulu Nation revered Carson and the group was inspiring new chapters worldwide (Ch.36). Also, Carson's son, Lumumba Carson, had started a highly influential Brooklyn group called Blackwatch. That group was one of the first to explicitly meld Black Nationalist politics with Hip Hop. Blackwatch spawned many activist rappers, including Lumumba Carson's own group, X-Clan, where Carson took on the moniker, Professor X. X-Clan's late '80s start had them reach #11 on Billboard's Rap/R&B charts, before their early '90s break up.[20]

Rap activists report that the music industry aided the more subtle attacks on rappers. For example, Public Enemy's former member, Professor Griff, said that people in the record industry tried to create a conflict between his group and X-Clan.[21] Time Warner did buy up a majority of rap labels and the CIA architect who headed Psychological Warfare, C.D. Jackson, also headed Time Inc. (Ch.20). Thus, the company had a long commitment to placing U.S. Intelligence agents and carrying out such operations against Black activist musicians as an extension of its Cointelpro tactics (also see Chs.6, 34).

In the late '90s, events supported Wu Tang Clan rapper ODB's claims that the FBI had targeted him. ODB, Wu Tang's more eccentric rapper, told friends and relatives that the FBI killed Tupac for being a rap activist. He changed his name in the futile hope of avoiding being framed or murdered due to his own activism. From 1998-99,

19 "U.S. Intelligence...Nation." On Carson as founding member of Republic of New Afrika, see Dasun Allah, "Sonny Carson Dies: Legendary Black Nationalist Figure in Bedford-Stuyvesant," *Village Voice*, 1/1-1/7/03. .villagevoice.com On, Zulu Nation, personal interview, this author heard Zulu nation founder Afrika Bambata say this at the Third Black Panther Film Festival at CUNY in New York City, 2002, then talked briefly with him afterwards. On Zulu's worldwide status see, Shaila Dewan, "At a Live Homage, Hip-Hop Is King but 'Rapping" is Taboo," New York Times, November 13, 2000, p.B3. Also see articles on Zulu Nation at .daveyd.com which said the Zulu Nation had 10,000 members.
20 "U.S. Intelligence had many...break up." Andy Soages, "Hip Hop Fridays: Vibes of the Pro Black: A Conversation of Brother J. of X-Clan Part 1 (May 27-30), 2005. Blackelectorate.com/articles.asp?ID=1382 .Blackelectorate.com
21 Personal interviews with June of Shaka Shakur's Maroon Records and "Panther Cub" Orlando Green, who also organizes the Hip Hop Convention .hiphopconvention.org 3/4/06. In an interview with Davey D, Proorfessor Griff also claimed that Public Enemy's former Def Jam label claimed that the group owed them $2 million. He further said that the industry changed the laws making sampling of other's music require royalty payments and that this went into effect retroactively. http://odeo.com/audio483066/view

police arrested ODB four times around the country on trivial charges, suggesting their use of the FBI harassment arrest strategy. In the summer of '98, strangers broke into ODB's New York home and shot him, but he survived.[22]

Later, possibly using a version of the U.S. Intelligence threat-timing tactic, police orchestrated their most blatant and deadly attack on ODB and his rapper cousin, Fred Cuffie, on Martin Luther King's birthday. As mentioned, it was later revealed that the NYPD rap intelligence unit had a file on Cuffie (Ch.30). On that mid-January night in '99, two plainclothes New York Street Crime Unit cops wearing bulletproof vests and driving an unmarked car in Brooklyn, sirened ODB to pull over. One of the officers put a gun to the head of ODB's passenger, Cuffie. The other cop told ODB to get out of the car, according to the rappers. Out of fear, ODB stepped on the gas and fled. The cops then fired at the rappers.[23]

A different group of uniformed cops then came upon the rappers, surrounding ODB's car just outside his aunt's boarding home. These Street Crime Unit cops that had shot at the rappers likely didn't want to reveal their identity after their apparently unprovoked murder attempt. While the new group of cops didn't find a gun on ODB or Cuffie, the Street Crime cops claimed ODB was driving with his headlights off and that the rapper fired at them first. A police source said ODB's lights were on and a grand jury ruled in favor of ODB and Cuffie's account. Months after that New York shooting, police arrested ODB and held him on $115,000 bail for wearing a bulletproof vest. [24]

In 2000, *The Village Voice* said the FBI had paid an undercover agent to become a Wu Tang Clan manager. *The Voice* reported that a confessed bank robber and Ecstasy drug-dealing young Mafia kingpin, Michael Caruso, had gone undercover to work for the FBI. The *Voice* said Caruso's work appeared to include becoming a personal manager for Wu Tang Clan. Caruso said he managed two Wu Tang rappers. The FBI said they and the Bureau of Alcohol, Tobacco and Firearms

22 "In 1999, events…survived." Peter Noel, "A Bullet for Big Baby Jesus," *Village Voice*, 2/2/99, pp.45-6.
23 "Possibly using…fled." Most details of this event described in Noel, *Village Voice*, 2/2/99, pp.45-6. On cops shooting at ODB in Street Crime Unit, see *Vibe*, May 1999. Noel, *Village Voice*, cited a Criminal Court complaint saying that these cops were part of the Street Crime Unit.
24 "Other cops…vest." Patrice O'Shaughnessy, "Rapper Vows Suit, Sez Cops Did Him Dirty in Shooting," New York's *Daily News*, February 5, 1999, p.4. *Vibe*, May 1999. Noel, *Village Voice*, 2/2/99, pp.45-6. On arrest for vest, Associated Press, "Rapper's in the Clink," New York *Daily News*, 3/11/99, p.3.

(ATF) were investigating Wu Tang on suspected gunrunning, but the FBI never charged anyone with a crime.[25] *The Source* rap magazine ran an interview of Caruso joking about the charge of his FBI spy work months later, but Caruso failed to say that Wu Tang immediately fired Caruso after reading the *Voice* article, and the interviewer failed to mention it.[26]

From 1999-2004, police subjected ODB to trivial arrests, and prison doctors reportedly forced medications on ODB in jail. Still, most of his solo CDs topped the pop music sales charts. In 2004, ODB died just before his 36th birthday. It mysteriously took over a month for a coroner to announce that ODB died from a heart attack due to mixing cocaine with a prescription painkiller.[27] Sonny Carson's business partner, Papa Wu (a.k.a. Freedom Allah), disagreed with the coroner's report, saying that his brother ODB was drug free at the time of his death. Papa Wu also implied political reasons for his brother's death, saying that he and ODB were attending activist rallies together at that time.[28]

Large police groups such as the Policemen's Benevolent Association (PBA) and the Fraternal Order of Police (FOP) also helped local and federal intelligence agencies target Black activist celebrities. *The Village Voice* said the PBA tried to ban entertainers throughout New York City, including Rage Against the Machine and New York rapper Mos Def, because of their support for political causes. Most of the PBA and FOP censorship took place in the New York area, but they had a strong national reach. The PBA even protested a Bruce Springsteen tour when he sang about police brutality against Blacks. *The Voice* also said that the FOP "compiled a list of hundreds of artists, celebrities, and venues" working on Black activism nationwide, especially rap groups aiding Mumia.[29]

---

25 "Also, in 2000…a crime." Frank Owen, "The Rap Group and the Rat; Gunrunning, the Feds, and the Wu-Tang Clan," *The Village Voice*, May 30, 2000, pp.43-48. Caruso disclosed being the personal manager for two Wu Tang rappers. "Music Matters; Family Ties," *The Source*, October 2000, p.56

26 "Music Matters; Family Ties," *The Source*, October 2000, p.56. Frank Owens, "Letters: Response," The *Village Voice*, June 13, 2000, p.6.

27 Nolan Strong, "Ol' Dirty Bastard Dead," 11/12/04. Roman Wolfe, "Ol' Dirty Died From Cocaine and Prescription Painkillers," 12/15/04. Both from allhiphop.com/news/*AllHipHop.com*: News. The listed painkiller was Tramidol.

28 Odd names do run in the family but his appears to have a positive purpose. Remmie Fresh, "Family, Friends, Say Goodbye to Ol' Dirty Bastard," allhiphop.com/news/*AllHipHop.com*: News 11/19/04.

29"Police groups…Blacks." Chisun Lee, "Taking the Rap; City Clubs Ban Hip Hop Radicals," *The Village Voice*, 9/12/00, pp.47-8. pp.47-8. See quote on FOP and PBA by Police lieutenant Eric Adams, president of 100 Blacks in Law Enforcement Who Care.

The PBA particularly focused on banning the annual activist conference Black August that often set up concerts in New York City and Havana, Cuba. At the 2000 event in New York, the PBA effectively pressured venue owners to cancel their deals with Black August organizers, reportedly due to the presence of Dead Prez, an activist rap group they had hounded. Dead Prez had collaborated with Fred Hampton, Jr. and supported his National People's Democratic Uhuru Movement and Prisoners of Conscience Committee.[30]

Other rap shootings suggest that U.S. Intelligence continued murderous attacks on rappers in many cities nationwide. For example, One of the top rap activists, Boots Riley, formed The Coup. Riley also served on the central committee for the Progressive Labor Party, headed the International Committee Against Racism, and helped publicize campaigns by organizations such as the Women's Economic Agenda Project, the International Campaign to Free Geronimo Pratt, and anti-police brutality groups. While Riley's rap group, The Coup, had never got close to top ten pop chart sales, their star was rising with the help of their newest member and hype man, Tarus Jackson. Riley started appearing on various national news shows as he and Jackson did a 36-city, three-week tour by mid-November 2005. Just at the end of it, two gunmen forced their way into Jackson's home and murdered him.[31]

30 "The PBA...Committee." On PBA hounding Dead Prez, Chisun Lee, "Taking the Rap; City Clubs Ban Hip Hop Radicals," *The Village Voice*, 9/12/00, pp.47-8. On Dead Prez supporting Uhuru Movement, this writer saw him speak of his support at the 3rd Black Panther Film Fest, NYC, 2003.
31 "Other rap...him." On Riley's activism, see speakoutnow.org/People/BootsRiley.html On Jackson and his murder, see Houston Williams, "Paris Not Dead, Member of The Coup Killed," 11/17/05 allhiphop.com/news/ allhiphop.com/hiphopnews

NYPD VS HIP-HOP SUMMIT RAP MOGULS RUSSELL SIMMONS AND SEAN "PUFFY" COMBS

"1. We want freedom and the social, political and economic development and empowerment of our families and communities; and for all women, men and children throughout the world. 2. We want equal justice for all without discrimination based on race, color, ethnicity, nationality, gender, sexual orientation, age, creed or class 3. We want the total elimination of poverty. 4. We want the highest quality public education for all... 6. We want universal access and delivery of the highest quality health care for all...10. We want the progressive transformation of American society into a Nu America as a result of organizing and mobilizing the energy, activism and resources of the hip-hop community at the grassroots level throughout the United States..."

—Excerpt of Hip Hop Summit Action Network's "What We Want."

In 1999, after Tupac and Biggie's murders, rap mogul Russell Simmons and many activists convened "Hip-Hop Summits" to end any perceived conflicts between East and West Coast rappers, and to create unity amongst rappers. Simmons had a vast influence amongst rappers that stemmed from his co-founding of one of the most successful rap labels, Def Jam Records. Def Jam launched top rap groups, including the group Run-DMC headed by Simmons' brother, Joseph "Reverend Run" Simmons. Def Jam also produced Public Enemy, LL Cool J, the Beastie Boys, DMX and Jay-Z.

By 2001, Russell Simmons turned the Hip-Hop Summit conferences into an organization called the Hip-Hop Summit Action Network (HSAN). HSAN's Board of Directors consisted of a multiracial group of top rap record label owners. These included a Def Jam director, Kevin Liles, and Damon Dash of rapper Jay-Z's Roc-a-Fella Records, as Simmons' co-chairs. The board also included Bad Boy Entertainment founder Sean "Puffy" Combs (later changed to P. Diddy) and white Warner executive, Lyor Cohen. Political leaders such as former Congressional Black Caucus leader and NAACP Director Kweisi Mfume and NAACP director-turned Nation Of Islam leader, Benjamin Muhammad (formerly Chavis) also sat on the board. The board further included Columbia University professor Manning Marable, *who was a Democratic Socialist and radical activist.*

HSAN developed an ambitious 15-point goal statement similar to the Black Panthers Ten Point Program, called "What We Want." While not containing all of the overt socialist politics nor the militant self-defense tactics of the Panthers' Program, their 15-point goal statement included Panther-like radical leftist ideas such as "the total elimination of poverty...racism and...bigotry." It also called for universal health care, equal justice without discrimination, African American reparations, voter enfranchisement and the end of companies' environmental polluting of poor neighborhoods.[32] HSAN further tried to effect electoral politics by registering close to 100,000 new voters a month from 2003-2004.[33]

While HSAN lacked many of the Panthers' activist community survival programs, its directors' and rapper volunteers' vast wealth, influence, leadership and experience made HSAN an imposing force. Queens, New York native Russell Simmons had enormous success by the turn of the century. In 2001, his various companies' annual sales had reached close to $500 million.[34] Russell Simmons also gained huge wealth by starting the Phat Farm clothing line and Rush Communications, which made $192 million in '01. The *New York Times* called Rush Communications "one of the biggest Black-owned companies in the world."[35] Simmons used his mogul status to get mainstream media coverage of his activist speeches nationwide.[36]

Most of the chart-topping rappers in the country worked with the Hip Hop Summit Action Network in various ways. And many of them appeared to be subjected to corrupt attempts by police, the FBI and government prosecutors to put them in jail. While Simmons sold his portion of Def Jam for $100 million in 1999, he stayed linked with many Def Jam artists who spoke at HSAN conferences. The NYPD had many of these rappers on the NYPD rap intelligence database and the rappers came under attack amidst government foul play.

The government put large resources into attacks on HSAN board director Sean Puffy Combs. As the rap mogul owner of Bad Boy Records, Biggie Smalls's label, Combs had an estimated worth of $400 million dollars by 2001, [37] a portion of which he had donated to activist

32 "By 2001,... neighborhoods." Hip-Hop Summit Action Network, hsan.org/Content/main.aspx?pageid=27
33 Kristin Jones, "Rocking the Hip-Hop Vote," *The Nation*, 12/1/03, p.7-8.
34 Lola Ogunnaike, "Soldier of Fortune," *Vibe*, December, 2002, p.101
35 Felicia Lee, Hip Hop is Enlisted in Social Causes," *New York Times*, p.B9.
36 For one of many examples, Baltimore news channels covered his speech against Bush's Patriot Act and interviewed him on 4/17/03.
37 Scott, Murer of Biggie Smalls, p.192. Katherine Finkelstein, "Hip Hop Star Cleared of Charges in Shooting at Manhattan Club," The New York Times, March 17, 2001, p. A1, B2. Peter Noel, "The 'Bad Boy' Curse," *Village Voice*, April 3, 2001, p.45

groups in the late '90s.[38]   U.S. Intelligence appeared to target Combs with much fewer assaults but similar tactics as used on Tupac. These included an early FBI investigation and arrest.[39] *Highly suspected police intelligence agents such as Suge Knight also tried to draw Combs into a feud by criticizing his appearance on many of his rappers' recordings and blaming Combs for murders of Death Row associates, which became the* "East/West conflict." By the fall of 1999, Combs was helping Simmons with some aspects of organizing HSAN. Combs' huge finances and high esteem for producing rap talent made him a formidable HSAN member. In October of '99, gunmen inexplicably shot at Combs' recording studio.[40]

But the most infamous incident involving Sean Puffy Combs came in December of 1999. Closer scrutiny of this attack suggests that U.S. Intelligence first attempted to murder Combs in the guise of a robbery, and then they used many government resources in an attempt to imprison Combs. As mentioned, the NYPD rap unit already had a profile on Combs. Combs had helped launch the career of film and music star, Jennifer "J-Lo" Lopez, and had a relationship with her in '99. One of Combs' new rappers, 19 year-old Jamal "Shyne" Barrow, accompanied them and their bodyguards when they went to a Manhattan dance club one night. Original accounts of what transpired indicated that an argument with several people in the club led a stranger to throw a stack of money at Combs. A fight ensued, and gunshots wounded several bystanders.[41]

Prosecution ended up keeping their top witness, Mathew "Scar" Allen, from testifying in person. Witnesses said that Allen, a convicted felon wanted on three unrelated warrants, started the altercation with Puffy. But the judge allowed prosecutors to present Allen's absent testimony against Combs in court through videotape. He also allowed Jennifer Lopez's absent testimony supporting Combs by this means. Witness Tavon Terrence Jones described seeing a man with no resemblance to Puffy Combs shoot in the crowded bar. Other witnesses said that this shooter was Allen. Jones said

38 He donated a lot of much money, giving $500,000 to the largely Black college he attended, Howard University, $50,000 to the 100 Black Men think tank, as well as $125,000 for his after-school and summer programs out of the Harlem YMCA. He further donated a100 computers in Harlem and fed 30,000 as part of an Atlanta project started by civil rights leaders. Scott, Murder of Biggie, pp.166. Peter Noel, "Guns, Bribes, and Benjamins," *Village Voice,* December 12, 2000, p.53. Karen Hunter, "Wrist Slapped Puffy a Magnet for Tribulation," *Daily news,* 1/15/01, p.8. The 10 Black Men think tank rejected Puffy's donation to avoid bad publicity since a member of the think tank, attorney Johnnie Cochran, represented Puffy.

39 Cathy Scott, The Murder of Biggie Smalls, pp.94, 129. *Rock and Rap Confidential* Dave Marsh reported that New York cops put rappers under surveillance and quoted hip-hop journalist, Davey D, about national rap surveillance and banning of rap shows. On FBI arrest, see Randall Sullivan, *LAbyrinth* (New York: Atlantic Monthly Press, 2002), p.289. Cathy Scott reported the criminal mischief conviction as '96, Cathy Scott, *The Murder of Biggie Smalls* (New York: St. Martin's, 2000), pp.188-9.

40 See "Puffy's Studio Hit by Street Shooting," MTV.Com news, cited in Tina Johnson, "Kurupt's Security Guard Killed, Two Other Injured in Studio Shooting," mtv.com/news/articles/1431071/19991018.story.jhtml .

41 "Combs hadahd helped...bystanders." Dan Barry and Juan Forero, "Between High Life and Street Life," The New York Times, December 29, 1999, p.B1.

he heard the man [Allen] talk in the bathroom of robbing Combs.[42]

That prosecution only had the top shooting suspect as their main witness, combined with more evidence gathered by Combs' lawyers, further supports that U.S. Intelligence was the top suspect in setting up the incident. The longtime New York District Attorney, Robert Morgenthau, notorious for aiding U.S. Intelligence in trials against Assata Shakur in the '70s and Tupac Shakur in the '90s, initially filed many charges against Combs *regarding the nightclub shooting*. Morgenthau eventually dropped all but a gun possession charge.

Combs' high-powered legal defense team then revealed various links between U.S. Intelligence and the witnesses that prosecutors used for that lone charge. Morgenthau's prosecutors claimed that a "street person" saw a Black man in Puffy Combs' car throw a gun out the window when driving away from the club incident. Combs' lawyers, Benjamin Brafman and Johnnie Cochran, said this street person gave the gun to a friend. "That friend is apparently a career informant who was working with a task force of federal and city agents…this professional informant, in turn, gave the weapon to Detective Andrew Vargas, who lists his law enforcement address [as] 26 Federal Plaza—the building in which the New York office of the Federal Bureau of Investigation is located," said Brafman and Cochran.[43]

Several other aspects of the trial support that U.S. Intelligence set up the incident. First, the FBI agent who was at least found to have passively watched Biggie's murder, Det. Oldham, said he was watching the Combs trial (Ch.27). *Oldham surely participated in the rap unit targeting political rappers with his involvement in photographing Biggie just before his murder that aided the cover-up of Tupac's murder.*[44]

Also, a television news report said that in no other gun possession case in the country had prosecutors called so many witnesses to testify.[45] A veteran cop with the NYPD's anti-gang unit said, "Morgenthau wants Puff Daddy [Combs]." The cop provided his own half-revealing reason, saying that since the sensational Tupac "rape" trial the "attention-grabbing Morgenthau seems eager to send an A-list celebrity like Combs to prison." As with Tupac, Morgenthau rejected any deal that didn't involve jail time.[46]

42 "Prosecution ended…robbing Combs." Katherine Finkelstein, "Judge in Combs Case Permits Statement by Missing Witness," *New York Times*, 3/6/01, B2.
43 "The DA…Cochran." Peter Noel, "Daddy Under the Gun," *Village Voice*, January 9, 2001, p.21.
44 Nick Broomfield, *Biggie and Tupac*, 2002.
45 Heard by this writer on WB11 News at 11p.m., 3/14/01.
46 "A veteran…time." Noel "Daddy Under the Gun," *Village Voice*, p.21

Furthermore, police tested Comb's and rapper Shyne Barrow's hands for gunpowder residue after their arrests, but they failed to process the test kits. Prosecutors said that they did this because the tests are unreliable. Defense lawyers said it underscored their clients' innocence.[47] On March 16, 2001, the court acquitted Sean Puffy Combs of all charges. The court acquitted Shyne Barrow of the most serious charges: attempted murder and intentional assault in the first degree. But his conviction on three lesser assault charges, including reckless endangerment and possession of a weapon, led to the judge giving him a 10-year jail sentence.[48]

Despite the trial outcome, and similar to what happened to Tupac, "gold-digging" lawsuits piled up against Combs and other rappers. Prosecutors or government-linked defense attorneys may have influenced these seemingly specious suits as part of a "harassment lawsuit strategy" (Ch.15). Shooting victim Natania Reuben had testified against Combs, yet she also undermined her credibility by filing a $150 million lawsuit against Combs before any trial verdict. Reuben's lawsuit and other claimants' suits amounted to $850 million of lawsuits against Puffy by that time.[49]

Within the next few years, police focused on top rap producer Russell Simmons, who had founded the Hip-hop Summit Action Network. Russell Simmons experienced police attention after his HSAN conferences drew tens of thousands, many of whom registered as new voters in 2004.[50] That year, police pulled over his wife's car near their house and arrested her when they allegedly found a bag of weed in a passenger's purse. The police revealed that this wasn't an incidental arrest when they asked her whether Russell was home.[51] Kimora Lee Simmons later received six months of probation as a first time offender when she pled guilty to careless driving for not pulling over fast enough in that incident.[52] Such police focus works as a not-so-subtle warning that if the targeted person continues their leftist activism, police will continue their harassment.

47 "Furthermore, police…innocence." Barbara Ross and Leo Standora, "Puffy Linked to Gunshot," *Daily News*, January 10, 2001, p.7.
48 "On March…sentence." Katherine Finkelstein, "Hip Hop Star Cleared of Charges in Shooting at Manhattan Club," *The New York Times*, March 17, 2001, p. A1, B2.
49 "Shooting victim…time." Katherine Finkelstein and Dexter Filkins, "Combs Trial Jurors Consider Gun Case Against Rap Star," *New York Times*, 3/15/01, p.B3.
50 Jody Miller and Ellen Golden, "Record Breaking Houston Hip-Hop Summit Registers & Encourages Over 20,000 Youth to Vote," 2/3/04. Also see, Jody Miller and Ellen Golden, "St. Louis Hip-Hop Summit Announces 114,000 New Voter Registrations in Missouri," 2/23/04. businesswire.com/news/home/20040823005288/en/St.-Louis-Hip-Hop-Summit-Announces-114000-Newhsan.org
51 "That year…home" Nolan Strong, "Kimora Lee Simmons Arrested," 7/28/04, *All HipHop.com*: News.
52 Clover Hope and Clarence Burke Jr. "AHH Stray News: Kimora Pleads Guilty," 8/10/05 allhiphop.com/news/allhiphop.com/hiphopnews

THE NYPD VS. ACTIVIST LATINO GANGS

As detailed earlier, the CIA collaborated with special units in New York City. Researchers and other historians of the era cited memoirs of officers in the New York Police Department's Bureau of Special Services showing that they did CIA work.[1] Another possible example of CIA collaboration with the NYPD started by the end of the '90s. News groups revealed that Republican Mayor Rudolph "Rudy" Giuliani began a hugely expensive NYPD program called "Operation Condor." In 2000, New York's murder rate, which had been decreasing (along with virtually all major cities nationwide), increased by about 13%. This increase happened after Condor began, and it occurred just after Condor added $100 million to overtime undercover police work over the course of the year.[2]

The same American officials involved in New York's Condor had been involved in a murderous South American operation of the same name, globally targeting leftists from that continent.[3] *The New York Times* noted that William Casey of the CIA later started the Manhattan Institute in 1978, which they cited as shaping George W. Bush's political views. *The Times* also said that the Manhattan Institute "has become the nation's most influential, though not best known—as befits a CIA operation—right wing think tank."[4]

Another *New York Times* article about the New York-based Manhattan Institute suggests that Mayor Giuliani's use of the name Operation Condor in 2000 was likely no coincidence. In the fall of 2002, *The Times* reported that the Manhattan Institute had regularly advised

1 See, for example, an NYPD BOSS undercover agent's memoir on his duel work with the FBI against Malcolm X, Tony Ulasewicz, with Stuart McKeever, the President's Pirvate Eye (Westport Connecticut: MACSAM Publishing), p.145, cited in James Douglas, "The Murder and Martyrdom of Malcolm X," James DiEugenio and Lisa Pease, eds, *The Assassinations: Probe Magazine on JFK, MLK, RFK and Malcolm X* (Los Angeles: Feral House, 2003) p.390-1. One historian said BOSS was known amongst Intelligence as "the little FBI and the little CIA." Frank Donner, Protectors of Privilege (Berkeley: University of California Press, 1990), p.155.

2 "Another possible…year." William K. Rashbaum, "Rising Murder Rate Defies Latest Push Against Crime," *The New York Times*, April 5, 2000, p.B3. On the decreasing murder rates in "New York and other cities nationwide," see Yale Law School Professor John Donnohue, Letter to the Editor: "Rudolph Giuliani, Nobel Nominee," *New York Times*, 6/6/05. He and MIT Professor Steve Levitt published this research that showed other reasons for the crime drop nationwide in their best-selling book, FreakonomicsFreakanomics. On Condor adding $100 million to overtime undercover…Kevin Flynn, "Feeling Scorn on the Beat and Pressure From Above," *The New York Times* on the web, December 26, 2000, posted on nytimes.com/2000/12/26/nyregion/police-feel-scorn-on-beat-and-pressure-from-above.html?searchResultPosition=5. nycpba.org/press-nyt/00/nyt-001226-morale.html

3 The Chilean Condor work later advised Giuliani on New York's Operation Condor. CIA director Allan Dulles and fellow CIA associates, particularly Reagan/Bush's future CIA director, William Casey, worked on transporting the Nazis to Latin America with Sunrise and bringing many Nazis to the U.S. with other operations, such as Paperclip (Ch.19). Paperclip partly worked through a front group directed by Casey—The International Refugee Committee in New York. Thierry Meyssan, "The Center for Security Policey: Washington's Manipulators," *Voltaire*, 11/13/02 voltairenet.org/article30118.html Meyssan citation for this appeared to be "Group Goes from Exile to Influence," *The New York Times*, 11/23/81.

4 "Bush Culls Campaign Theme From Conservative Thinkers," *The New York Times*, 6/12/00.

Mayor Giuliani's administration and was leaving to advise conservative opposition politicians in Latin America. The Manhattan Institute also advised NYC Mayor Bloomberg's Police Department. [5]

While one of the phases of Operation Condor in South America targeted influential targets such as popular Chilean folk singer Victor Jara, New York's Condor appeared to target popular rappers and other leaders particularly feared for their potential to mobilize world opinion or organize broad opposition.[6] The New York Police Department began their Operation Condor after they "reformed and decentralized" the Street Crime Unit, which had started in 1971, the year that the NYPD's Panther-targeting BOSS disbanded. As detailed earlier, BOSS agents and leaders had also worked for both the FBI and the CIA (Chs.3, 4). CIA documents showed this work with local police Intelligence Divisions.[7]

In 2000, undercover Condor agents (dressed in street clothes) replaced the plainclothes Street Crime unit cops. Statistics on the NYPD's Condor suggest that one of its goals was harassment arrests. Since Condor's inception coincided with the forming of the Hip-Hop Summit Action Network, rappers appeared to be one of the activist-linked groups of color that it targeted. Operation Condor also coincided with the increased work of the NYPD's rap intelligence unit in 2000.[8] With their rap intelligence unit and its overlapping units, local and federal, the NYPD vastly increased the number of rappers they arrested from 2000 to 2003. The fact that judges dismissed many of these charges adds weight to the notion that the NYPD was pursuing a harassment arrest strategy.[9]

---

5 "Another...Department." Anthony DePalma, "The Americas Court a Group that Changed New York," *The New York Times*, 11/11/02. On Manhattan Institute advising Bloomberg's police, Nicholas Confessore, "Giuliani Guide is Bloomberg Gladfly," *New York Times*, 10/25/05.

6 "What Prof. McSherry reported...politicians." J. Patrice McSherry, "Operation Condor: Deciphering the U.S. Role" from her website, Crimes of War. See, Amnesty International, *Report on Torture* (U.S. Edition, Farrar, Straus and Giroux, 1975), pp.206-7, cited in Chomsky and Herman, *The Washington Connection and Third World Fascism*, p.9.

7 See p.27 of CIA documents known as "Family Jewels" at gwu.edu/~nsarchiv/NSAEBB/NSAEBB222/index.htm

8 "Statistics on Condor...crime." "NYC Police Suspend Extra Patrols for 10 Days," American Civil Liberties Union News, Source reportedly *The New York Times*, October 12, 2000, nytimes.com/2000/10/12/nyregion/police-suspend-extra-patrols-for-10-days.htmlhttp://archive.aclu.org/news/2000/w101200z.html

9 "The NYPD...them." See, for example, "Operation Lockdown," *The Source*, March 2004.pp.107-127. That article cites many of the notable rap arrests in a timeline and short essays from 1986 to 2003. Adding them up, significantly more arrests occurred in the four years between 2000-03 then occurred in the 14 years from '86-'99. Also see, "Actual Facts," *XXL* magazine, July 2000, p.35. Of the many other examples besides Tupac, Biggie, and ODB targeted in California, "Oakland hometown favorite, Seagram Miller, a.k.a. Seagram, age 26 was shot in the head...[after] illustrating the dangers of the violent and criminal lifestyle he'd denounced." "Bits and Pieces," *The Source*, October 1996, p.6. And Oakland graffiti artist and rap collaborator Mike "Dream" Francisco, who had organized the first-ever Bay Area gallery installment—a response to the Rodney King verdict called "No Justice No Peace," was fatally shot. Leah Rose, "360: Street Dream" *XXL* magazine, p.36.

Outcry from New Yorkers and many police officers walking the streets ended New York's Condor in 2001. Nevertheless, newly elected Republicans had appeared to continue Giuliani's practices through other means. Condor appeared to use the tactic of throwing a wide net over the city's people of color and training its undercover cops to use particularly brutal force. Condor's sweep contributed to 60,000 arrests in 9 months, with 40,000 for drug misdemeanors and 7,000 for violations, offenses "that do not rise to the level of a crime."[10]

The more famous cases of brutality likely became so because they weren't political targets and the media allowed their coverage. Under Condor, the Street Crime Unit's brutality, such as the 41-bullet murder of unarmed Amadou Diallo in 1999, continued. For example, in 2000, police murdered Patrick Dorismond, reportedly after an undercover cop offered him drugs, beat him when he refused, and then allowed arriving cops to shoot him. Other examples include police firing 50+ bullets at the vehicle of Sean Bell and others attending his bachelor party unarmed.[11]

The Manhattan Institute's Operation Condor-type policies appear to have been even more prevalent before it took on the official name. It would seem as though the Institute's focus on opposing Latino leftists continued inside the United States. New York Mayor Giuliani Administration's police worked with federal agents to target the Latino activist-converted gang, the Latin Kings, in the mid-1990s. Called "the largest and most powerful street gang in New York," the 3,000-member Latin Kings changed its name to the Almighty Latin King and Queen Nation in 1994. The Latins Kings' transformation into a leftiest political group was aided by the influence of The Yound Lords, a former Latino activist group that modeled themselves after the Black Panthers.[12]

A *Village Voice* article provided details that supported civil rights lawyer Ron Kuby's description of how the NYPD used what was likely a harassment arrest strategy on Latin Kings' leader Antonio "King Tone"

10 "Statistics on Condor...crime." "NYC Police Suspend Extra Patrols for 10 Days," American Civil Liberties Union News, Source reportedly *The New York Times*, October 12, 2000, hnytimes.com/2000/10/12/nyregion/police-suspend-extra-patrols-for-10-days.htmlhttp://archive.aclu.org/news/2000/w101200z.html
11 "Under Condor...Dorismond." Bill Vann, "The Killing of Patrick Dorismond: New York police violence escalates in wake of Diallo verdict," March 22, 2000, wsws.org/articles/2000/mar2000/nyc-m22.shtml Veronica Belenkaya, Alison Gendar, Mike Jaccarino, and Robter F. Moore, "Sean Bell is killed after cops blasted 50 bullets in 2006," *New York Daily News*, 11/24/15.
12 "Called the largest...group." For example, see Jennifer Gonnerman, "'Throne Behind Bars; The Latin King leader on love, law enforcement, and landing back in jail," *Village Voice*, 4/7/98, p.61. and, see, Big Noise Films, *Black and Gold: The Latin King and Queen Nation*, AK Press Catalog, 2003, p.155.

Fernandez. Kuby said the NYPD's tactics included falsifying information and evidence to arrest King Tone a half dozen times without landing a single conviction. Kuby also told the *Voice* that police targeted King Tone because *The New York Times* was giving him publicity for turning the group into "a progressive revolutionary force."[13] Former Young Lords member and Latin King advisor, Vincent "Panama" Alba, said that after the group's activist conversions, the NYPD started arresting Latin Kings and Queens in even larger numbers with street sweep-type roundups.[14]

Many other New York community activists said the NYPD and FBI teamed up to target King Tone and the Latin King and Queen Nation because of their activist conversion. Another former Young Lord, Richie Perez, who moved on to chair the National Puerto Rican Resistance organization, said police targeted King Tone after he started settling conflicts peacefully. Father Luis Barrios, a priest and professor at John Jay College, stated that the government didn't mind when the Kings were killing each other but once they turned to activism the FBI started a massive undercover surveillance of the group.[15]

King Tone claimed police initially sought to kill him and then settled on keeping him in prison for many years, starting in the later '90s. King Tone said that *The New York Times* noted how strangers who shot at him were caught with a 9-mm handgun and a fully loaded machine gun but were released from jail with no charges. Yet cops searched Tone's car, arrested him because they found a bullet shell in his trunk, and put him on trial for possession of ammunition. On a different occasion they arrested Tone and 24 other Latin Kings. After their search turned up empty handed, they ended up charging them with disorderly conduct and unlawful assembly. Bail before their court dates was set at $15,000 for Tone and $500 for the others.[16]

In May 1998, the NYPD initiated their largest attack on King Tone and the Latin King and Queen Nation. At 5 a.m., in reportedly the largest coordinated New York City raid since the prohibition of <u>alcohol in the 192</u>0s, 1,000 U.S. Marshals spanned out across NYC and

13 "Civil rights…force.'" Gonnerman, *Village Voice*, 4/7/98, p.61.
14 Personal interview, Vincent Panama Alba, 10/15/96 and 5/15/98. Arrest of King Tone and 23 other Latin Kings was also reported in Jennifer Gonnerman, "Thrown Behind Bars," *The Village Voice*, 4/7/98, p.61.
15 "Many other…group." *Black & Gold: The Latin King and Queen Nation*, a documentary, Big Noise Films, 1999.
16 "King Tone…court dates." *Black & Gold: The Latin King and Queen Nation*, a documentary, Big Noise Films, 1999. Arrest of King Tone and 23 other Latin Kings was also reported in Jennifer Gonnerman, "Thrown Behind Bars," *The Village Voice*, 4/7/98, p.61.

arrested Latin King and Queen leaders in what they called "Operation Crown." They found no drugs or guns in that raid, yet they arrested the 90 top male and female Kings and Queens for drug dealing and "criminal association." A judge set Tone's bail at $350,000. Community activists such as Father Douglas, Richie Perez, and Black Liberation leader-turned rap producer, Sonny Carson, put up their cars and payroll checks as collateral for Tone's bail.[17] Prosecutors used similar tactics against "King Tone" Fernandez as they used against Tupac, and Tone received a 10-15 year prison sentence.[18]

The U.S. Intelligence war on the Almighty Latin King and Queen Nation continued amidst the NYPD's Operation Condor in 2000, as did the targeting of the activist-converted United Blood Nation and rappers.[19] New York's *Daily News* noted that Latin King and Queen "elder spokesman" Hector Torres took part in a seminar at John Jay College of Criminal Justice in May of 2001, in which he warned of ways police try to turn people of color against each other. He claimed that police were waging a fake war on gangs to justify a war on youth of color. In that *Daily News* article Torres announced his nationwide travels to help gangs transform "into positive political voices for disenfranchised communities."[20]

David Cohen, a CIA loyalist to the Bush family, proceeded to run a global police operation out of New York after Republican Mayor Bloomberg appointed him to head New York's police intelligence.[21] From 1991 to 1995, Cohen had been the CIA's deputy director of the Directorate of Intelligence. He then headed their Directorate of Operations, overseeing the CIA's global network of offices and personnel until 1997. Cohen also said that for several years in the '90s he was the highest-ranking CIA agent working in New York City.[22]

One of Cohen's first actions in 2003 was to dismantle the New York "Handschu" restrictions on police intelligence that Barbara Handschu, lead lawyer for the group of activists that included Afeni

17 "In May...bail." *Black & Gold: The Latin King and Queen Nation*, Big Noise Films, 1999.
18 Personal interview with Hector Torres, 9/12/98. Hector Torres, called the "elder spokesman" for the Latin Kings and Queens, also worked for New York activist Reverend Al Sharpton. In describing how King Tone's probation officer didn't believe Tone's probation should be violated, Torres described a similar situation as had happened to Tupac before his sentencing hearing.
19 Robert Gearty and Bill Hutchinson, "Sweeping Up Street Gang," Daily News, May 9, 2001, p.7.
20 "New York's *Daily*...color." Maki Becker, "Latin King vows to aid gang kids," *Daily News*, 7/9/01.
21 "Bush family...intelligence." "A Spymaster Joins the NYPD," *The New York Times*, 1/23/01, p.B3.
22 "He spent...City." David Cohen, "The Cohen Declaration: Facing 'Heightened and Unjustifiable Risk'" *The New York Sun*, 12/5/02.

Shakur, had fought for years to attain.[23] Also by 2003, New York upped the number of officers in the state's Joint Terrorist Task Force (JTTF) from 17 to 120, and the JTTF included officers from 35 other agencies. Cohen vastly expanded the NYPD intelligence division to global proportions, including 74 overseas offices.[24]

His office also targeted a throng of anti-Republican activists. Eighteen months after the Republican National Convention for the presidential election of 2004, *The New York Times* published an exposé that New York Police used undercover agents to infiltrate the 100,000+ protesters at the Republican convention. These undercover police agents purportedly started conflicts that police used as an excuse to conduct mass arrests at that and other protest events.[25]

Further details of Cohen's expanded NYPD intelligence division show its global dimensions, as well as its focus on Black and activist American neighborhoods. Cohen increased one intelligence unit from a handful of cops to 600 officers working from Brooklyn's "Park Slope to [the country of] Pakistan." [26] The largely white Park Slope Brooklyn activist neighborhood borders the Bedford-Stuyvesant area that spawned top rappers from Biggie Smalls to Jay-Z. As rap had become popular amongst most countries, the nationalized rap intelligence unit had potential for an international reach, and NYPD detectives started working in the international police offices of Interpol from Tel Aviv to London, France and Canada.[27]

With the "Project Crown" Latin King and Queen arrests, the U.S. Intelligence war on activist-converted gangs appeared even larger and more overt than their war on rappers. This war on gangs grew in direct proportion to the increasing threat to the racist, conservative U.S. Intelligence interest of keeping the ethnic communities politically inert so they couldn't erode wealthy white dominance of political power.

---

23 Cohen's declaration, New York Sun, 12/5/02. "Red Squad" and "restrictions modified and eased," Benjamin Weiser, "Threats and Responses: Law Enforcement" *New York Times*, 2/12/03, p.17. Also, Associated Press, "Judge Backs Expanded Police Surveillance," *New York Times*, 3/22/03, p.2.

24 "By 2003…Pakistan.'" Brad Hamilton, " 'Blue Spies' for City: Kelly's Anti-Terrorism Cops Go Global for Higher Intelligence," *New York Post*, 6/29/03, News, p.3. On FBI overseas offices, see Raymond Bonner, "World Briefings: Australia: FBI Opens Office," *The New York Times*, 11/9/06, p.A22.

25 Jim Dwyer, "New York Police Covertly Join In at Protest Rallies," *The New York Times*, 12/22/05, pp.A1, B10.

26 "By 2003…Pakistan.'" Brad Hamilton, " 'Blue Spies' for City: Kelly's Anti-Terrorism Cops Go Global for Higher Intelligence," *New York Post*, 6/29/03, News, p.3

27 "The largely white…Canada." Brad Hamilton, " 'Blue Spies' for City: Kelly's Anti-Terrorism Cops Go Global for Higher Intelligence," *New York Post*, 6/29/03, News, p.3

EPILOGUE

As an entertainer, Tupac Shakur was prolific. Considering that Tupac died several months after his 25th birthday in June of 1996, his rate of creative output appears historically unmatched. Two of his five chart-topping CDs (which sold the most worldwide in a week) came out when he was alive.[1] He produced five solo rap CDs (and his fourth recording was a double CD) and one group CD before he died. Death Row released the fifth CD just after his murder. Tupac had left hundreds of unreleased songs. Afeni Shakur then produced, or allowed production of, ten CDs of his unreleased recordings (four single CDs and three double CDs). Several of these posthumous CDs topped the pop music charts and most of them sold over a million copies, contributing to the $12 million his estate made in 2003 alone.[2]

Tupac also worked on a vast amount of art forms in his short life. He produced dozens of music videos and acted in six films, five of them in lead roles. He further wrote a book's worth of poetry. His first manager, Leila Steinberg, produced Tupac's book of poetry, *The Rose That Grew From Concrete,* releasing it after his death (many celebrities read or interpreted these poems for 2 CD releases of the same name).[3] Since Tupac Shakur's death, U.S. Intelligence has appeared to put vast resources into continuing the cover-up around his life and death. Police detective Russell Poole, the lead detective in Tupac's murder investigation, had to resign from the Los Angeles Police Department and hold a press conference to get his information to the public.[4]

---

1 "Considering that Tupac...when he was alive." On over 30 million copies sold, see John Jurgenson, Hartford Courant, "New CD extends Tupac's lucrative post-death career," The Mercury News, 12/18/04, MercuryNews.com. On the third no.1 CD since death, see Ben Sisario, "Tupac Is Back, Again," New York Times, 12/23/04, p.B2. Also see "Tupac has a platinum 2003" which says two of his CDs, Better Dayz and Resurrection both went platinum. rapnewsdiret.com

2 Afeni Shakur kept them listed mostly under his industry spelling, 2Pac. She named her production company after Tupac's middle name, Amaru. These were, in chronological order, 2Pac, R U Still Down? [Remember Me] (Interscope, double CD, 1997); 2pac and Outlawz, Still I Rise (Interscope, 1999); Tupac Shakur, The Lost Tapes (Herb N'Soul: 2000); 2Pac, Until The End of Time (Amaru Entertainment, double CD, 2001); 2Pac, Better Dayz (Amaru Entertainment, doble CD, 2002); Tupac: Resurrection (Amaru Entertainment, 2003); 2Pac, Loyal to the Game (Interscope, 2004). Tupac's finished CDs while he was alive include his solo CDs: 1991's 2Pacalypse Now (Interscope), 1993's Strictly 4 My N.I.G.G.A.Z, 1995's Me Against the World (Interscope), February of 1996 release All Eyez On Me (Death Row) and November of 1996 release under the pseudonym Ma.k.a.veli, The Don Kiluminati: the 7 Day Theory (Death Row). Tupac Shakur, The Rose that Grew from Concrete (New York: MTV/Pocket Books,1999). CD, Tupac Shakur, The Rose that Grew from Concrete (Amaru/Interscope, 2000). forbes.com/2003/10/24/cx ld_1024deadcelebintro.html#523a5750223c . en.wikipedia.org/wiki/Forbes%27_list_of_the_world%27s_highest-paid_dead_celebrities#2003_list

3 Tupac Shakur, The Rose that Grew from Concrete (New York: MTV/Pocket Books,1999). CD, Tupac Shakur, The Rose that Grew from Concrete (Amaru/Interscope, 2000). Films include: Juice, Poetic Justice, Above the Rim, Bullet, Gridlock'd, and Gang-Related.

4 Police Detective Russell Poole said this on film in Nick Broomfield, Biggie and Tupac (documentary, 2002). Randall Sullivan, LAbyrinth: A Detective Investigates the Murders of Tupac Shakur and Notorious B.I.G., the Implication of Death Row Records' Suge Knight, and the Origins of the Los Angeles Police Scandal (New York: Grove, 2003).

Award-winning documentary filmmaker Nick Broomfield made a film focused on Poole, titled *Biggie and Tupac*. Veteran journalist Randal Sullivan wrote his book *LAbyrinth: A Detective Investigates the Murders of Tupac Shakur and Notorious B.I.G., the Implications of Death Row Records' Suge Knight and the Origins of the Los Angeles Police Scandal* about Poole.[5]

Three of Hollywood's biggest stars have attempted to portray Russell Poole based on Sullivan's book. In the summer of 2003, many media sites announced that Sylvester Stallone was slated to write, direct, and star in a film with Stallone playing Det. Poole. Producers apparently cancelled Stallone's project before completion.[6]

Some years after Stallone's project was announced, Steven Spielberg's DreamWorks lined up Leonardo DiCaprio to play Detective Russell Poole. Randall Sullivan said that he saw the LAPD get the movie canceled. Regarding that cancellation, Sullivan further stated that the LAPD "is the most politicized police department in the country and its relationship with financial powers and political powers [locally and nationally] are… unprecedented."[7]

The latest attempt to put Det. Russell Poole and his findings about Tupac and Biggie's murders on screen, *City of Lies*, featured Johnny Depp playing Poole. The film already had trailers in many major movie theater chains in the summer of 2018. Producers Global Road scheduled its release on the anniversary of rap icon Tupac's fatal shooting in early September. By early August, Global Road announced they put the *City of Lies* release date on indefinite hold.[8]

A former FBI agent who worked on the case of the Biggie Smalls murder investigation discussed the 2018 attempt to release a film on the subject. He said *A City of Lies* release "would shut down all the different task forces that LAPD had with the FBI as well as other federal agencies."[9] It had a limited release in Italy in 2019 and was finally released in March of 2021.

By 2015, Russell Poole had contributed to a book by Michael Carlin and R.J. Bond, *Tupac 187*, and was reportedly co-writing another

5 Nick Broomfield's documentary, *Biggie and Tupac*, Lionsgate, 2002. youtube.com/watch?v=GX_rM1Uwo9o for full movie. For excerpt of Broomfield quoting Poole, see trailer for Drugs as Weapons Against Us: youtube.com/watch?v=0MamdDXe5fs 3:22-3:33

6 Gary Susman, Sylvester Stallone will direct a Biggie-Tupac film," Entertainment Weekly, 6/6/03. ew.com/article/2003/06/06/sylvester-stallone-will-direct-biggie-tupac-film/

7 Rohrlich, *The Daily Beast*, 8/23/18.

8 Justin Rohrlich, "Inside the Shocking Death of Johnny Depp's Biggie-Murder Movie 'City of Lies,'" *The Daily Beast*, 8/23/18. thedailybeast.com/inside-the-shocking-death-of-johnny-depps-biggie-murder-movie-city-of-lies

9 Rohrlich, "Inside the Shocking Death…" *The Daily Beast*, 8/23/18.

book with Carlin, titled *Chaos Merchants*. By the end of July, 2015, Poole and Carlin had secured a meeting with members of the Los Angeles Sheriff Department to discuss reopening the investigation of Tupac and Biggie's murders. When Poole attended that meeting, officials said he had a fatal heart attack, also described as an "aortic aneurysm."[10]

Michael Carlin stated that he ended up not being able to make that meeting. He said that he found out from a source inside the Sheriff's Department that Poole arrived in that meeting room and found former police officer Reggie Wright Jr. there. Wright had headed Death Row Records Security that included dozens of moonlighting LA cops. Poole had found evidence of Wright's involvement in Tupac and Biggie's murders. Carlin said his Sheriff's Department source claimed that police choked Poole unconscious and then used a defibrillator to cause Poole's heart attack, leaving burn marks on Poole's chest.[11]

In 2017 A&E released a documentary series, *Who Killed Tupac?*, co-produced by Tupac's stepbrother, Maurice "Mopreme" Shakur, who Tupac was very close to all his life (this documentary also featured me, *FBI War on Tupac…* writer John Potash). In that series, Civil Rights attorney Benjamin Crump and his fellow researchers said that 28 people close to Tupac and his murder investigation have had mysterious deaths from 1996 to 2017.[12]

Benjamin Crump and one of his researchers, author Lolita Files, also interviewed former police detective Greg Kading. Despite much skepticism regarding Kading from people close to Tupac and Biggie Smalls, mainstream media gave Kading a massive spotlight for years regarding a book he wrote and film based on it—*Murder Rap*. That book made the claim that Bad Boy Records owner Sean Puffy Combs paid Crips gang members to kill Tupac. Russell Poole commented on Kading's book, saying:

> "Greg Kading has no credibility on this subject matter. He became a task force member on the Biggie case 10 years after the fact. Kading left the LAPD in disgrace for his false testimony on a federal murder & racketeering case United States v. George

10 Andrew Buncombe, "Biggie Smalls murder detective Russell Poole dies from heart attack while still probing unsolved murder," *The Independent*, 8/21/15. independent.co.uk/news/people/news/biggie-smalls-murder-detective-russell-poole-dies-from-heart-attack-while-still-probing-unsolved-10466388.html
11 Michael Douglas Carlin video, posted by him, 6/30/17. youtube.com/watch?v=4rhTHTNigpQ
12 Benjamin Crump, *Who Killed Tupac?* Episode 1 "Murder in Vegas/Crips Vs. Bloods," A&E, aired on 11/21/2017.

Torres-Ramos CR06-656(A) SVW. Guilty verdicts were overturned in part due to Kading's testimony. He said LAPD cleared him of those charges, but that is not entirely true. Kading also had some help writing this book from disgraced *LA Times* reporter Chuck Phillips. Kading forgets there were actual eyewitnesses to the Biggie killing. He spends a lot of time talking about things he knows nothing about. This is a desperate attempt for Kading to salvage his reputation. Suge Knight is a suspect, but not for the reasons Kading talks about. In closing, Kading never attempted to interview me regarding the Biggie investigation. He makes a lot of false statements about me, and my part in the investigation."[13]

The documentary series, *Who Killed Tupac?* Episode 2 "East Coast vs West Coast" presents footage of attorney Ben Crump interviewing Greg Kading near the start of the 43-minute episode. Kading's top piece of evidence was an audiotaped confession by imprisoned Crips gang member Duane "Keefe D" Davis, who said Combs gave Harlem drug dealer Eric "Zip" Martin $1 million, who then gave that to Davis to kill Tupac and Death Row Records director Suge Knight. The rest of the episode presented interviews with dozens of others in an attempt to investigate this claim as part of the purported "East Coast vs. West Coast" conflict and whether there was any substantiation to back Kading's claims.

People close to the situation, such as Comb's former top bodyguard, Eugene Deal, refuted Kading's claims. Deal said Combs refused involvement in violence or illegalities for fear of losing white music executives' collaboration. Researchers such as Randall Sullivan said Keefe D Davis was in jail facing a possible decades-long prison sentence and "that confession was obtained to get leniency on a major drug charge."

By the end of the episode, Ben Crump and author Lolita Files's questioning forced Kading to admit on film that, "Keffe couldn't be incriminated for anything he said and he would get leniency for the

13 Russell Poole, 1/26/13. Amazon comments section, *Murder Rap: The Untold Story of the Biggie Smalls and Tupac Shakur Murder Investigations*. amazon.com/Murder-Rap-Untold-Biggie-Investigations-ebook/product-reviews/B005SGYSWM/ref=cm_cr_getr_d_paging_btm_next_13?ie=UTF8&reviewerType=all_reviews&pageNumber=13

drug charge... he was never prosecuted." Longtime attorney Crump explained how such jailhouse informants are very often only "trying to tell police what they want to hear" in these situations to get such leniency.[14]

A&E's *Who Killed Tupac?* documentary series explored most of the major theories about the entertainment icon's death, concluding with Prof. Michael Eric Dyson stating that Tupac "was a war reporter for... the war on Black and brown people." It further presented Civil Rights activist and one-time presidential candidate, Rev. Al Sharpton. Sharpton also founded the National Action Network (NAN) that has included the late Coretta Scott King and Martin Luther King III in its leadership. NAN has 89 chapters nationwide. Sharpton said "Tupac is today as strong a symbol of the movement that we're all still engaged in, as any artist out there... which made him dangerous." [15]

Chokwe Lumumba

Before Russell Poole died, an important figure in Tupac's life, his national attorney Chokwe Lumumba, had transitioned into mainstream politics. Lumumba had been the second vice-president for the Republic of New Afrika and then the founding National Chairman of the New Afrikan People's Organization (NAPO). In 2009 he won a Jackson, Mississippi city council position. In 2013 he was elected as Jackson's mayor.[16]

As mayor, Chokwe Lumumba won praise from Blacks and whites in Jackson, particularly due to his pragmatic approach. For example, he passed a tax increase to fix potholes and sewers, winning a 90% approval for the tax. More progressive media groups such as Democracy Now radio program fondly called Lumumba "America's most revolutionary mayor."[17]

In February of 2014, after less than a year in office, Chokwe Lumumba suddenly died. The coroner first said the death was neither due to a heart attack nor a stroke, but was still due to "natural causes," though he felt fine while at work several hours earlier in the day. Hinds

14 Benjamin Crump, Randall Sullivan, Eugene Deal, and Greg Kading, *Who Killed Tupac?* Episode 2 "East Coast vs West Coast," A&E, aired on 11/28/2017.
15 Michael Eric Dyson and Al Sharpton, *Who Killed Tupac?* Episode 5 "Time For Justice," A&E, aired on 12/17/2019. nationalactionnetwork.net/chapters/
16 Caldwell, Earl; Rackley, Lurma; Walker, Kenneth (December 1994). *Black American Witness: Reports from the Front.* Lion House Publishing. p. 348.
17 Buchsbaum, Herbert. "Jackson Mourns Mayor With Militant Past Who Won Over Skeptics." *The New York Times*, The New York Times, 10 Mar. 2014, nytimes.com/2014/03/10/us/jackson-mourns-mayor-with-militant-past-who-won-over-skeptics.html. "Chokwe Lumumba: Remembering 'America's Most Revolutionary Mayor.'" *Democracy Now!*, democracynow.org/2014/2/26/chokwe_lumumba_remembering_americas_most_revolutionary.

County Supervisor Kenny Stokes said, "We're going to ask a question: Who killed the mayor? So many of us feel, throughout the city of Jackson, that the mayor was murdered." An independent autopsy was conducted but the findings reportedly weren't conclusive.[18]

Still Lumumba's legacy lives on. In 2017, Lumumba's son, Chokwe Antar Lumumba, won the mayoral election in Jackson.

Afeni and Mutulu Shakur

Afeni's activism on behalf of Geronimo Pratt (changed to Geronimo Ji-Jaga) helped gain his release from jail with a judicial finding of false imprisonment in 1997. Afeni further tried to help gain the release of her former partner Mutulu, who had also worked on Tupac's gang peace truce movement. Mutulu gained peace truces between the Bloods and the Crips in the national prison system. This might be the top reason the Board of Parole continues to illegally reject Mutulu's release despite his prison sentence having been completed February 10, 2016.

In 2018, after another rejection for parole, Mutulu filed a lawsuit. In that suit he and his lawyer stated that the parole commission "has failed to adopt or apply any known standards on the meaning of frequent rule violations. A handful of old telephone rule violations over 30 years do not show Plaintiff frequently violated prison rules or is likely to re-offend if released on parole."[19]

Afeni further stayed active, building the Tupac Amaru Shakur Foundation and the Tupac Amaru Shakur Center for the Arts. The latter served as a theater, music, and poetry camp for kids. She further used the income from Tupac's estate, reported at $900,000 per year, to buy a 50-acre ranch in the area she grew up in—Lumberton, North Carolina. She lectured in the vein of her friends and comrades, Chokwe Lumumba and Watani Tyehimba, stating that we need to "take back the land." She further continued to fight for the estimated 100+ Tupac recordings she had never received, filing a lawsuit in 2013.[20]

In 2004, Afeni married a preacher named Gust Davis. In 2005, Davis proceeded to buy a very large organic farm in Lumberton. In

18"Saying Goodbye and Thank You to the 'Judicial Genius' Chokwe Lumumba." *New York Amsterdam News: The New Black View*, amsterdamnews.com/news/2014/mar/06/saying-goodbye-and-thank-you-judicial-genius/.
19Sha Be Allah, "Tupac's father, Mutulu Shakur, files lawsuit against the U.S. government for illegally holding him in prison," The Source, 3/29/18.
20 Rob Kenner, "You Are Appreciated: Remembering Afeni Shakur," *Complex* 5/9/16. complex.com/music/2016/05/afeni-shakur-legacy-obituary. Jordan Darville, "Two new Tupac albums are reportedly in the works," The Fader, 10/1/18. thefader.com/2018/10/01/new-tupac-albums-death-row-settlement

March of 2015, Afeni separated from Davis, leaving him on the ranch while she lived on a houseboat in Sausalito, California.[21] In April of 2016, Afeni filed for a divorce from Davis.[22]

In May of 2016, a friend of Afeni Shakur called 911 reporting that Afeni felt ill. *The New York Daily News* said that the "Marin County sheriff's deputies and firefighters responded to Shakur's houseboat." Why, when someone is feeling ill, would police respond instead of just paramedics? *The Daily News* quoted Marin County Sheriff's Lt. Dough Pittman as saying, "At this point, there is nothing to indicate to us that there was any foul play, nothing suspicious about this other than this being sadly a natural event." It's uncertain if anyone questioned anything being suspicious for him to respond that way.[23]

More importantly, while Afeni was estranged from and divorcing Gust Davis at the time of her death, he was trying to take half of her regular $20,000 monthly allowance from Tupac's estate.

Furthermore, once the coroner had completed their autopsy, Afeni's body should have gone to her surviving adult daughter Sekyiwa. Yet the government authorities gave Afeni's body to her estranged former husband. Davis flew to California and authorities gave her body to him.[24]

It's a wonder if Afeni's marriage to preacher Gust Davis went bad on its own, or if he was another case of U.S. Intelligence trying to control her. As detailed earlier, evidence supports U.S. Intelligence previously placed Kenneth "Legs" Saunders in Afeni's life to control her. Was U.S. Intelligence concerned that Afeni's permanent break from Davis would mean their losing any control?

Other factors also suggest U.S. Intelligence foul play. First, there were several important anniversaries on the year of her death, raising the question of a possible "threat-timing" around it. Huey Newton and Bobby Seale founded The Black Panther Party for Self-

---

21 Gust Davis worked as a minister and bizarrely called himself "Prophet Gust Davis" on one Facebook page. He called himself Dr. Gust Davis on another page, despite no signs of ever having received a doctorate. On separation and divorce, Krista Caproni, "Afeni Shakur is Getting Divorced with No Prenup; Husband Wants $10K a Month," The Source, 3/18/16. thesource.com/2016/03/18/tupacs-mom-is-getting-divorced-with-no-prenup-husband-wants-10k-a-month/ On Davis, 2paclegacy.net/gust-davis-afeni-shakurs-husband-what-you-need-to-know-about-him/

22 "Tupac's Mom: Husband Wants a Piece of Tupac's Pie in Divorce," TMZ, 3/18/16. tmz.com/2016/03/18/tupacs-mom-divorce-alimony/

23 Nancy Dillon, Meg Wagner, and Brian Niemietz, "Afeni Shakur, mother of hip-hop legend Tupac, dead at 69," The New York Daily News, 5/4/16. nydailynews.com/entertainment/music/afeni-shakur-mother-tupac-dead-69-article-1.2622887

24 Flo Anthony, Nancy Dillon, and Brian Niemietz, "Tupac Shakur's step dad agrees to move out of disputed property," The New York Daily News, 8/14/17.

Defense, 50 years previous, and various anniversary celebrations were planned. Similarly, a film studio gained international distribution for a widely anticipated Tupac biopic movie, *All Eyez on Me*. Afeni Shakur was listed as Executive Producer on that film.[25] The movie's September 2016 release coincided with the 20th anniversary of Tupac's death and the year of his 45th birthday.

Tupac's Legacy

Now Tupac's half-sister, Sekyiwa Shakur, her children, his stepbrother Maurice "Mopreme" Shakur, and his extended family of comrades are left to carry on his legacy.

Since Tupac's death some top universities have held classes on Tupac's body of work. These include Harvard University, the University of California-Berkeley, Boston University, and the University of Washington.[26]

Many influential people have hailed Tupac, including Professor Michael Eric Dyson calling him a "20th century prophet;" Prof. Nikki Giovanni, "a great mind… [who was] assassinated;" actor Jim Belushi, "I loved Tupac… a wonderful man;" rapper Nas, "a God;" rap producer Dr. Dre "Incredible;" rapper Eminem, "a superstar in every aspect of the word;" boxer Mike Tyson, "a heart as big as this planet;" actor Jada Pinkett Smith, "he had so much charisma;" film producer Neil Moritz, "Dynamic, bold, powerful, magnetic;" Janet Jackson, "I adored him;" Tom Whalley, "I never worked with anyone who could write so many great songs so quickly;" actor Tim Roth, "fucking amazing!" NBA star Kevin Durant, "He would have been a Ghandi or Martin Luther King."[27]

And many have cited his global influence, as seen through dedications on every continent. These include a statue in Germany, his likeness plastered on a wall in Libya, and murals of him in Brazil,

25 Nancy Dillon, Meg Wagner, and Brian Niemietz, "Afeni Shakur, mother of hip-hop legend Tupac, dead at 69," *The New York Daily News*, 5/4/16. nydailynews.com/entertainment/music/afeni-shakur-mother-tupac-dead-69-article-1.2622887
26 Travis Hay, "UW class dedicated to slapin gangsta-rapper Tupac Shakur," *The Seattle Post-Intelligencer*, 12/3/03 seattlepi.com/ae/music/article/UW-class-dedicated-to-slain-gangster-rapper-Tupac-1131215.php
  Rich Barlow, "A Class That Explores the Gospel According to Tupac Shakur," *BUToday*, 2/27/19. bu.edu/articles/2019/a-class-that-explores-the-gospel-according-to-tupac-shakur
27 "Holla If Ya Hear Me: Michael Eric Dyson Talks Tupac's Prophetic, Self-Destructive Work," *The Source*, 12/21/17. thesource.com/2017/12/21/holla-hear-tupac-shakur/
  and David Fear, "Tim Roth on 'Tin Star,' Tarantino and Tupac," *Rolling Stone*, 9/29/17. rollingstone.com/tv/tv-features/tim-roth-on-tin-star-tarantino-and-tupac-253513/
  and "Jim Belushi: I Loved Tupac," *Larry King Now*, 12/8/17, youtube.com/watch?v=pjPxTrLWnFM
  and Joi-Marie Mckenzie, "Tupac's 45th Birthday: 45 Celebrity Quotes to Remember Tupac Shakur," *ABC News*, 6/16/16. abcnews.go.com/Entertainment/tupacs-45th-birthday-45-celebrity-quotes-remember-tupac/story?id=39902842

Australia, Spain, Peru, Korea, France, Mexico, Wales, and Sierra Leone.[28]

Besides his catalogue of hundreds of songs, a book of poetry, six movies, dozens of videos, and a film script, Tupac's legacy includes interviews that so many of his fans have pored over around the world. Many have repeated Tupac's quotes, including "I'm not saying I'm going to change the world, but I guarantee that I will spark the brain that will change the world."

Tupac's political role-playing and attempt to appeal to the masses had him simplify the complex politics he learned in his teen years. Some of his most repeated quotes are "Death is not the greatest loss in life. The greatest loss is what dies inside while are still alive. Never surrender!" And, "We can never go nowhere unless we share with each other." May his ideals live on in all of us.[29]

For the reasons mentioned above, virtually all media organizations have long maintained various degrees of censorship over many of these issues. Gaining justice and a final peace on these issues may take a variety of tactics for which some of the organizations described in this book may be consulted. Defying imperial forces' "divide and conquer" strategy and salvaging a humane way of life will require a concerted effort by all racial and ethnic groups to oppose malevolent multinational corporate forces and their mercenary government puppets rather than each other.

28 Agence France-Presse, "Why Tupac still reigns in hip hop 20 years after his death, and why his legacy is at risk," *South China Morning Post*, 9/13/16. scmp.com/culture/music/article/2018867/why-tupac-still-reigns-hip-hop-20-years-after-his-death-and-why-his
29 Norbert Juma, "14080 Tupac Quotes on Life, Love, and Being Real That Will Inspire You," *Everydaypower.com* everydaypower.com/tupac-quotes/

CREATE THE WORLD YOU WANT TO SEE AT MICROCOSM.PUB™

SUBSCRIBE!

For as little as \$15/month, you can

support a small, independent publisher

and get every book that we publish—

delivered to your doorstep!

www.Microcosm.Pub/BFF

MORE UNCENSORED HISTORY FROM WWW.MICROCOSM.PUB